M000286668

American Scots

American Scots

The Scottish diaspora and the USA

Duncan Sim

DUNEDIN

Published by
Dunedin Academic Press Ltd
Hudson House
8 Albany Street
Edinburgh EH1 3QB
Scotland

ISBN 978–1–906716–33–2
© 2011 Duncan Sim

The right of Duncan Sim to be identified as the author of this book
has been asserted by him in accordance with sections 77 & 78 of the
Copyright, Designs and Patents Act 1988

All rights reserved.
No part of this publication may be reproduced or transmitted in any form
or by any means or stored in any retrieval system of any nature without
prior written permission, except for fair dealing under the Copyright,
Designs and Patents Act 1988 or in accordance with a licence issued by the
publisher or by the Copyright Licensing Society in respect of photocopying
or reprographic reproduction. Full acknowledgment as to author, publisher
and source must be given. Application for permission for any other use of
copyright material should be made in writing to the publisher.

British Library Cataloguing in Publication Data
A catalogue record for this book is available from the British Library

Typeset by Makar Publishing Production, Edinburgh
Printed in Great Britain by CPI Antony Rowe

FSC
www.fsc.org
MIX
Paper from
responsible sources
FSC® C013604

For my family

Contents

Acknowledgements

I have a large number of people to thank in relation to this book.

First, I would like to thank my employers, the University of Stirling (where I worked until December 2006) and the University of the West of Scotland (where I currently work). Both institutions have provided me with continuing support in all kinds of ways both during the research period and during the actual writing of the book. I am also particularly grateful to colleagues at both universities with whom I have been able to discuss issues arising from my research. In particular, I would like to thank Douglas Robertson and Ian McIntosh at Stirling, and Murray Leith at West of Scotland.

My research visits to the United States were funded by the Carnegie Trust for the Universities of Scotland and I am deeply grateful to them for their financial support.

During my time in the United States, I received outstanding hospitality from both the University of Colorado and New York University and my thanks go to all those members of staff there who helped me with my work. I would like to say a special thank you to Brian V. Klocke of Colorado, who transcribed all my Colorado interviews for me. I also received amazing hospitality from members of the Scottish diaspora itself and from the range of Scottish organisations with whom I came into contact. Again, my thanks.

The book has been published by Dunedin Academic Press. I am grateful to the staff at Dunedin, to Joanna Chisholm who advised on practical matters of text preparation, and to Euan Hague of DePaul University, Chicago, who read the text and provided valuable advice, pre-publication.

Finally, my greatest debt is to all those individuals who gave up their time to be interviewed by me. I am deeply grateful to them.

University of the West of Scotland,
Paisley, January 2011

Introduction: the Scottish diaspora

This is a book about the Scottish diaspora — or at least a part of it. Estimates of the size of the diaspora vary and nobody really knows how many people across the globe claim Scottish ancestry. But Scottish politicians Kenny MacAskill and Henry McLeish (2006) suggested that estimates range extremely widely from forty to eighty million, in comparison to a 'home' population actually residing in Scotland of barely five million. On the other hand, the Scottish Diaspora Forum, which was part of Scotland's 2009 Year of Homecoming, referred in its online publicity to a diaspora of 'more than thirty million'.[1] Either way, the numbers are huge, relative to the size of the population in Scotland itself.

Although the Scottish diaspora may be found in all parts of the world, the largest groupings are generally acknowledged to be in North America and Australasia. Data from the 2000 United States Census, for example, showed that 5.4 million people in the US claimed Scottish ancestry, representing 1.7% of the population. More recently, the 2006 American Community Survey indicated a total of six million people with Scottish ancestry, also representing 1.7%. This is a significant number and this book therefore focuses on the Scottish diaspora within the United States, because of its size and importance.

Perhaps the main theme of the book — the continuing importance to the diaspora of being both American *and* Scottish — is demonstrated by the T-shirts belonging to one of the people interviewed as part of the research. He was a businessman, working in the oil industry, and was also a senior office-bearer in the local St Andrew Society. While having a very clear picture of modern Scotland himself, nevertheless he believed in the importance of heritage and tradition:

---

1 http://www.homecomingscotland2009.com/media-centre/diaspora_forum.html; accessed April 2011

I'm an American, of Scottish ancestry. I have some shirts: 'America first, Scotland forever'. It's the origins of my family, that's why it's forever. I don't think it would have changed if my family would have been German. My lines happen to be Scottish and that's where I've focused. I know people who are just as strong about their family origins in other countries. My family is Scottish (C4).

This chapter begins by exploring the concept of 'diaspora' before discussing the extent to which the Scots fit the generally accepted diaspora 'norms'. The chapter also describes the organisation of the book.

The idea of 'diaspora'

The term 'diaspora' is derived from the Greek word for a scattering, as of seed, and was initially used to refer to the population of Jews exiled from their homeland in Israel. The word became more widely applied to include those who were deported or exiled from a state, or to those who migrated for economic reasons to find employment or for political reasons as part of a process of empire-building. It is now commonly used in English to describe long-term expatriates and their descendants living in significant numbers in countries or regions other than their home.

Safran (1991, pp. 83–99) suggested that there are certain defining characteristics of diasporas, including dispersal to two or more locations, a collective mythology of homeland, an alienation from the country to which they have migrated, the idealisation of a return to their homeland and an ongoing relationship with their homeland. Other researchers such as Butler (2001, pp. 189–219), however, have suggested that there is some disagreement over Safran's list and, in particular, over the issue of return to the homeland. For example, some diaspora communities, particularly those who have migrated of their own free will, may opt for a permanent settlement elsewhere. As a result, Butler argued that there is agreement only over three basic features of diaspora, although she would add a fourth.

The first agreed characteristic of diaspora is that there should be a minimum of two destinations as the word 'diaspora' suggests a scattering, rather than a transfer from a homeland to a single destination. Secondly, there should be some sort of relationship to a real or imagined homeland and, thirdly, there should be a self-awareness of the group's identity.

Butler's suggested fourth characteristic is the existence of the diaspora over at least two generations.

Van Hear (1998) agreed with Butler that a diaspora should exist over more than one generation, being semi-permanently located in another country, while accepting some movement will be ongoing between the homeland and the new country of settlement. He also suggested that the idea of a diaspora implies a degree of exchange (social, economic, political or cultural) between its members.

Butler devoted some consideration to the actual means by which diasporas have become dispersed. She suggested there are six types. The first is *captivity*, which includes enslavement and would relate, for example, to the forced migration of black people from Africa to the American South. The second is *state-eradication exile* and refers to state-sponsored genocide, where there have been attempts to exterminate whole tribes, cultures or communities. The third is *forced and voluntary exile*, which differs from the previous form of forced exile in that the homeland still continues to exist, thus allowing for the possibility of return. The eviction of Highlanders from Scotland during the Clearances would be an appropriate example of this form of dispersal. Butler's fourth category is simply *emigration* and refers to individual initiatives, often involving a move to find employment. This is distinguished from *migration*, which is a more general term, referring to more widespread migratory patterns and practices. Such migration would involve whole groups or tribes rather than individuals. Finally, Butler referred to the *imperial diaspora*, which originated as a mode of conquest, in which a colonial power sent its nationals to administer and control its conquests. Here, relocation was a direct result of formal state policies. Van Hear concurred broadly with Butler that there are a significant number of components in the making of diasporas. However they are initially created, they develop through accretion, as a result of steady, gradual migration over years or generations.

In more recent years, the expansion of diasporas may simply be a by-product of globalisation and the growth of globally powerful cities, which act as magnets to migration. Thus:

> members of diasporas are almost by definition more mobile than people who are rooted in national spaces. They are certainly more prone to international mobility and change their places of work and

residence more frequently. In previous eras, and still in some places, their cosmopolitanism was a distinct disadvantage and a source of suspicion. In the age of globalisation, their language skills, familiarity with other cultures and contacts in other countries make many members of diasporas highly competitive in the international labour, service and capital markets. (Cohen, 1997, pp.168–9)

Diasporas therefore act as a bridge between the *particularism* involved in reaching for identity or a grounding in a place — and the *universalism* implicit in globalisation. They cut across nation states, being communities not necessarily of place but of interest, shared opinions and beliefs, tastes, ethnicities and religion, as well as cuisine, lifestyles, fashion and music.

Two of the integral components of diasporic analysis are the relationships between diasporas and their host countries, and between diasporas and their homelands. In relation to the former, Berry (1992, pp. 69–85) has identified five types of relationships that may exist. These include *acculturation*, where relations exist between the diaspora and the host society but there is a strong maintenance of separate cultural identity; *assimilation*, where the diaspora is subsumed within the host society; *segregation*, where relations with the host society are fairly minimal; *marginalisation*, where the diaspora loses its own identity but fails to become part of the larger society; and *integration*, where participation in the larger society occurs while the diaspora also succeeds in maintaining its self-identity. The position of the Scottish diaspora within the United States may, as will be seen later, be described as one of integration.

Even where diasporas fail to become integrated, they change over time and are affected by the larger society in which they are located. Stuart Hall (1990) wrote of how cultural identities may be historical but nevertheless undergo constant transformation, being subject to the continuous play of history, culture and power. Diaspora identities therefore are those that are 'constantly producing themselves anew through transformation and difference' (Hall, 1990, p. 237). I will explore later in this book how the Scottish diaspora in the US has itself changed, inventing its own traditions which are related to but different from the traditions of the Scottish homeland. Tartan Day, which is discussed in Chapter 4, is perhaps a prime example of this.

The relationships between diasporas and their homelands may vary considerably in their intensity. For some expatriates the relationship may merely be a sentimental one, particularly if members of the diaspora have opted for permanent settlement elsewhere. Indeed, Brah (1996) argued that the concept of diaspora may not necessarily involve a homing desire at all and cultural identification may be the most significant aspect. For others, however, the relationship with the homeland may be a highly political one, with members of the diaspora communities actively seeking to influence events within their homeland (Shain and Barth, 2003, pp. 449–79). Many nationalist movements, for example, may look to their diasporas for support.

Butler (2001, p. 205) made the point that the views of the homeland held by members of the diaspora change significantly over time and may begin to diverge markedly from reality. Thus 'diasporan representations of the homeland are part of the project of constructing diasporan identity, rather than homeland actuality'. This echoes the work of Handlin (1973), who suggested that the upheavals and hardships involved in migration cause many migrants to look back fondly to their previous life, even though they may know that it is a past which is already changing and to which they can no longer belong. This divergence means that those still living in the homeland are often slightly bemused by the views of those in the diaspora. Some of this bemusement is explored in this book in relation to the Scottish diaspora. Scots living in Scotland are sometimes puzzled by American Scots who appear to take a greater interest in Scotland and its history and culture than they do themselves, becoming in a sense, 'more Scottish than the Scots'.

This rather uncritical and nostalgic gaze on the homeland sometimes leads to a rather obsessive fascination with it. Radhakrishnan (2003, p. 128) suggested that this may be unhealthy:

> The diasporan hunger for knowledge about and intimacy with the home country should not turn into a transhistorical and mystic quest for origins. It is precisely this obsession with the sacredness of one's origins that leads people to disrespect the history of other people and to exalt one's own. Feeling deracinated in the diaspora can be painful, but the politics of origins cannot be the remedy.

Some countries with large diasporas, however, have come to view them as important resources and sources of influence. Some diasporas may participate in the affairs of the homeland and there may be a significant flow of political and policy influences in both directions. For example, Pires-Hester (1999, pp. 485–503) wrote about the relationship between the government and inhabitants of the Cape Verde islands and their descendants in the United States. There was an apparent shift from simply ignoring the Cape Verdean diaspora to seeing it as an important resource for levering investment and influence.

Closer to home, the then president of the Republic of Ireland, Mary Robinson, in an address to the Houses of the Oireachtas in 1995 argued strongly that Ireland should cherish its diaspora. She spoke of the huge numbers of Irish people living across the world, but particularly in America, and suggested that Ireland needed to respond to desires for dialogue, interaction and practical links involving trade and business. In some respects this proved to be a double-edged sword, with the Irish diaspora becoming closely involved with Ireland's internal policies and politics, most notably in fundraising activities. Many of these funds were raised specifically for the support of the Irish Republican Army and its activities in Ulster.

Such political involvement has not been a characteristic of the Scottish diaspora, which, over many years, has tended to have a more historical or even sentimental focus. So what is the Scottish diaspora like? How does it fit into the diasporic models described here?

The Scottish diaspora

It is important, first, to distinguish between different members of the diaspora. There are substantial numbers of individuals in the USA (and elsewhere) who were born and brought up in Scotland and have migrated as adults, often for employment reasons. While such individuals clearly form a part of the diaspora, their identity is essentially a Scottish one and they would not normally see themselves as 'American Scots'. The bulk of the Scottish diaspora in the USA comprises descendants of original settlers who are Scottish through ancestry, and it is essentially they who form the six million who self-identify in the various censuses and surveys. The diaspora is not therefore homogeneous. The research reported in this book covers both groups, although the majority of those interviewed were descendants and thus American born.

No matter whether emigration from Scotland was recent or in an ancestral past, it may perhaps be explained in three main ways, using Butler's (2001) categorisation.

First, a significant proportion of Scottish emigration was 'forced and voluntary exile', where Scots left their homeland for economic or political reasons. Perhaps the most significant event or series of events relate to the Highland Clearances, where thousands of Highlanders were forcibly removed from their crofts and smallholdings by landowners in the eighteenth and nineteenth centuries. Additionally, some left of their own accord, either because they feared forced clearance or because it was becoming increasingly difficult to farm relatively poor land. The Clearances have been well documented (Devine, 1994; Richards, 1999, 2000) and hold a significant place in Scottish popular history. Perhaps because many present-day American Scots owe their origins to the Clearances, they are similarly regarded in the United States, although sometimes linked to a 'romanticised, sentimentalised *Brigadoon* type of picture of Highland society' (Shepperson, 1981, pp. 229–52). Other examples of forced exile from Scotland relate to political events such as the conflicts involving the Covenanters in the seventeenth century, or the Jacobite risings of 1715, 1719 and 1745 (Pittock, 1998), after which defeated Jacobites fled or were expelled to the colonies. Flora MacDonald, who emigrated to North Carolina following her involvement in the escape of Bonnie Prince Charlie after Culloden, is a prime example.

The second explanation for Scottish emigration relates simply to individual initiative and there are large numbers of Scots who emigrated for economic reasons, often establishing significant business enterprises in the countries to which they migrated. American examples include Andrew Carnegie from Dunfermline, who made his fortune in the steel industry before becoming a leading benefactor; Alexander Graham Bell from Edinburgh, the inventor of the telephone and founder of the Bell Telephone Company; David Dunbar Buick from Arbroath, who established the Buick Motor Company; and Allan Pinkerton from Glasgow, who founded the private detective agency which bears his name. In other fields, famous Scottish emigrants include Mary Garden from Aberdeen, the opera singer, and John Muir from Dunbar, who established the American conservation movement and the country's first national parks. Other significant examples elsewhere in the world include William Jardine and James Matheson from Sutherland, who established the Jardine Matheson company, responsible for the economic development of Hong Kong; and George Stephen from Dufftown in Banffshire, who was responsible for the construction of the Canadian Pacific Railroad.

Finally, it is also the case that some Scots emigrants would be classified as part of an 'imperial diaspora', helping to administer the British Empire, and forming a disproportionately large part of the British army over the years (Fry, 2002).

Because of the different reasons behind Scottish emigration, Vance (2005, pp. 156–79) suggested that Scots might not legitimately be considered a diaspora, as the term has connotations of victimhood and hence forced migration. However, I would argue that the term has been interpreted in a range of different ways within diaspora studies (as acknowledged by Vance himself) and its use in this book is therefore legitimate.

Certainly a range of authors recognise the different ways in which diasporas form, not all of which are related to victimhood. Cohen (1997) divided diasporas into five categories. Like Butler, he identified those who were forced into exile as a key part of the diaspora — what he referred to as a 'victim/refugee' diaspora. Those who migrated on their own initiative are a 'trade/business/professional' diaspora, and he also recognised the 'imperial/colonial' diaspora. His additional categories are a 'labour' diaspora, which includes people who migrate as indentured labour or as guest workers, but this category may not be applicable to Scots. His fifth category is a 'cultural' or 'postmodern' diaspora, which differs from the others in that cultural ideas may be exported, not solely through physical migration but also by means of the airwaves. Thus ideas, literature and music, for example, may be exported from Scotland and raise the profile of the homeland.

It is already clear that the Scottish diaspora is an extensive one. What kind of relationship currently exists between it and the homeland? Is it one of sentiment and nostalgia, as researchers on diasporas suggest is often the case? How has the Scottish diaspora itself changed over time? And is there any sense of a desire for a return home, as is often the case within diasporas?

MacGregor (1980, p. v), writing as an American Scot himself, suggested that there are, in fact, three Scotlands which he distinguished as:

(1) the never-never land of *Brigadoon*, where kilted Rockettes dance
in the moonlight on heather hills, and men, having greeted the dawn
with a quaich of Scotch, sally forth to shoot a deer or two for breakfast;
(2) the Scottish Homeland, an area of just over thirty thousand square
miles inhabited by five or six million people on the northern part of the
island we call Britain; and (3) the Scottish Diaspora, consisting of the
vast millions of people of Scottish birth or ancestry dispersed throughout the world (in the United States alone an estimated five times as
many as in the Homeland) who look to the Homeland with that deep
affection and occasional exasperation that people never bestow on
anyone but their mother.

Although the *Brigadoon* version of Scotland may still have some currency,
it is becoming harder to take it seriously, even in the diasporic context.
As is evident later in this book, the Scottish diaspora is becoming increasingly better informed about modern Scotland, thanks to the internet and
to cheap transatlantic air travel. The key relationship is therefore between
the second and third of MacGregor's Scotlands — between modern-day
Scotland and its diaspora. This is explored in more detail in Chapter 6.

The relationship between diaspora and homeland is not an easy one.
Some writers, for example, have sought to explore in great — and often
sympathetic — detail the confused feelings which many overseas Scots
have towards their identity. Some of the most successful have been
writers of fiction. The Canadian Scot, Hugh MacLennan, for example,
in *Scotchman's Return* published in 1960, recounted the experiences of a
fourth-generation Canadian as he travelled round Scotland. He recalled
his father, who had a strong sense of his own identity:

> It mattered nothing that he was a third-generation Canadian who had
> never seen the Highlands before he visited them on leave in the First
> World War. He never needed to go there to understand whence he
> came from or who he was.

At the end, however, he returned 'home', which turned out to be in Canada,
asking in the process:

> Am I wrong, or is it true that it is only now, after so many years of not
> knowing who we were or wanted to be, that we Canadians of Scotch
> descent are truly at home in the northern half of North America?
> (MacLennan, 1960, p.12)

Another Canadian writer who has explored this theme is Alistair MacLeod. His best-selling novel *No Great Mischief* recounted the story of a Scottish-Canadian family over several generations, recalling at intervals their Gaelic heritage and the ties that bound them together as a family, as well as to the Scottish homeland. At one point, the narrator's sister visits Scotland, where she meets an old woman gathering shellfish at low tide:

> And then, she said, she met the woman face to face, and they looked into each other's eyes.
>
> 'You are from here,' said the woman.
>
> 'No', said my sister, 'I'm from Canada.'
>
> 'That may be', said the woman. 'But you are really from here. You have just been away for a while'. (MacLeod, 2001, p. 147)

On accompanying the woman to her cottage, the narrator's sister is able to speak in Gaelic to the woman's husband, having maintained a knowledge of the language over several generations in Canada.

Both authors capture the sometimes uncomfortable relationship between the diasporic Scot and the homeland — an uncertainty as to whether he or she still belongs there, yet accompanied by a remarkably strong sense of affinity for the country and its people.

Researching the American Scots

The inclusion of questions on ancestry in the American Census demonstrated clearly that this is an important issue for large numbers of Americans, who have a continuing identification with their heritage. There is a strong desire to be 'from somewhere'.

As far as the Scots are concerned, the continuing strength of the Scottish connection coincides with important changes within Scotland itself. In 1999, the establishment of a devolved Scottish Parliament in Edinburgh gave Scotland the opportunity to administer and legislate in a number of areas for the first time since the Union of the Scottish and English Parliaments in 1707. Successive Scottish administrations since 1999 have recognised the importance of engaging with the Scottish diaspora, perhaps taking their cue from Ireland's success in this regard. In 2009, Scotland hosted a national Homecoming event, timed to coincide with the tercentenary of the birth of Robert Burns, to which members of the Scottish diaspora were invited. It has therefore been a particularly appropriate time to undertake research within the Scottish diaspora to explore the ongoing strength of the connection with the Scottish 'homeland'.

Chapter 2 includes data from the 2000 US Census (the most recent from which statistics are available at the time of writing). It showed that the main areas of America where significant numbers of people claim Scottish ancestry are New England and the north west of the country. There are, additionally, areas of America, such as North Carolina, where there has been a significant history of Scottish immigration and where Scottish traditions are still extant. It was decided to focus on the north east and the north west of the United States and the research reported in this book results from two periods of study undertaken, in New York and in Colorado.

Within these chosen study areas there are a number of Scottish organisations. These include St Andrew societies in both New York and Colorado; bodies responsible for organising and/or participating in Highland Games, Tartan Day and a range of social events; several Scottish Country and Highland dancing societies; several pipe bands; branches of An Comunn Gàidhealach, the organisation responsible for promoting the Gaelic language; and Scottish football supporters organisations. There are also significant numbers of individuals who are involved in business in both the United States and Scotland. These various organisations and individuals provided a number of points of initial contact and they were then able to suggest further contacts.

Much of the initial contact was made by email, sometimes followed up by telephone. Individuals were generally very welcoming and delighted to participate in the research. The secretary of the St Andrew Society of Colorado, for example, suggested that I write a short piece for the next society newsletter, explaining the research and asking for those willing to be interviewed to contact me; the publication of the article in the news-letter led to several further contacts being made. When I was in both Colorado and in New York, I was able to attend a number of social events, including weekly country dance classes, a ceilidh, a St Andrew's Night Dinner, Tartan Day events including the New York parade, and a soccer match. All of these occasions provided me with further contacts.

In Colorado, a total of twenty-one separate interviews were achieved, but in five cases they involved couples who chose to be interviewed together and, in one instance, the teenage son of the family also participated. Thus, a total of twenty-seven individuals participated in the interviewing process. In addition, social contact with a large number of other individuals helped to provide valuable contextual information.

In New York a total of fifteen interviews were conducted, involving eighteen people. Two further interviews were conducted in Scotland, involving individuals with interests in the Scottish-American diaspora.

A summary list of the interviews is contained in the Appendix. Each interview is allocated a reference number and these numbers are used to identify quotations in the text. Interviews that took place in Colorado are prefixed with a letter 'C', those in New York with an 'N' and those in Scotland with an 'S'. Within quotations, questions or comments by the interviewer (myself) are indicated by the use of the letter 'I'. Respondents are indicated by 'R'. Where more than one person was interviewed, they are referred to as 'R1', 'R2' etc.

The interviews themselves were semi-structured and explored a number of areas, as follows:

- basic data on the individual interviewee, including place of birth, age, marital status, household or family structure, and occupation;
- family history, including information on immigration — by the interviewee or their ancestors — reasons for immigration, the area of Scotland where the family had originated and the existence of any previous connections with America;
- involvement with Scottish organisations or related activities, such as dancing or Gaelic learning;
- current links with Scotland, including visits 'back home', the nature of these visits, the places visited and any links with Scotland still extant;
- issues of identity, including the meaning of 'Scottishness', the importance of the Scottish identity, exploration of genealogy, and the profile of Scots within America;
- the growing significance of events such as Tartan Day;
- knowledge of Scotland today, including awareness of constitutional change and the Scottish Parliament, and the ways in which individuals kept 'in touch' with Scottish affairs, usually through use of the internet;

- future intentions — which might include a possible return to Scotland at some point or, if the interviewee intended to remain in America, the future pattern of contact with their Scottish 'heritage'.

Although I sought to retain the same broad format for all interviews, the conversations sometimes ranged widely and the interviews were kept as informal as possible, in order to encourage respondents to talk. The interviews were held in a wide range of locations, including individual homes, in offices, or in other public or semi-public places, including dance studios, cafés, a hotel and even in the street.

There are obvious dangers in using quotations from interviews as part of our discussion, as interviewees' experiences may not necessarily be representative of the diaspora as a whole and may lapse into anecdote. This 'anecdotalism' is a recognised problem with qualitative research. In fact, analysis suggests that, while individual experiences may have varied, there was often broad agreement on attitudes to Scotland and to ongoing links with the homeland. There is therefore no reason to think that the quotations used were unrepresentative. The analysis of the transcribed interviews followed broadly the interview structure described above and the results of the interviews are described in subsequent chapters.

A plan of the book

This is not really a history book — although there is a fair bit of history in it. It is rooted more in sociological analyses of identity, nationality and belonging. It is similar in its approach to Reginald Byron's (1999) important study of Irish America. Noting that much of what had previously been written on the Irish in America was historical, Byron took inspiration from American sociologists Herbert Gans, Richard Alba, Stanley Lieberson and Mary Waters and, through a mix of interviews and participant observation, constructed a unique portrait of the Irish-American community primarily in Albany, New York. His work is a fascinating mix of personal histories and present-day experiences.

This book seeks to do likewise for the Scots. It focuses specifically on the United States, while recognising that there is a large Scottish community elsewhere in North America. And in focusing on the Scots, it does not deal with the Scots-Irish. This group — also very large in the US — comprises emigrants from Northern Ireland, who had previously emigrated from

Scotland; in moving to America, they had therefore undertaken a complicated 'double migration'. They have already been described in some detail elsewhere by other writers (for example, Leyburn, 1989; Webb, 2004).

The plan of the book is as follows. After discussion of the concepts and interpretations of 'diaspora' in the Introduction and their applicability to the Scottish diaspora, Chapter 1 examines the growing interest in genealogy, in 'roots' and in identity and ethnicity within America. Initially, such interest was more common within the black communities but white people are also increasingly searching their ancestries and there is a growing 'white ethnic' movement. At one time, hyphenated identities within America were seen as being less important than the creation of a single American identity through the common 'melting pot'. But such hyphenated identities are now a key part of American society, and while these identities may sometimes be dismissed as merely symbolic, nevertheless for the individuals concerned they are of major personal significance.

Chapter 2 explores in some detail the Scottish-American communities which have developed. The Scots have become very scattered across the continent and this chapter describes aspects of the history of Scottish settlement, from initial concentrations in areas such as the Carolinas to the movement westwards. Information from the US censuses provides more detailed information on the various Scottish communities within the country. The development of these communities is illustrated with reference to the individual family histories of those interviewed as part of the research, including family migration and ongoing present links with Scotland.

Chapter 3 explores the continuing significance of Scottish-American organisations. Members of the diaspora have a reputation for establishing Scottish societies, in whatever country they live and the internet reveals a huge range of Scottish organisations across the globe. The chapter explores the extent and nature of the involvement of American Scots with such organisations, and the size and relative health of the organisations concerned.

One of the most important expressions of identity for American Scots is the annual Tartan Day parade and its related celebrations, and these parades have come to occupy a significant place in the calendar. Chapter 4 explores the impact of Tartan Day and its associated events, informed by the New York City research, conducted at the time of Tartan Day in April 2007.

The next three chapters all focus in different ways on the relationship between the diaspora and the homeland, and the ways in which this may be changing. Chapter 5 deals with the markers of national identity, which are sometimes rather unclear — relating as they do to birthplace, ancestry, place of residence, upbringing and education, or simply to commitment to place. American Scots tend to assert their 'Scottishness' through their ancestral links and this chapter explores these issues of 'Scottishness' and Scottish identity and how American Scots seek to maintain this.

Chapters 6 and 7 reflect the considerable changes that have taken place in Scotland itself in recent years, most notably through political devolution and the establishment of the Scottish Parliament. Chapter 6 explores the extent to which American Scots are aware of how modern Scotland has developed and their continuing relationship with the country. Chapter 7 explores the relationship between Scotland and its diaspora from the Scottish 'end'. It describes the Scottish government's initiatives to encourage reverse migration and to tempt emigrants back to Scotland. It also describes various 'homecoming' events including the major national Homecoming event held during 2009.

Finally, *American Scots* concludes in Chapter 8 by reflecting on the growing importance of heritage and 'roots' to Americans, the growth in hyphenated identities, and the long-term relationship between Scotland as 'home' and the Scottish diaspora.

Chapter 1

Hyphenated identities in America

America is an obvious country in which to study diasporas, because of the large number of immigrant groups which have located there. After the founding of the independent United States in 1776, many of these groups began to cast off their immigrant identities to become 'Americans', encouraged by a government that saw the importance of forging a single nation out of a quite disparate collection of citizens.

In the early twentieth century, this notion came to be referred to as the 'melting pot', whereby immigrants of various nationalities and origins were 'melted' or 'smelted' into American citizens. In the latter part of the century, however, the melting pot appeared to work less successfully and many groups began not only to seek to retain their identities and ethnicities but also actively to explore their heritage and ancestries. For black people, the publication of Alex Haley's best-selling novel *Roots* in 1976 encouraged a heightened awareness of their heritage but the book impacted also on white communities.

This chapter therefore explores the concept of white ethnicity and the continuing search for an 'ethnic past'. It also considers the position of the Scots in America. Are they simply an assimilated grouping within the 'WASP'[1] population, or are they too a clearly identifiable expatriate minority increasingly seeking to explore their ethnic heritage?

The American melting pot

The concept of the melting pot has frequently been employed to describe the way in which millions of immigrants of diverse origins have successfully come together to create the country that is now the United States of America. It is not completely clear where the term originated, although

1 'White, Anglo-Saxon and Protestant.'

Schlesinger (1991) suggested that the similar term 'smelting pot' was used during the nineteenth century by the American writer Ralph Waldo Emerson.

The origin of the more usual phrase is generally attributed to Israel Zangwill, an English writer of Russian-Jewish origin, whose play entitled *The Melting Pot* opened in Washington in 1908. The play tells the story of a Russian-Jewish composer, whose aim is to write a symphony expressing the vast interweaving of races and groupings in the United States. It was a huge success, with President Theodore Roosevelt attending its opening and praising its sentiments.

This interweaving was traditionally seen as extremely important within the US, as former ethnic and cultural ties were loosened and immigrants became assimilated into a wider American society. This process of assimilation was essentially one of boundary reduction, as individuals blended into a single socio-cultural group. Yinger (1981, pp. 249–64) suggested that the extent of assimilation was a function of the strength of four interdependent sub-processes, and he identified these as: amalgamation (biological), identification (psychological), acculturation (cultural) and integration (structural).

Amalgamation tended to occur late in the assimilation process, for example as a result of intermarriage, usually after other sub-processes such as acculturation had occurred. The psychological process of *identification* occurred when individuals from separate groups came to think of themselves as belonging to the same society — a new society, blended from their societies of origin. *Acculturation* was the process of change towards greater cultural similarity, brought about by contact between two or more groups. It was a process more likely to affect smaller groups who may have had to concede more as they became part of a new cultural entity. Finally, *integration* occurred when different groups entered into sets of shared interactions, for example as part of a single workforce. These four processes operated in complex ways and the speed of the overall assimilation was in turn dependent upon a range of variables.

Yinger identified these variables as including: the comparative size of the groups involved, the nature and recency of the contacts between groups, the geographical concentration or dispersal of the various groups, degrees of cultural or racial similarity or dissimilarity, the legal and political status of the groups, and levels of prejudice and discrimination. The under-lying implication of the operation of these variables was that the closer an immigrant group was — racially or culturally — to the Anglo-Saxon core group (or WASPs), the easier and speedier was the process of assimilation.

Gordon (1964) distinguished between what he termed 'Anglo-conformity', the process by which immigrants renounced their ancestral culture in favour of the behaviour and values of the WASP core group, and the melting pot idea, whereby there was a biological merger of the Anglo-Saxon peoples with other immigrant groups and a blending of their respective cultures into a new indigenous 'American' culture. Gordon suggested that the ethnic identity of individual Americans could be portrayed as a series of concentric circles. At the centre was the individual, whose first circle represented his or her national origin, be it English, German, Irish etc. Subsequent circles represented religion (Roman Catholic, Protestant, Jewish etc.) and race, while the outermost circle, surrounding everything else, was 'nationality' which was, of course, American.

He acknowledged that, for many immigrants to America, rates of assimilation would vary markedly, depending on the link between ethnic group and social structure. Thus, within any ethnic group, there develops a network of organisations and social relationships which allow, in dif-ferent ways, members of that group to remain within the confines of that group. In the case of religious and family relationships — and, to a certain extent, relationships linked to recreational activities — he suggested that these are 'ethnically enclosed' and different ethnic groups do not mix much. Relationships linked to political and economic activities, however, are much more ethnically mixed. Thus the speed of assimilation must be affected by the extent of involvement in, for example, the labour market. This would correspond to Yinger's (1981) definition of integration as occurring when immigrants become involved in a single workforce.

Politicians have viewed assimilation as important in creating a single American society, reflecting the national motto of *E Pluribus Unum*. During the First World War, for example, there were some concerns that European immigrants might be unwilling to fight for America, preferring instead to express their sympathies with their homelands. There was considerable anti-German hysteria after America entered the war, with concerted attempts to erase German cultural heritage from within the country

(Brown, 2005, pp. 527–32). Thus, there were fears that the 'melting pot was failing to melt' (Jones, 1974, p. 4) and President Woodrow Wilson expressed his concern about the issue, arguing strongly against 'hyphenated Americans' like Irish Americans or Italian Americans. He stated bluntly in 1915 that: 'America does not consist of groups. A man who thinks of himself as belonging to a particular national group in America has not yet become an American' (quoted in Gordon, 1964, p. 101).

Theodore Roosevelt similarly argued that people had to make a choice. He suggested that people could not: 'hoist two flags on the same pole without one underneath; and the hyphenate would always tend to fly the Stars and Stripes beneath a foreign flag' (Jones, 1974, p. 5).

For Roosevelt, the issue was of major concern. He argued that a 'hyphenated' American was not a true American and to permit individuals to remain as German Americans, Irish Americans or any other combination would lead to a 'tangle of squabbling nationalities', eventually bringing the country to ruin (Gjerde, 1998).

In the event, the politicians did not need to worry and the American war effort was not compromised. But it was certainly true that, for many immigrants at that time, consciousness of now being American was not well developed. It grew once they had settled in the USA, if only as a means of working out relations with each other and Americans generally.

As a country, therefore, America was never at ease with multi-culturalism. Indeed, it is an excellent example of how the potential divisiveness of a multi-ethnic society has been avoided through the forging of a brand-new — American — identity. The major vehicle for this process was the education system, where people were 'Americanised' and taught to follow the American Dream. Carlson (1987) argued that the process had been pernicious and that the pursuit of homogeneity had had a negative impact on those who found it hardest to assimilate, particularly black people. Weed (1973) agreed, suggesting that there was a 'pervasive blindness' to American cultural diversity, such that the persistent reality of America's cultural pluralism was made to seem divisive.

Stratton and Ang (1998, p. 137) demonstrated the tensions inherent within this pursuit of a unified national identity in the face of a social reality that was so clearly multi-cultural. 'Multi-culturalism', they argued, 'is alien to the way American national identity is imagined' and they pointed to significant differences of approach between the two immigrant nations of America and Australia. In the latter case, there was a positive encouragement of multi-culturalism, whereas in America migrants were left to find a place in the new society and become absorbed. They suggested that some immigrant groups tried to resolve the tension through having different sets of identities. Being a good American tended to be seen in terms of loyalty and patriotism and not necessarily in cultural terms. Cultural distinctiveness could therefore be pursued outside the general paradigm of a 'universal all-American-ness'. The hyphenated American, they argued, was a coupling of two separate identities, one culturally particular, the other presumed to be ideologically universal.

The pursuit of a homogeneous America was encouraged following the First World War through immigration legislation. The Immigration Act of 1924 was the first permanent limitation on immigration — a tightening up of the Emergency Quota Act of 1921 — and it confirmed a 'national origins quota system'. Essentially, the quota of immigrants allowed from any single country was to reflect the proportions of that nationality already resident within the USA. Additionally, no 'alien ineligible to become a citizen' was to be admitted, a provision aimed principally at the Japanese. A consular control system of immigration was established, involving the issuing of immigrant visas at US consular offices abroad. Steinberg (1981) argued that this represented a major watershed in American ethnic history, as it resulted in a generation that grew up in the interwar period which had no direct ancestral memories relating back to their countries of family origin.

As a result, researchers such as Child (1943) could suggest that the second generation of immigrant groups were essentially integrated within American society, while Steinberg (1981) believed that immigrants were unlikely to survive as distinct cultural or ethnic identities:

> Unlike some plural societies that were formed out of a fusion of neighbouring territories with distinct ethnic populations, pluralism in the United States evolved out of the displacement of masses of individuals. As transplanted minorities, ripped from their cultural moorings and lacking a territorial base, cultural survival would have been problematic under the best of circumstances. (Steinberg, 1981, p. 43)

The 1924 legislation had provided generous quotas for immigrants from Britain but, in practice, the quotas were not filled, a result in part of the

Great Depression just a few years later and the reduced employment opportunities available in the United States. Where emigration from Britain to North America did occur, it seems to have been directed more towards Canada during this period (Van Vugt, 1999).

Certainly, by the 1970s, Dinnerstein and Reimers (1975) believed that the USA was on the threshold of the disappearance of the European ethnic minorities. They argued that the longer that groups lived in the USA, the more they relinquished their Old World cultures and languages, and the more that immigrant organisations lost both members and vitality as the old immigrant neighbourhoods decayed. Indeed, Stein and Hill (1977) argued that the Americanisation of immigrants was the whole point. People came to the United States because of the 'American Dream', not for a dream of cultural pluralism. Thus the melting pot was the compelling image and metaphor of the Dream.

Much of this assimilationist literature examined the role of the melting pot, with perhaps an underlying assumption that, ultimately, full integration would happen and immigrants would become assimilated into American ways and customs. In point of fact, these ways and customs tended to be historically Anglo-Saxon or WASP in nature and so the process was, as Gordon (1964) suggested, one of 'Anglo-conformity'. In a later work, he argued that the assimilation process involved a number of major variables, including changes to the immigrant group's cultural patterns, intermarriage, the development of the same sense of 'peoplehood' as the host society, and the importance of the immigrant group not raising issues or demands that might result in conflict. In the USA, this, he believed, meant adapting to Anglo-Saxon norms:

> ... it is clear that in the assimilationist process, most of the 'melting' is to be done by the immigrants and their descendants, who are to melt into the dominant ethnic culture (white Protestant), rather than contribute to a new amalgam composed of equal or proportionate contributions from each group. Viewed from this standpoint, the invitation to assimilate is an invitation not to pool one's ethnic background into a common 'American culture' but, rather, to submerge its identity into that of another ethnic group. (Gordon, 1978, p.157)

Greeley (1974) therefore believed that the process of assimilation had created a fair degree of ambivalence among the immigrant population. On the one hand, there was a pride in the heritage of one's own group, but on the other a resentment in being trapped in that heritage. Those who were most successful in becoming American and who developed the great-est sense of patriotism were those who were proud of their uniqueness, yet simultaneously wanted to be like everyone else, only more so. In an earlier work, Greeley (1971) suggested that there were six steps in ethnic assimilation. There was a period of *cultural shock* on first arriving in the United States, followed by *emerging self-consciousness*, when leaders began to organise schools, churches and welfare groups. During the third stage, the immigrant group started to climb the social ladder and there was a gradual *assimilation of the élite*, who began to 'get on' in society, followed by a fourth stage of *militancy*, when the group began to exert influence politically, socially and economically. Having thus succeeded in entering American society, the fifth stage was one of *self-hatred*, as the group began to become critical of its past ethnic background. Finally, in the sixth stage, of *emerging adjustment*, another generation, more secure in itself, might become more comfortable about its background and ethnicity, while not necessarily becoming militantly aggressive about it. Greeley (1971) recog-nised that young people at the time he was writing were beginning to show a greater interest in their ethnic origins.

Immigrants with a WASP background, understandably, have found the whole process of assimilation easiest, but may be unwilling actu-ally to admit other immigrants into their social structures. Gordon (1964) suggested that there have been difficulties on both sides with some minority groups keen to retain their own clubs, organisations and communal institutions, while WASPs are sometimes reluctant to admit minority members. For second-generation groups, born and brought up within the USA, this apparent rejection may ultimately lead to a return to a minority ethnicity. Indeed, it has been suggested that some people only really became aware of their ethnicity and nationality after they arrived in America and encountered expatriate societies (Krickus, 1976). Immigrants, therefore, dealt with the upheaval of entering a new life by looking backwards, so that 'yesterday, by its distance, acquires a happy glow' (Handlin, 1973). Alternatively, for some immigrants, their ethnic awareness may have been heightened by the experience of being excluded from parts of mainstream American society.

This exclusion appears to have operated to a much greater extent in the lower socio-economic groups. For example, Japanese Americans tend not to belong to expatriate societies and quickly become integrated into American society (Montero, 1980). However, the process is accelerated as people move up the socio-economic ladder and move away from Japanese affiliations and traditions.

By the 1970s, therefore, the picture that emerges is of a country that has actively encouraged immigrant groups to become assimilated into a new — American — society, to be 'Americanised' as it were, and to leave behind previous ethnic identities. Yet the situation is not really that straightforward. No matter the speed of assimilation, America throughout the twentieth century has been a multi-cultural, ethnically diverse nation, yet has apparently been unwilling to embrace fully its diversity. Although the decline in immigration from the 1920s onwards may have hastened the decline of overt ethnicity, it could not prevent future generations from beginning to search for their roots.

'Beyond the melting pot'

Reference has been made above to the difficulties facing many immigrant groups in 'melting' into a dominant Anglo-Saxon culture within America. Even where assimilation was achieved, it was not necessarily without some sacrifice and a sense of loss, and so it became common for second-, third- and fourth-generation immigrants to attempt to rediscover something of their ethnic background. Thus: 'Children of parents who carried little ethnic baggage in their search for upward mobility deeply miss the expressive emotional satisfactions of some form of ethnic belonging' (De Vos, 1995, p. 30).

While the melting pot did occur in the sense that diverse immigrant groups acquired the same basic language and values, it may not have occurred in the sense that many people still seem to draw resources — symbolic, material or political — from ethnic identifications (Eriksen, 1993). There has therefore been a revival of the ethnic group within American society, not as some survival from the age of mass immigration but as a completely new social form (Glazer and Moynihan, 1963).

Glazer and Moynihan's landmark study showed that, despite assimilation, many individuals continued to have an awareness of their historical identity and to be members of a recognisable ethnic or national group.

In addition, they were often thought of by others as being members of such groups and had developed identifiable attributes which had served 'to mark them off by more than simply name and association, in the third generation and even beyond'. Ethnic groups, Glazer and Moynihan (1963) suggested, had developed rather like an extended family or tribe, aided by various types of immigrant social organisation. While it was true that the assimilation process had led to a decline in certain such organisations, others had been ingenious in remoulding and recreating themselves. Many American cities, such as New York where their study was based, are often perceived as rather anonymous places, and so the ethnic group could serve an important social function, helping people make friends and giving their social activities a structure. As a result, a substantial amount of New York city life was lived within 'ethnic bands'.

Not all hyphenated Americans would feel comfortable with their respective ethnic organisations. Glazer and Moynihan (1963) pointed to the Irish-American identity, often fostered by Irish organisations, which tended to portray the Irish as friendly, witty, generous, physically coura-geous and fond of a drink. Some people might feel that they had a need to live up to this image, although it was a very proletarian image and not one which necessarily reflected the experience of middle-class Irish Americans. Nor was it necessarily an accurate picture of 'homeland' Irish. Even today, when Irish Americans meet 'homeland' Irish, who have trav-elled to America for St Patrick's Day parades, the two groups are often uncertain what to make of each other (Dezell, 2002).

This is an issue that has resonance for research into Scottish Americans, of course, as there are often similar differences between the social attrib-utes of Scottish Americans and 'homeland' Scots. The introduction of Tartan Day in America in 1998 has served to highlight some of these differ-ences, as described in later chapters. Glazer and Moynihan (1963) did not actually discuss the position of Scottish Americans whom they included within the wider British grouping.

The continuing strength of ethnic distinctions highlighted by Glazer and Moynihan (1963) has prompted social scientists to rethink models of ethnicity which are rooted in assumptions about the inevitability of assimilation. New ideas about ethnicity have therefore stressed the fluid and dynamic nature of ethnic identification, resulting in a model:

that emphasises the socially 'constructed' aspects of ethnicity, that is, the ways in which ethnic boundaries, identities and cultures are nego- tiated, defined and produced through social interaction inside and outside ethnic communities. (Nagel, 1994, p. 1001)

Nagel (1994) showed that, increasingly, hyphenated Americans were *choosing* to retain their ethnicity, rather than being assimilated into an undifferentiated American society. Individuals might not necessarily join defined ethnic organisations, participate in events or socialise with others from the same background but they might still *feel* a sense of belonging to a particular ethnic group and declare themselves to be a member.

Waters (1990) found, in her research, in San Jose and Philadelphia, that individuals constructed their ethnic identification using knowledge of their own background and their ancestors. Clearly, people may have ancestors from a range of different backgrounds but individuals make choices, sifting through their family backgrounds before naming the ancestry of their choice. Such an ethnic identification should not be seen as being in any way anti-American. Waters noted that many young people were increasingly exploring their ethnic roots, while simultaneously being patriotic Americans. Being American was thus a primary identity, about which people rarely had to think. But being a hyphenated American was a way of differentiating oneself from other Americans and giving oneself a more individual identity.

Other writers have spoken of the value of ethnic groups in providing a form of support for individuals which American society as a whole cannot always provide. As people have become wealthier and upwardly mobile, many have moved from older, ethnically distinct neighbourhoods into suburban housing estates. Modern suburban living, however, may some- times be socially unsatisfactory and so ethnic organisations can help to provide the additional social networks and support, which give people a continuing sense of 'belonging'. Novak (1971) referred to the 'Saturday ethnics', meaning those who shop for ethnic food and participate in ethnic organisations only at weekends. There is also perhaps a wider and habitual rootlessness within American society, with people constantly 'on the move' across the country. Americans appear to have few roots (Hughey and Vidich, 1998, pp. 173–96) and those they do put down are often shallow and temporary. Ethnic organisations can help to counteract this, by providing opportunities for social support, which provide a basis for both personal identity and communal solidarity. Indeed, Novak (1971) saw ethnic groups as extremely important:

> Diversity of ethnic consciousness is exciting and valuable. It is so utterly refreshing to meet people in touch with their roots, secure in them even if long ago having transcended them. (Novak, 1971, p. 250)

The persistence of ethnic identification is not therefore dependent on factors such as class, education or income. Improved education appears not to have led to a diminished ethnic consciousness, nor has increased wealth. Indeed, contacts made through involvement with ethnic organisations may activate a new and positive appreciation of personal ethnic identity (Parenti, 1967, pp. 717–26).

That said, the continued strength of ethnic groups may sometimes be seen as indicative of a lack of faith by certain ethnic groups in an 'American' future. Stratton and Ang (1998) have argued that national unity is key and tolerance of diversity is a means of guaranteeing that unity. But tolerance may depend on the extent to which an ethnic community 'deviates' from an accepted American 'norm'. This implies that white ethnic groups are easier to tolerate than black ones and that race is central to the 'problematics of national identity'.

'Symbolic' white ethnicity

I have already established that, despite the processes of assimilation which have continued for many years and despite the encouragement given by politicians to the notion of the melting pot, ethnic identification has continued to be an important aspect of American society. Such an ethnic awareness might be expected where black people are concerned, not least because of their long experience of being excluded from many areas of society. Race is therefore a significant factor in ethnic identification. What is less clear, however, is why such ethnic identification continues to be important for white people and indeed why there has been an upsurge in interest in ethnic roots among various white communities.

One explanation (Nagel, 1994) related directly to the black experience. Thus, as desegregation and affirmative action programmes got under way in the 1960s and 1970s specifically to counteract historical disadvantage amongst black people, it led to a complementary awareness raising of white ethnicity. The result was a white anti-bussing movement and a backlash against affirmative action. Similar white backlashes have been experienced in relation to Native Americans whose ancient hunting and fishing rights have become the subject of legal protection. The publication of Alex Haley's book *Roots* in 1976 and the success of the subsequent television adaptation gave black people a heightened awareness of their ethnic heritage and many began searching for information on their ancestral past. But the book's publication coincided with the US bicentennial and a nationwide interest in the country's history and origins. Thus *Roots* also had an impact on the white communities who began similar searches for their heritage.

Ethnic identification may also be assisted in other ways. First, Congress passed the Ethnic Heritage Act in 1974, which supported the funding of initiatives that promoted the distinctive cultures and histories of the various ethnic groupings within the country. This was a recognition of cultural pluralism at the highest levels of government (Halter, 2000).

Second, cultural pluralism may have been assisted by the religious freedom enshrined within the United States constitution. Although the country has tended to encourage ethnic assimilation and frown on multiculturalism, nevertheless there has always been a system of denominational pluralism (Greeley, 1974). Because individual religions needed to be respected, there has been no established church, and religion and state are kept constitutionally separate. This means that, when immigration occurred, immigrant groups were free to retain their own systems of worship and establish churches to meet their needs. There is no doubt that these churches have helped to retain separate ethnic identities over the years.

The process of assimilation itself may also have played a part. Light (1985), for example, has argued that the growth of many ethnic organisations was due to assimilation of immigrants and not their exclusion. He suggested that Irish immigrants were drawn out of local neighbourhoods and helped to become involved in a wider social context. As they came into contact with others with an Irish background, they began to form Irish societies, but these had social and charitable aims and were not intended as any sort of backlash against assimilation itself.

I have already referred to the process of suburbanisation and how some people living in distant suburbs may feel isolated and socially dissatisfied.

Waters (1990) suggested that they may feel that they are somehow missing out on the 'ethnic experience' of being in an inner city neighbourhood, while many people may experience difficulties in dealing with an increasingly anonymous world. Hence:

> the difficulty many people feel in identifying with a large, heterogeneous, rapidly changing society. They seem surrounded by anomie, alienation and an unqualified *Gesellschaft*, with its emphasis on universality, rationality and instrumental values. An ethnic attachment, it is argued, helps one to preserve some sense of community …. (Yinger, 1981, p. 258)

Finally, the Second World War proved something of a watershed for European ethnics (Alba, 1985). Some, in fighting for the United States, had taken arms against their homeland. After the war, there was perhaps a realisation that they had become transformed from an immigrant group into an integral part of the labour force and there had been a demographic transition from immigrant to second generation. A continued ethnic identification could be seen as a reaction, in trying to keep certain memories and social interactions alive.

It is clear therefore that there has been a continuance of white ethnic identification and that there are a number of possible reasons for its persistence. What then are the characteristics of this white ethnicity? First, and perhaps most obviously, is its voluntary nature. Unlike black people who do not have a choice, white people can choose which ethnic group with which to associate. Thus ethnicity can be flexible and symbolic and voluntary for white middle-class Americans, but not so for black or Hispanic Americans. White ethnicity does not bring with it the social costs involved in being black.

That said, however, it is recognised that belonging to a white ethnic group can be important in countering racism. Novak (1971) argued that white people who are confident and comfortable about their own ethnic inheritance are less likely to have any concerns about black ethnic consciousness, or to see it as any kind of threat. Thus:

> the new ethnicity is the nation's best hope for confronting racial hatred.
> A Pole who knows he's a Pole, who is proud to be a Pole, who knows
> the social costs and possibilities of being a Polish worker in America,
> who knows where he stands in power, status and integrity — such a

> Pole can face a black militant, eye-to-eye. A Pole uncertain whether
> he is American or Polish, WASP or racist, worthy or despicable, feels
> emotions too confused for compromise, emotions most easily dis-
> charged as hate. (Novak, 1971, p. 250)

A second aspect of white ethnicity relates to its selectivity and choice. Many white Americans have very mixed ethnic backgrounds and so individuals could, legitimately, claim to belong to several different ethnic groups. But usually one particular group is selected and becomes the group recorded 'officially', for example, in the Census questions on ancestry. Greeley (1974) recalled a colleague with French, Dutch, Scots, Irish and Sioux Indian ancestry, but who claimed his ethnic identification as 'Irish'. It is not at all clear how individuals with mixed ethnic origins 'choose' their ethnicity, nor is it clear whether such a choice leads in turn to attitudes and behaviour thought to be appropriate to that choice. Some ethnic groups become 'popular' with a high rate of identification, often at the expense of identification with other ancestries (Waters, 1998). As a result, the Irish, being a 'popular' ancestry, are a larger group than might be expected, while the Scots are probably smaller.

Some people appear to 'shop' for ancestries that suit them:

> We might half seriously speak of 'dime-store ethnicity' as characteris-
> ing the predominant form of ethnicity in contemporary American life.
> Many attributes of a multitude of ethnic cultures are offered for con-
> sumption. One selects, tries, likes or dislikes, and returns for the same
> 'purchase' or an alternate. Ethnicity is assimilated into the syncretic,
> fluid nature of American culture in general (Stein and Hill, 1977, p. 22).

The issue of choice is nicely illustrated by Hollinger (1998), who referred to the work of Alex Haley himself, the author of *Roots*. Haley had an Irish ancestor, who had contracted a mixed-race marriage several generations previously. Had he therefore chosen to follow his father's genealogy rather than his mother's, he would probably have ended up in Ireland and not in Gambia.

Business has not been slow to appreciate the importance of ethnicity and it has been increasingly promoted through food, drink and advertising; Irish theme pubs are an obvious example (Halter, 2000). Such promotions may portray one ethnicity as being particularly desirable and may therefore influence individual ethnic choice.

Waters (1990) identified a number of possible factors that may influence such choices. These include knowledge about one's ancestors, one's surname, perhaps one's physical appearance (although this may be rather unreliable), and, interestingly, the subjective rankings which people have regarding different ethnic groups. Some groups, she suggested, are seen as having low status and — of relevance to this present study — she placed the Scots in this category, although the reasons for this are not made clear. She stated that the Scottish side of many people's ancestry was suppressed because of its low status and its popularity declined during the period from the 1920s to the 1970s.

However the choice is made, it is clear that individual's ethnic identification does not necessarily coincide with his or her origins, nor indeed with their 'ethnic culture' (Greeley, 1974). The inter-relationships between heritage, culture and identification are therefore extremely complex ones.

A third issue for white ethnics is the political one. White ethnic groups within America have often played an important role in maintaining a particular heritage, when that heritage was under threat in the European homeland. Many immigrant groups came from nations in Europe which were struggling to become states and the ethnic organisations that they founded in America became important in assisting nationalism at home (Portes and Rumbaut, 1990). Thus, the Germans who travelled to America in the nineteenth century emigrated from a part of Europe which did not become a German nation until the mid- to late-nineteenth century. The same would be true of the Italians.

Lithuanian Americans could speak their language in America at a time when their country and its language and culture was threatened by Russian expansion and the absorption of their nation into the Soviet Union. Indeed, the first Lithuanian-language newspaper was actually produced in the United States. After the First World War, the Polish Central Relief Committee within the US pressed for Polish liberation, while Czechs and Slovaks campaigned similarly for the establishment of their new nation in the wake of the collapse of the Austro-Hungarian Empire. After the Second World War, American Jews were hugely influential in the establishment of the state of Israel.

Interestingly, Portes and Rumbaut suggested that British Americans were relatively apolitical and, while retaining an interest in events at home, had no intention of 'revamping either the English or the American political system'. In their work, however, they equated 'British' with 'English'; one might speculate as to whether the same would be true for the Scottish or the Welsh Americans, who might possibly have supported nationalist movements in their home countries. Certainly, the Irish Americans retained an interest in supporting Irish Home Rule against the British government, some raising funds for the Irish Republican Army. The point was recognised by Nagel (1994) in her reference to the work of Trevor-Roper (1983) and the 'invention' of some Scottish traditions. As she pointed out, the fictive aspects of Scottish ethnicity do not necessarily lessen the reality of Scottish nationalism within the United Kingdom.

Despite the continued strength and importance of white ethnicity, one need not necessarily conclude that assimilation is somehow not working. White ethnicity has had periods of political importance elsewhere and there is also no doubt that certain ethnic groups have influenced the American political system by block voting. Politicians frequently refer to the Jewish or Irish vote. But in the main it is essentially a voluntary — or leisure-time — activity by third- or fourth-generation middle-class Americans and cannot be seen as some kind of threat to American society.

White ethnicity therefore can be seen as essentially 'symbolic' in Gans' (1979) phrase, characterised by a nostalgic allegiance to the culture of the immigrant generation or that of the 'old country', a love and pride in a tradition that can be felt, without having to be incorporated into everyday behaviour. People may even desire to return to some kind of imagined and rather sanitised past, conveniently cleansed of the complexities that accompanied them in the real past. People eventually realise, of course, that this 'myth of return' (Anwar, 1979) can probably not be achieved and so individual wishes are then displaced on to churches, schools and even the mass media, asking them to recreate a tradition or, rather, create a symbolic tradition. This symbolic ethnicity is new in that the social life associated with it takes place without ethnic clustering. Individuals are not therefore interested in recreating an ethnic neighbourhood but with finding ways of maintaining and expressing an identity. Gans (1979) suggested that, as ethnic neighbourhoods within America are dispersed, the homeland countries take on the role of substitute community, to satisfy people's identity needs. Interest in these old countries is usually historical and often focuses on those countries as they were at the time of ancestral departure.

Indeed, part of the lure of this real or imagined past may be precisely because it is no longer available:

> In a country long devoted to dulling the sense of the historical past and denying the continuity of experience from Europe to America … groups of people now seek to define themselves through a deliberate exclusion from the dominant native stock which, only yesterday, had been taking pains to exclude them. These ethnic groups now turn back — and as they nervously insist, 'with pride' — to look for fragments of a racial or national or religious identity that moves them to the extent that it is no longer available. Perhaps, also, *because* it is no longer available. (Howe, 1977, p. 18; emphasis in original)

Greeley (1971) identified four elements in this revival of interest in one's 'homeland'. These were:

- an increase in the 'high culture' of the various ethnic traditions. This involves explorations of literature, music and the other arts associated with the 'homeland';
- visits to the 'homeland' and in particular to the localities from which one's ancestors originally came;
- an increased use of ethnic names; and
- an increased interest in and use of original ethnic languages.

A similar list was compiled by Zelinsky (2001), suggesting how individuals expressed their ethnicity. Language, religion, food, music and dance, dress, social practices and even the built landscape (individuals' homes) were all examples of personal expressions of ethnic and cultural heritage. Ethnic festivals, ethnic 'villages' or city enclaves, literature, film and television were external representations.

Steinberg (1981) has pointed out the difficulties for ethnic groups in this process, in that the more they pursue their original culture, the less compatible this might be with American culture. There is therefore a dilemma of revivalism among groups who are in the process of assimilation. Ethnic identity, he believed, is also a distraction from issues of class, employment and wealth inequality and ethnic groups can become false havens from these wider and important questions. Similarly, Hollinger

(1995) pointed out that, as multi-culturalism has become more accepted within America, it has fostered a sensitivity to diversity such that the differences and divisions between groups are emphasised and disunity rather than ethnic harmony may be the result.

Nevertheless, symbolic ethnicity fulfils the 'particular American need to be "from somewhere"' (Waters, 1990, p. 150). It is something that is inherited through ancestry but is also a personal choice. It allows people to express their individuality without making them stand out as being exceptionally different from many other people. In other words, it is a solution 'to a dilemma that has deep roots in American culture'. This particular perspective was termed an 'ethnogenesis model' (Greeley, 1974) and presented specifically as an alternative to the idea of the melting pot and complete assimilation on the one hand, and cultural pluralism on the other. It may therefore be a useful complement to models of assimilation and acculturation, emphasising how American ethnic groups can be dynamic and flexible institutions for becoming part of American society.

How do the Scots fit in?

Within the general theme of assimilation, there is an underlying assumption that it has been much easier for those immigrants from a WASP background to blend or 'melt' into American society. Because America was once a British colony and the dominant language was English, there were fewer barriers of language, religion or culture placed in the way of immigrants from Britain and many writers have referred to the process of assimilation as being akin to 'Anglo-conformity'. But there is a tendency in much of the literature to use 'British' and 'English' interchangeably. Many American researchers (Glazer and Moynihan, 1963; Gordon, 1964), for example, appeared to assume a kind of Anglo-Saxon homogeneity and there was little recognition of the impact of assimilation on other national groups from the 'British Isles'. The Irish, it is true, were recognised as being significantly different — not least because they were predominantly Roman Catholic and, at one time, many would be Irish-speaking. But there is little consideration in the literature of the Scots, the Welsh or smaller groups like the Cornish or the Manx — in other words, the Celtic 'fringe'.

Even where writers did explore the position of the Scots, they were not always seen as being particularly distinctive from other British

immigrants. Berthoff (1953) described the importance of Scottish societies and Highland Games to immigrant Scots but concluded that 'British
Americans' assimilated well, because they had fewer economic, social
or language adjustments to make in comparison with other immigrant
groups. Yet many of the Scots immigrants, particularly in the South, were
Gaelic-speaking Highlanders who would have had to make substantial
adjustments, for complete assimilation to occur.

Indeed, many Highlanders were regarded as being quite different
to the WASP majority in America and were not necessarily regarded
even as 'white'. Newton (2001) argued that we are guilty of projecting
late twentieth-century attitudes about race backwards in assuming that
Highlanders were seen as white. In fact, 'whiteness' was a hotly contested
notion, with the granting of American citizenship in 1790 to 'free white
persons' being aimed specifically at people of English descent. Thus participation in American life became essentially grounded in racial terms and
Highlanders tended to be bracketed with the Irish and immigrants from
elsewhere in Europe as being 'non-white' (see Ignatiev, 1995).

Newton (2001, p. 225) continued:

> When commenting on the British forces that fought the Spanish
> in Georgia in 1742, James Oglethorpe wrote: 'The white people,
> Indians and the Highlanders all had their share in the slaughter.'
> This enumeration implies the perception of different racial groups,
> Highlanders not matching English people closely enough to share
> their distinction as 'white people'.

This view of Highlanders may have contributed to the perception of
Scottish ancestry as being of low status, as noted earlier. It may also have
led to a Celtic identity being seen as a significant ethnic 'other', reflecting
peripheral and marginal groupings around an English WASP core (Harvey
et al., 2002).

Indeed, Scots sometimes walked a very fine line, being careful not to be
seen as being too different from the WASP norm as to deter potential business customers, yet not being completely assimilated into the host society.
Many English people in America saw the Scots as a separate ethnic group
in any case and so this may have encouraged Scots to look to each other
for support and to develop their own distinctive social networks (Karras,
1992). Szasz (2000) noted how the Scots tried to resolve their identity

problem through a focus that, while 'British', was distinct from that of the English. This is not unlike the stance adopted by Welsh Americans, where the sharing of a common ethnic boundary, both with *and* against the English, was among the most important factor constitutive of Welshness (Jenkins, 1997). Thus in literature there was a focus on Scottish authors (such as Sir Walter Scott and Robert Burns), in music (the bagpipes), in costume (the kilt), in food (haggis, whisky and oatcakes) as well, of course, as the Presbyterian religion. Alba (1990) has confirmed that the Scots seem to be a group particularly sensitive to questions of ethnicity, with a greater interest than many other white groups.

The work of Neidert and Farley (1985) is relevant here, as an exploration into issues of status and achievement across a range of different ethnic groups. They took as their starting point a sample survey carried out in 1979 by the US Bureau of the Census. Those reporting Scottish ancestry represented the fifth largest group, after Germans, Irish, English and Afro Americans, and excluding those who did not report an ancestry. When educational attainment was measured, the Scots scored highly and, indeed, among third-generation men, Scots and Welsh, along with Russians and Asians, scored higher than the English. When occupational groupings were examined, Scots and Welsh, Russians and East Europeans were all working at significantly higher-status jobs than the English. Thus the Scots could be seen as relatively high status.

Indeed, Aspinwall (1984) drew attention to the education and technical skills possessed by many Scots and which could be realised in the US. Scots also had a strong work ethic and were seen as being sober and thrifty; they were 'thus committed to the realisation of an efficient moral social order'. Importantly, Aspinwall noted that, although Scots may have retained a strong affection for their homeland, they did not develop the intense nationalism which characterised some other immigrant groups. The fact that they mixed relatively well within American society allowed Charlotte Erickson (1972), analysing letters written by emigrants to their homeland, to describe the Scots as 'invisible immigrants'.

So, in terms of identity and how Scots may seek to position themselves within American society, the situation is a little unclear. Scots presumably benefit from being predominantly English-speaking and have been able to assimilate and be successful within America. On the other hand, they are able to emphasise their Celtic heritage sufficiently to create a distance between themselves and English immigrants. Scotland, like Ireland, may be viewed externally as a rather romantic country and there is evidence that it has become a more attractive and higher-status ethnic grouping than was once the case.

The number of Scots-born people in the United States has declined considerably since a peak of 350,000 in 1930. By 1970, the total had fallen to 170,000, yet this was precisely the time that there was a growing interest in white ethnic groups and 'Scottishness' appeared to become more popular. Many of these self-professed Scots were generations away from Scotland but they took over moribund organisations, and founded new ones, developed clan societies and established or re-established Highland Games. Berthoff (1982) has suggested that these 'new' Scots were more traditional than the old, and were not content solely to organise Burns Suppers or ceilidhs. They became immersed in cultural activities, studied Scottish literature and developed a whole range of sources of advice on genealogy, tartans and 'such fine points as the various ways in which to address a Highland chief' (Berthoff, 1982, p. 15). The closer ties with Scotland which these 'new' Scots have developed have had an impact in Scotland itself. Berthoff noted the way in which clan chiefs have gained a significance in America which they rarely possess at home, and the growth in clan gatherings and genealogical research into clan connections. The clan associations, suggested Berthoff, are a classic example of the symbolic ethnicity discussed earlier.

The symbols of Scottishness have increasingly been absorbed into the American mainstream. For example, for Irish Americans the St Patrick's Day parades constitute a 'memory site' *par excellence (Moss, 1995)*. But such celebrations are not limited solely to the Irish community. Once immigrants have settled and integrated into American society, their traditions and folkways enter local culture (Portes and Rumbaut, 1990). After a while, these traditions become institutionalised and are proudly presented as 'typical' of the local lore. St Patrick's Day parades, Chinese New Year celebrations, Mardi Gras carnivals and Mexican fiestas would all be examples of this process. Presumably, Tartan Day celebrations could now be added to the list.

Thus Scots may be regarded as thoroughly assimilated within American society, yet distinctly different; part of the American mainstream yet flamboyant and romantic; given to celebrating and dressing in distinctive ways, and yet for the most part being indistinguishable from other WASP Americans. Ethnicity for many Scottish Americans is clearly extremely complex but 'things Celtic have again become fashionable' (Ray, 2005a, p. 34).

Reflecting this 'fashion', there have now been a number of studies of the Scots in America. Some such as the research by Ray (2001a; 2005a), Hague (2002a; 2002b; 2006) and Basu (2007) is academic, while there is also work by individuals such as Herman (2001) and Hewitson (1993), which is aimed at a much wider audience. Some work such as the publications of D. A. Bruce (1996; 2000) and Thomson (1996) tend to be rather hagiographic. While very different, all these studies help to piece together a picture of the Scots within the USA.

Conclusion

I have sought to demonstrate in this chapter how immigrants to America initially went through a 'melting pot' process, by which their immigrant identities were essentially lost as they became assimilated into a wider American society. Since the 1960s, however, the descendants of those immigrants have shown an increasing interest in exploring their roots, adopting in the process 'hyphenated' and symbolic identities. The Scots have been no different to other groups in this regard.

I now move on to explore in more detail the background to Scottish immigration to America, illustrating the process through interviews carried out with a number of American Scots and their descendants.

Chapter 2

The Scottish communities in America

Background

There was comparatively little emigration from Scotland to North America before the late seventeenth century. Some political prisoners were exiled by Cromwell and a number of Covenanters[1] were sent to the American colonies. There were also emigrants to America who were fleeing religious persecution, resulting in attempts to found a Scottish Presbyterian colony in South Carolina in 1684 and a settlement of Scottish Quakers in New Jersey three years later (Harper, 2003).

Some Scottish entrepreneurs sought to develop trade links with the Americas, although these were not always successful. The English government's Navigation Acts attempted to prevent competing Scottish developments and both the English government and the English East India Company helped to undermine the 1695 scheme for an independent Scottish colony at Darien, in the isthmus of Panama. By 1707, however, the Treaty of Union between England and Scotland opened up the American colonies to Scottish trade, and Scotland (and Glasgow in particular) became heavily involved in the import of tobacco. This led to a significant Scottish trading presence in areas such as Virginia.

Subsequently, one of the most significant areas of Scottish settlement was the Cape Fear river area of North Carolina (Meyer, 1961). There were Highlanders in Carolina by 1729 or possibly earlier. Many were farmers, driven from the Highlands and Islands by poverty. Cape Fear became

1 The Covenanters signed the Scottish National Covenant in 1638, and promoted Presbyterianism as the form of church government favoured by the people of Scotland — in opposition to Episcopalianism, which was favoured by the Crown. These religious disputes formed part of the background to the English Civil War. After the restoration of Charles II to the throne in 1660, many Covenanters were forced into exile.

known as the 'Argyll colony' and in 1739 the ship *Thistle of Saltcoats* sailed from Campbeltown with 350 passengers to Cape Fear (MacDonald, 1992). The peak years of emigration were from 1768 to 1775, with the American War of Independence limiting numbers in subsequent years. Indeed, it has been suggested that, between 1760 and 1775, around 40,000 Scots emigrated to the United States, representing 3% of the entire population of Scotland in 1760 (Bailyn, 1986). There was significant emigration from the Highlands, presumably as a result of poverty and repression following the failure of the 1745 Jacobite Rising; the numbers were huge, even by today's standards. Between 700 and 800 people are reported to have sailed from Stornoway in a single day in June 1773. That same month, 800 left Skye for Carolina, while in October that year 775 sailed from Stromness in Orkney. The impact on the communities concerned would have been massive.

The overall estimate of the total number of Scots settling in North America prior to 1785 is around 150,000 (Dobson, 1994). As well as the Cape Fear valley, other areas of early Scottish settlement included the Mohawk and Upper Hudson valleys in New York, the Altamaha valley in Georgia and, of course, eastern Canada (Graham, 1956). There was also a steady trickle of Scots migrating to the Boston area. Thus the main focus of Scottish settlement within the United States was in the South and in New England.

A second wave of emigration from the Argyll islands and from Skye occurred around the end of the eighteenth century with emigration in the nineteenth century being linked to the Highland Clearances. Emigration then ceased at the outbreak of the American Civil War, although there was a further wave of emigration in the 1880s, following the 'crofters wars' and the Battle of the Braes in Skye in 1882, and the work of the Napier Commission into crofting.[2] Advertisements placed in British newspapers

2 The Napier Commission, which reported in 1884, investigated issues of high rents and
   insecurity of tenure in the crofting counties. Resultant legislation gave crofters security
   of tenure but some historians believe that this insulated crofts from normal economic
   trends and legally ensured that crofting land could not be developed into viable economic units (Gillanders, 1968). The crofting counties at this time were referred to as
   'congested districts' because there were too many people living there to be supported
   by local resources. These population pressures and the legislative changes relating to
   crofting led to further emigration.

by Carolina farmers invited crofter families to move to America. Between 1870 and 1920, 53% of all Scottish emigration was to the United States (Donaldson, 1966).

Emigration was helped by the establishment of shipping companies, often with Scottish support. The Cunard company was founded in 1840 with the backing of Glaswegians George Burns and David MacIver, and in 1856 both the Allan Line and the Anchor Line began operating between Glasgow and New York. By the 1880s, the Donaldson Line was sailing to Portland, Maine and to Baltimore (Aspinwall, 1985).

By this time, the Cape Fear valley was a significantly Scottish area:

> It is apparent from the emigration from Scotland to the Cape Fear valley in the late nineteenth and the early twentieth century that Scots still considered that area of the United States to be particularly Scottish. It is also apparent that the inhabitants of the Cape Fear valley continued to feel strong ties with Scotland and wanted to encourage fellow Scots to settle in North Carolina. The promise of a better life in Carolina was therefore still attracting Scots to the Cape Fear valley well into the present century. (MacDonald, 1992, p. 266)

Some lowland Scots were based in southern ports like Wilmington and Charleston, importing Scottish linen and exporting cotton, rice and tobacco (Dobson, 1994). Indeed, most Scots at that time were in the southern United States, and in 1790, for example, the states and territories with the largest Scottish populations were as follows: in North Carolina 10.8% of the population were Scots, followed by Georgia (9.9%), Kentucky/Tennessee (8.5%), South Carolina (8.5%) and Pennsylvania (8.4%). There was also significant settlement in New York (Archdeacon, 1983; Bailyn, 1986).

The large numbers of Highlanders moving to Carolina ensured the survival of the Gaelic language — at least for the immediately following generations. Gaelic was widely spoken in the eighteenth and nineteenth centuries and helped bind together people of Highland descent, giving them an important sense of community. It would also have helped immigrants through a period of significant culture shock. After all, many Gaelic-speaking families had come from small communities in the Highlands where Gaelic was the only language and where society, in terms of religion, dress and customs, was very homogeneous. The United States, with its variety of cultures, must have been extremely confusing (Newton, 2001).

From the 1760s onwards, some Highland immigrants to Carolina became slave owners and it seems clear that many slaves were taught the Gaelic spoken by their 'masters'. Scottish cultural traditions seem also to have made an impact on the slave communities, and Newton (2005) has explored the fusing of African and Celtic music traditions in this area.

Gaelic remained significant well into the nineteenth century but gradually died out as a language for everyday use. The last Gaelic sermon preached in North Carolina was delivered in Galatia, in Cumberland County, in 1860. By that time, only the old people in the community really understood the language (Dunn, 1953).

Not all Scots emigrants were farmers or traders, and there were significant numbers from the Lowlands, as well as the Highlands. Jones (1976), for example, has referred to Scots granite workers moving to America. He suggested there were significant concentrations of quarrymen in New England, at Quincy in Massachusetts and Barre in Vermont. There were also skilled Scottish weavers working in New England in the later nineteenth century (Allen and Turner, 1988).

The coal mines of Appalachia also attracted Scots migrants and by 1860 there were significant numbers of Scots miners in Allegany County in the ridge and valley area of western Maryland. In 1980, that county reported easily the highest percentage of Scottish ancestry in the state.

There was significant settlement elsewhere in North America, particularly in the Canadian maritime provinces. There had been Scottish settlement in Canada through the eighteenth century, but it was the voyage of the *Hector* from Wester Ross to Nova Scotia in 1773, with 200 Highlanders on board, which initiated large-scale Scottish settlement on the east coast of Canada (Harper, 2003). Canadian immigration was boosted after the American War of Independence, as a number of Highlanders involved in the conflict retained their loyalty to the British crown. After the war, many moved to what became British North America, to Nova Scotia, to Prince Edward Island and to Glengarry County, Ontario. There appears, however, to have been movement out of Canada as well. Donaldson (1966) has suggested that the United States became more attractive to some Scots after 1776, because of its republican government and more egalitarian society.

Perhaps the huge significance of Scottish — and particularly Highland — emigration to North America is best illustrated by an entry in

James Boswell's journal from his 1773 tour to the Hebrides:

> In the evening the company danced as usual. We performed, with
> much activity, a dance which, I suppose, the emigration from Skye
> has occasioned. They call it *America*. Each of the couples, after the
> common involutions and evolutions, successively whirls round in a
> circle, till all are in motion; and the dance seems intended to show
> how emigration catches, till a whole neighbourhood is set afloat.
> (quoted in Hunter, 1994)

This reference has become widely used in describing emigration from
Scotland. The Gaelic rock band Runrig, based in Skye, had great popular
success with their song 'A dance called America' and James Hunter used
it as the title for his 1994 book on Scottish emigration to North America.

As is evident from the statistics quoted above, most Scots in the United
States settled in the south and in the north east, while there was a subsequent westward movement in the nineteenth century. It is perhaps useful
to look in a little more detail at these areas.

Scots and the South

The size of the immigrant Scots communities in the southern states — in
the Carolinas and in Georgia — has had an ongoing historical impact on
the American South, where the political right has consciously sought to
adopt a specific Celtic identity.

One particular Scottish bequest to the South appears to have been the
Ku Klux Klan, founded in 1865:

> John C. Lester, the moving spirit in the creation of the new organisa-
> tion, tells us that the term 'Klan' was included in the title, because its
> founders were 'all of Scotch descent'. Most accounts of the origins of
> the Ku Klux Klan concentrate on the Greek dimension of the title,
> but the Scottish connotations may be of greater significance. (Hook,
> 1999, pp. 197–8)

James (1999) has confirmed the Scottish connection. He stated that the
Ku Klux Klan is said to have been formed by emigrant Scots cavalry officers within the Confederate army. Its oaths were imported from the Society
of the Horseman's Word, a nineteenth-century secret society operating in
north east Scotland, and the burning cross is taken from the fiery cross,
used as a call to arms to Highland clans in earlier times. The Confederate

flag itself, as James pointed out, does have a resemblance to the Scottish Saltire, showing Scottish history as a locus of Southern history. Thus the Klan deliberately invoked largely spurious images of Highland clanship and heritage, derived in part from a book by an American Scot, Thomas Dixon of North Carolina, entitled *The Clansman* and published in 1904. Dixon's book was drawn on by D. W. Griffith for his controversial film *The Birth of a Nation*, released in 1915 (Calder, 2006).

The Scots influence in the South may also be seen in relation to language. The word 'hillbilly' is of Scots-Irish origin, referring to supporters of William of Orange based in the hills of Appalachia. It first appeared in print in April 1900 in the *New York Journal*. Hillbilly music consisted of Americanised interpretations of Celtic traditional music (Sawyers, 2000). 'Rednecks' were originally Scots Presbyterians, the term originating in the Covenanters' use of red pieces of cloth around their necks as a distinctive insignia. The word eventually came to be slang for a Scots dissenter and gradually was applied to all Southerners and not merely those of Scots descent. Finally, the term 'cracker', which is often used to describe Southerners, derives from the Ulster Scots word 'craic', describing talk or conversation (Wilkinson, 2002).

The word 'cracker' has been used specifically by McWhiney (1988), who has asserted that Southern culture and Celtic culture are strongly related. He suggested that there was long-standing prejudice against Celts in the northern United States, with 'Yankees' preferring to adopt the customs and ways of English people, whom they saw as being 'their own kind'. In contrast, Southerners were aware of their Celtic heritage and tended to sympathise with the Celts against the English. This is, of course, a contentious stance to take and has been criticised by Berthoff (1986) and later by Hague and Sebesta (2008). The latter draw attention to the wider political agenda implicit in this construction of a Southern Celtic cultural and ethnic identity; it forms a critical plank of the neo-Confederate claim to a distinctive Southern ethnicity, which would deserve an independent state.

Similarly, some of the Scottish literature which was particularly popular in the South has gained political overtones. Sir Walter Scott was widely read and inspired people to give their homes, children and pets names that appeared in his books. Scott's books, with their romance, history, chivalry and old-fashioned social attitudes, appealed to the South. Southern readers in the nineteenth century could see parallels between a Scotland that was a 'stateless nation' subsumed within the larger United Kingdom, and the position of the Southern (Confederate) states within the Union (Gerber, 2006). Thus:

> the popularity and influence of Scottish-derived literature was not due to any actual persistent Scottish element in American folklife but rather to the ability of these texts to meet the contemporary needs of Southerners. From the time of Scott to ours, however, the South has been particularly drawn to employing Scotland, or at least certain representations of Scotland, for specific agendas. Many of these agendas are, explicitly or implicitly, based on the fiction of race (Newton, 2001, p. 255).

It is suggested therefore that the attraction of the Celtic image has much to do with finding ways to explain the distinctions between the South and the North of the United States. Celtic music, similarly, was popular and was influential in the development of country music, again a distinctively Southern form of music for many years (Sawyers, 2000).

Scott's work also had a darker side and we are reminded of how, on entering the Scottish Highlands in one of Scott's novels, he:

> instantly transports us back to the dark side of the never-never land of *Brigadoon,* a perpetual past without a future, a timeless black hole foreshadowing the bestial hillbilly fantasies of James Dickey's *Deliverance.*
> (Blaustein, 2003, p. 30)

The popularity of the Scottish heritage movement in the South is perhaps due to its double celebration of a 'reclaimed' Scottish ethnicity and its particular relationship to a southern regional identity. So Scottish and Southern themes have become intertwined, for example at Highland Games, where re-enactors combine Confederate jackets and caps with Scottish kilts, singers perform both Scottish and Confederate songs and bagpipers play renditions of *Dixie.* Crowds are left cheering, or in tears or both (Ray, 2003).

More recently, the Scottish connection has surfaced in Southern politics. In 1994, the League of the South was founded and has around 9,000 members. It calls for the South to secede from the Union and to re-form a Confederate States of America. The League emphasises its Celtic roots as part of its 'distinctiveness' from the rest of the US and in 1996 convened a

'Southern Celtic Conference' in Biloxi, Mississippi. The date of the event, 6 April, was chosen as that for America's National Tartan Day two years later. The League's assertion that Southern Anglo-Celtic culture is irreconcilable with the dominant culture in the rest of the US is used to justify demands for political independence. It illustrates 'a construction of place identity through the LS's recognition of the "Celtic" origins of the American South and its belief that these origins remain a fundamental influence on the USA' (Hague, 2002a, p. 151). It may be argued (Hague *et al.*, 2005) that the claiming of Celtic ethnicity is nothing more than an implicit appeal to white privilege.

Sebesta (2000) noted the way in which Scottish symbols have been increasingly used by the neo-Confederate movement. Films such as *Braveheart* and *Rob Roy* (both released in 1995) have been enthusiastically reviewed by the neo-Confederate press, with parallels drawn between the Scottish Wars of Independence featured in *Braveheart* and the case for political independence for the South today. There is now a Confederate tartan, designed in 1995 and approved by the Scottish Tartans Authority. Sebesta saw dangers in these trends, with Scottish cultural themes becoming synonymous with those of white supremacy. The image of tartan itself may therefore become tainted in the eyes, for example, of black Americans. Indeed, Ray (2001b) pointed out that the creation of the tartan is:

> an amazing blend of simplified visions of 'Highlandness' and 'southernness' through which a southern identity becomes an unproblematic outgrowth of Scottish origins to heritage enthusiasts, rather than an identity chained to slavery and Jim Crow. (Ray, 2001b, pp. 133–4)

Roberts (1999) has highlighted similar dangers, with some Southerners seeing Scottish events such as Highland Games being celebrations of white culture. She described the Jefferson County Games in Florida, where several participants arrived in Confederate uniform. Other Highland Games are held in places associated with white supremacists, such as Stone Mountain, Georgia, 'where the Klan reignited itself in 1915'. One of the largest Highland Games held in the United States is at Grandfather Mountain in North Carolina. Scottish author Billy Kay (2006) has written of his discomfort at the military ethos of these Games and at its torchlight procession, with its overtones of the Ku Klux Klan.

That said, however, other researchers are at pains to emphasise that Scots are not necessarily 'closet Klansmen' and cannot be held responsible for those who choose to associate with them. Ray (2001a) has stated that she has found only seven supporters of the League of the South in nine years of research. The Confederate flag may sometimes appear alongside the Scottish Saltire at Highland Games, but there are differences in their symbolic power.

In short, there is no doubt that the impact of Scots on the American South has been significant and this is increasingly demonstrated through political developments such as the League of the South. But although the neo-Confederates may adopt Scottish or Celtic symbolism, there is no evidence that the gesture is reciprocated.

Scots and the North East

Within the north east of the United States, Scots immigrants were often highly concentrated. For example, there was a long-standing Scottish presence in New Jersey, dating from the mid-seventeenth century, when the area between Newark and Trenton was laid out by Robert Barclay, a Quaker from Kincardineshire in north east Scotland (Landsman, 1982). A century later, John Witherspoon, a minister from Paisley, who was later to sign the Declaration of Independence, travelled to New Jersey to become the president of the newly established College of New Jersey, later to become Princeton University.

During the nineteenth century, the New Jersey town of Kearny, near Newark, was an important focus for Scottish immigration, as a direct result of Scottish companies establishing factories there. Two firms engaged in the manufacture of thread, Clark's and J. & P. Coats, of Paisley, near Glasgow, set up factories in the nineteenth century, and they were later joined by Michael Nairn & Co., a manufacturer of floor coverings from Kirkcaldy, who opened a factory in Kearny making a flooring called 'Congoleum'. Singer Sewing Machines also had a major presence.

The impact of the Scottish influx can be seen in the town's ongoing social life. Kearny became a centre of American soccer, reflecting the strong Scottish interest in the sport (Allaway, 2001). There are still a number of local shops selling Scottish produce. And in 1932 the Scots American Athletic Club of Kearny was established, remaining to this day an important social contact point for Scottish expatriates. Interviews in 2007 with club members revealed this:

> **R1:** This club originated in 1932 and it was in a house at one time. Then all the old timers bought this place here and made a club out of it. It's been a real good club this … The membership's about 420 so it's quite healthy.
>
> **R2:** The club started with Scottish industry coming over to this area. Coats and Clarks were here and they built, I think, three or four factories in the Kearny area and they brought lots of people over with them. And then Nairns Congoleum came over and they brought people. So with the workers coming over here, they brought some of their family members along too, and that's really the start of the club.
>
> **R1:** And Singer Sewing Machines.
>
> **R2:** Singer Sewing Machines, yes — their building was the exact same as the one in Clydebank, except they didn't have the tower and the clock on it. (N7)

Another interviewee spoke of travelling to Kearny to watch Scottish football (soccer) matches on satellite television:

> Some of the satellite companies were providing information but there was nowhere necessarily in the city [New York] to go and see it. Sometimes we had to go out to Kearny. So, Kearny, a Scottish community, had a Scots club which at the time coincided with the Rangers Supporters Club in terms of the building they used. And there was a Celtic Supporters Club out there as well and still is. So, you know, a real Scottish community transplanted to America, rather than an American community with a Scottish influence I think. (N5)

Many of the migrants from Scotland to New Jersey came from the Paisley and Glasgow areas of Scotland and this pattern of localised emigration was common. Within Connecticut, for example, the growth of weaving in the late eighteenth century was boosted by a significant influx of weavers from Ayrshire — and Kilmarnock, in particular (Stone, 1979). There were also significant numbers of farmers, some of whom established new agricultural settlements (Beals, 2005).

By the nineteenth century, the development of manufacturing in the north and north east attracted significant numbers of Scots, who made an important mark on American industry. Key figures included Andrew

Carnegie who emigrated from Dunfermline to Pennsylvania and who created US Steel; Alexander Graham Bell, from Edinburgh, who emigrated to Boston and founded the Bell Telephone Company; and David Dunbar Buick from Arbroath, who established the Buick Motor Company in 1903 in Detroit.

Scots and the West

As the United States spread westward, so too did Scots migrants. There were many settlements of Scots in Illinois, Minnesota, Wisconsin and the Dakotas in the late nineteenth century, although the biggest concentration was in the Pacific north west, around Seattle (Aspinwall, 1985).

In Chicago, nineteenth-century expansion attracted Scots migrants but they seem not to have settled as a group. They seldom congregated in distinct neighbourhoods and did not form a distinct political bloc, like the Irish (Rethford and Sawyers, 1997). That said, Scottish organisations became important for maintaining a Scots identity, with the Illinois St Andrew Society holding its first formal meeting in January 1846. The Chicago Caledonian Club was established in 1865, the Caledonian Society of Chicago in 1884 and various pipe bands were set up, such as the Stockyards Kilty Band. Meanwhile, in the 1860s, the city's first 'Scotch' Presbyterian church was established.

Later organisations had a remarkably local focus. An Orkney and Shetland Society was established in 1885 and an Elgin Scottish Society in 1904. These societies reflected the origins of Scots immigrants to Chicago at the time but their membership was so limited that they cannot have lasted for very long.

Scottish social and religious life was closely tied to charitable effort, and towards the end of the nineteenth century the Scots community raised funding for the establishment of a residential home for elderly Scots. This was opened initially in 1901, moving in October 1910 to a new building, called 'The Scottish Home'. The establishment still exists.

Elsewhere in the Mid West, many of the Scots immigrants were farmers and, as a result, settled in a rather scattered way across the countryside. In Indiana, for example, although there were some Scottish settlements in Pleasant Township (Switzerland County) and the village of Scotland in Greene County, the Scots did not settle in large cohesive groups (Mork,

1996). Indeed, many Scots organisations within Indiana, such as the Scottish Society of Indianapolis Pipe Band, and other cultural, music and dancing organisations seem generally to date only from the 1980s. This suggests that it is only relatively recently that the Scots communities have felt the need to organise on a social basis.

Indeed, some Scots seem to have taken some care to ensure their integration and acceptance into American society, leaving their Scottish identity behind them. Van Vugt (2006) has described the experiences of the Scot James Westwater who settled in Columbus, Ohio. He spent his first earnings on new clothes which helped him to fit in with his fellow workers, and in the evenings 'he studied and practised hard to become more American ... Soon he had American friends who considered him one of them.'

In Milwaukee, Wisconsin, although there were some Scottish organisations with charitable aims established in the nineteenth century, they appear to have had only limited impact on city life:

> such activities in general represented the charitable, social and sporting concerns of men, for whom ethnic concerns represented an embellishment to daily activities, rather in the same fashion as the kilts they wore at their meetings — periodic moments of *auld lang syne* for men well integrated into wider Milwaukee society, rather than the very stuff of which their 'society' was made, as was the case among the Germans.
> (Conzen, 1976, p. 170)

Further west, the Scots like other migrant groups continued to be quite dispersed. In Minnesota, there were large numbers of both Scots and Welsh farmers, while Scots also became involved in the fur and timber trades (Forrester, 2003). Indeed, in both America and Canada, companies such as the Hudson Bay Company and the North West Company actually instructed their employees to become friendly with native Americans, so as to encourage the fur trade (Gibson, 2003). Some Scots ended up taking Indian wives, whom they later took back to Scotland.

Many Scots moved westwards, specifically because of advertising campaigns that encouraged settlement (Rubinstein, 1981). Scots became cattle and sheep ranchers and many place names reflect the influence of Scots. Scottish cowboy Jesse Chisholm, for example, gave his name to the Chisholm Trail, which ran from Texas to Dodge City, while McDonald

Peak and McDonald Lake in Montana are named after Angus McDonald, whose family were ranchers (Didcock, 2007). There was also some Scottish investment in railroad development in the West (Szasz, 2000).

There is some evidence that Scots immigrants became rather socially isolated as they moved west (Erickson, 1972). In the cities, there were Scots charitable societies but in rural areas, as noted above, there were simply not enough people to form these. As a result, there were no obvious ethnic leaders to interpret American society for them, no institutions they could join, no church in some settlements and so a feeling of loss of identity.

Even in some of the western cities, the Scots were not particularly in evidence and the English and the Irish tended to be the two largest groups, although in some places such as Denver there was also a substantial German presence. By 1890, there were around 1,000 Scots in Denver (Leonard and Noel, 1990). As in Chicago, Scottish societies were established, including a Caledonian Club and St Andrew Society.

Unusually perhaps, there was some concentration of Scottish settlement in Denver. William J. Palmer and William A. Bell of the Denver and Rio Grande Railroad laid out a Scottish village in North Denver, with curving streets named West Argyle Place, West Caithness Place, West Douglas Place, West Dunkeld Place and Fife Crescent. The local park was called Highland Park. Some Scots-Irish settled in this area known as Highlands, although they soon became outnumbered by other immigrant groups.

Like the English, the Scots became assimilated into the dominant culture and possibly they made less of their ethnicity than other groups. One of the few traces left of Denver's Scottish pioneers is a bronze statue of Robert Burns, installed in City Park in 1904 by the Colorado Caledonian Club. A similar statue was erected in Gilchrist Park in Cheyenne, Wyoming, in 1927.

The demographic background

Analysis of the decennial United States Census provides detailed information on the numbers of Scots-born people within the United States and, more recently, on those claiming Scottish ancestry. Hutchinson's (1956) analysis of the Census has shown that the numbers of Scots in the United States (either born in Scotland or with Scottish parentage) was between

700,000 and 800,000 at every Census from 1910 to 1950 inclusive, with the exception of 1930. That year, the number rose to 899,591 and may reflect increased migration from Scotland at a time of high unemployment. The numbers consistently represented around 2.4% of white people born abroad.

The overall pattern of settlement suggested a concentration on the Atlantic seaboard, with the highest numbers of both first- and second-generation Scots (in both 1920 and 1950) being in Rhode Island, Massachusetts, and New Jersey. That said, there were also some concentrations of Scots in the west in Wyoming, Utah and Nevada.

Data on the occupations of Scots were not collected separately until 1950. In that year, the highest percentages of Scottish males were in private household work, skilled labour and service work and the professions; indeed, males of Scottish parentage were particularly strongly represented in the professions. The lowest percentages were in agriculture and unskilled work. Occupational specialisations showed Scots as building managers, toolmakers, welfare and religious workers, accountants and auditors. The pattern was not unlike other British groups, although with fewer self-employed in manufacturing and retailing.

For women, the highest percentages were in domestic and other services and skilled labour; the lowest percentage was in agriculture. There appeared to be more Scottish women in the professions and in clerical work than many other immigrant groups (Hutchinson, 1956).

In 1980, for the first time, the US Census asked a question specifically about ancestry, rather than merely birthplace and parentage. Farley (1991) has suggested that the addition of this question has been of limited value in that it fails to distinguish between those who identify strongly with a group, and those who are casually reporting some awareness of their family history. He has also pointed out that only those individuals who are better educated will have the awareness and knowledge to respond to the question.

Nevertheless, for those of us with an interest in people's multiple identities, the Census results are fascinating. In total, 10,049,000 people reported either single or multiple Scottish ancestry. This placed the Scots in seventh place, after those claiming English, German, Irish, Afro American, French and Italian ancestry (Momeni, 1984).

The number of people claiming single Scottish ancestry was 1,172,904 and the number claiming multiple Scottish ancestry was 8,875,912, together accounting for 4.4% of the population. Although there was evidence of a concentration of Scots in the traditional areas of settlement such as the Carolinas and the Atlantic seaboard, there were significant concentrations in the west, confirming the substantial westward movement of Scots immigrants over the years. Some 91% of those claiming Scottish ancestry had three or more generations' residence in the United States, so the grouping was very long established.

The states with the highest percentage of people with Scottish ancestry in the population were:

Maine	1.57%
Wyoming	1.28%
Vermont	1.16%
Idaho	1.14%
New Hampshire	1.06%
Alaska	1.05%
Montana	1.02%

The counties with the highest percentage of Scottish ancestry in the population were:

Mono (main town: Mammoth Lakes), CA	3.43%
Wasatch (Heber City), UT	3.37%
Lewis (Lewiston), ID	3.23%
Moore (Southern Pines), NC	3.19%
Butte (Arco), ID	3.17%

In numerical terms, the counties with the largest Scottish-ancestry population were:

Los Angeles (CA)	33,447
Wayne, Detroit (MI)	14,695
Orange (CA)	13,972
New York City (NY)	13,670
San Diego (CA)	13,077

The cities with the largest percentage of population claiming Scottish ancestry were:

Seattle	7.5%
Portland, Oregon	7.4%
Salt Lake City	6.8%
Kansas City	6.1%
Denver	6.1%

This demonstrates clearly the westward movement of the Scottish population over the years (Lieberson and Waters, 1988).

Interestingly, North Carolina, which was such an important area for early Scottish settlement in the Cape Fear river valley area, had relatively low figures for Scottish ancestry, with only 0.8% of the state population claiming it. Although Scots emigrated from the UK at a much higher rate than the English or the Welsh, they often came as individuals or in small family groups and this helped ease their way into American society. There has therefore been relatively little residential clustering of Scots families and Scots have intermarried with people of other backgrounds to a considerable extent. The result is that the distribution of Scots is much like that of the US population as a whole, 'a reflection of Scottish geographical as well as social assimilation' (Allen and Turner, 1988, p. 45).

The 2000 United States Census confirmed some of the trends first evident in 1980. It was notable that the numbers claiming Scottish ancestry had fallen to 5,406,421, representing 1.7% of the population. Although this was a significant reduction, possibly caused by the death of older American Scots offset by only a small number of new Scottish immigrants, nevertheless the Scots moved down only one place in the ancestry table, to eighth place, being now overtaken by the Poles.

The Census provided interesting social and economic data on the American Scots. Generally, they were well educated with 88.6% possessing a High School Diploma, well above average. They were relatively well off, with above-average income levels and low levels of poverty. On the other hand, only 65% were part of the civilian labour force, around the national average and suggesting an ageing population. The median age of Scottish Americans was 39.5, above the national average of 33.0, and 58.9% of those born in Scotland were now naturalised, significantly above the average for all foreign-born residents of 40.5%. The picture that emerged therefore was of a relatively well-established, prosperous, but ageing group of people.

The states with the largest percentages of Scottish Americans were:

Maine (4.8%)

Vermont (4.6%)

New Hampshire and Utah (both 4.4%)

Idaho, Oregon and Wyoming (all 3.2%)

Montana and Washington (both 3.0%)

Colorado (2.7%)

Massachusetts (2.6%)

Alaska (2.5%)

Once again, there was a strong pattern of concentration in New England and the north west United States.

At the time of writing, the 2010 US Census has taken place but data on ancestry will not be available for some time. The figures described above are now considerably out of date and must be treated with some caution.

Family histories

So far, this chapter has described migration from Scotland to America and provided statistics on the present whereabouts of those people claiming Scottish ancestry. In order to put some flesh on these historical and statistical bones, it is helpful to explore some of the personal experiences of those people interviewed as part of this research.

Of the forty-seven people interviewed, twenty-six had been born in the United States, eighteen in Scotland and three elsewhere — in Canada, in England and in Africa (where her father was working at the time, but she was brought up in Scotland). Interestingly, most of the Colorado interviewees were American born, while most of those interviewed in New York were born in Scotland. This may reflect New York's role as a melting pot, still attracting immigrants from Scotland.

The age range of interviewees was rather limited. With the exception of one teenager who took part in an interview with his parents, only one other person was aged under thirty. Twenty people were in their fifties and eleven people were in their seventies or eighties. It was therefore a rather middle-aged sample but personal observation confirms that this is representative of those expressing a Scottish identity in America. Those born or brought up in Scotland tended to be at the upper end of the age range, suggesting that there is now rather limited migration from Scotland to America to 'renew' the expatriate community, although there were a few 'newer' migrants in the New York sample. There were a number of younger people involved in some of the Scottish organisations observed, but conversation with them established that they had an interest in some of the activities, such as music or dancing, but that they had no personal Scottish connection.

Areas of employment varied considerably. Not all interviewees provided details of their jobs but it was clear that a significant number worked for private-sector companies, in pharmaceuticals, computing, engineering, finance and the law. There were also a number who worked in the public sector or in public service, including education (school and university), health and social care, and local government. Thirteen people were retired, a reflection of the age range of the sample, and one person was still at school.

In the case of those interviewees born or brought up in Scotland, decisions about migration to the United States had obviously been taken personally. In the other cases, emigration had taken place often several generations previously. Nevertheless, despite the historical distance involved, almost everyone interviewed had some knowledge of their family history and several had undertaken some genealogical research. They were able therefore to speak with some authority about their family background and migration to America.

Not everyone was able to indicate precisely the place of origin of their family but most had reasonably clear ideas. A number had Highland origins, in Sutherland, Rum, Inverness, Oban and Skye. Other places mentioned were Kincardineshire, Aberdeenshire (Banchory and Maud), Perth, Stirling, Edinburgh, Glasgow, Culross (Fife), Dunbartonshire and Ayrshire.

Reasons for emigration varied but several people suggested that their ancestors had been forced to move because of their role in conflicts or rebellions. The Covenanters and the Battle of Culloden in 1746 (which ended the Jacobite Rising) were both mentioned:

> My family history goes back to the early 1700s here in the United States. Most of my lines are Scottish but not all. Several lines are Scotch-Irish, which came through Ireland on their way to the States from Scotland. I haven't found out exactly why each of the lines came but a lot of it had to do with the religious conflicts in the early 1700s and of course we also know about the English versus the Highlanders

during the mid 1700s also. I believe there was a little bit of both in the exodus. Several lines went to Ireland in response to Culloden. And a loss of land. That's my perception of why the families came here. (C4)

OK. Let me say I'm sort of the family genealogist and … I am aware of ten or eleven family lines coming from Scotland, most of which I know to be Ulster Scots who immigrated to Ulster after the Jacobite rebellion of 1745. Had a generation of children in Ireland and then all moved to North Carolina. There are two of the lines for which I don't have much information. But all of the ones I know about have that pattern. (C12)

I have four separate clans in my history. They have traced back one of them, my Johnstone clan. He would be my seventh great-grandfather and was a Covenanter and was imprisoned at Dunnottar Castle for refusal to sign the Covenant. He was tortured and escaped twice. His name is on a plaque in the towers at Dunnottar Castle along with 164 others. He was sent to America on a prison ship as an indentured servant in the mid 1600s. As fate would have it, when he got to the States, his ship was blown off course and landed at the wrong port. The person he was indentured to was nowhere to be seen so he just started off a free man. He ended up and stayed in Virginia. (C13)

In some cases, ancestors had left the Highlands as a result of the Clearances, when crofters were forcibly evicted by their landlords, often to make way for sheep:

As near as I can determine, my family was McDonald. And they were cleared from the Island of Rum some time in the 1860s probably. And it's not clear what happened when they came to this country. They actually came to Nova Scotia first and then … went west, different families, in the 1870s and 1880s and eventually settled in Wyoming and northern Colorado, that part of the world. (C11)

Thus many individuals had emigrated in a series of stages. The most common was a move from Scotland to Ireland, before onward migration to the United States and some people referred specifically to their families being 'Ulster Scots' or 'Scotch-Irish'. Several emigrants to Ireland had found the initial move unsuccessful, because of the subsequent poverty which they experienced — notably the potato famine in the 1840s — and they moved on to America:

R: Actually, my husband's family came from Ireland. His great-grandfather came over in 1846 due to the potato famine. He was sixteen years old at that time. He came into Nova Scotia and then worked his way down into the United States, came into Ohio. One of the things we are still trying to verify, he worked in carpentry, and he supposedly worked on Fort Kearney in Nebraska. Because the labour was contracted for those things by the government, we haven't been able to find the contract firm. His name was Samuel Pollock. Eventually he went back to Michigan and settled in Coldwater. The family had been there for many years in the 1800s and had remained in the same area all that time. Just recently my husband's brother died, so there is no longer a family member in the town. My husband and I and my children had all moved away from them.

I: You said they came from Ireland originally. Had they moved to Ireland from Scotland before that?

R: The Pollock name had to originate in the Glasgow area ... We can't prove the information we have found ... but we do know that the family came originally from the Pollok area.[3] We know that they went over there in the early 1700s into Ireland, most of them.

I: When they left Ireland it was because of the famine?

R: Yes. (C14)

Several emigrants had gone initially to Canada which had remained British after 1776 and so had continued to be a relatively popular destination for migrants. Many subsequently moved south into the United States:

Both my mother's side and my father's side are Scottish. We tracked that down. My father's side are McIntoshes and came from the Highlands, the Inverness area and it looks like they came over around 1801 to Canada, to Pictou in Nova Scotia. They were farmers. They came down into Iowa and then into South Dakota and finally in the 1820s into Colorado, to do farming. (C8)

....

I have Scottish on both my mom and my dad's side. My mother's grandfather was born in Halifax, Nova Scotia. He is also a Johnstone. We don't know when they came to Nova Scotia. He emigrated into

3 Pollok is an area in the south west of the city of Glasgow.

Montana in about the late 1800s and married an Irish woman. My grandma was their child and my mom was theirs. (C13)

Even some more recent migrants had initially moved to Canada:

When I lived in Glasgow I had done my National Service for two years and I did seven years in the Territorials. I worked for Glasgow Corporation as a mechanic on the buses. I just couldn't see myself getting on. It wasn't a challenge ... I thought I should better myself and I moved to Toronto ... [My] landlady was English. And there were eighteen guys all off the boat from Britain — Irish, Welsh, Scots and English. They all lived in one house and they all had the same ambition — to hustle and to get something. (C9)

These more recent migrants to America had moved either for job reasons, essentially a perceived lack of opportunity in Scotland in the 1950s, or, in one case, because of marriage to an American soldier.

In the case of those interviewed in Colorado, there was a frequent pattern to migration in that the initial place of arrival in the United States was rarely the place that the family settled. There was considerable subsequent movement, from the east coast to the west. Some families were farmers and saw agricultural opportunities in the west. Others had more specific reasons for moving, relating to relocation by an employer or, in one case, because of a connection with the Mormon Church in Utah. Some families had moved following fighting in the war of 1812 or the American Civil War:

My family ended up in Kentucky because they fought in the war of 1812. They fought under General 'Lighthorse' Harry Lee and to pay them for their services in the military they gave them land grants in Kentucky and that's how I was born in Kentucky. So the Patersons were awarded land in Kentucky, large tracts, and they settled there. (C1)

....

I: Were they farmers in Carolina?

R: For the most part, yes. A number of them were slave owners and had plantation kind of arrangements.

I: At some point there was presumably quite a lot of intermarriage then within the community, which is why these various lines come together in the Carolina area?

R: Certainly that happened within Carolina. However, there's a general migration pattern in the United States of people from the eastern sea-board, the Scots in particular. The ones from North Carolina that are in my family moved to Mississippi or Alabama or perhaps Kentucky. From there later generations moved to Texas. And from there even later generations moved to Oklahoma. I see intermarriage among Scottish lines in some of those later generations at least in Alabama and Mississippi. Those were in the early to mid 1800s.

I: How did you actually end up in Colorado?

R: Job really. We're pretty migratory in the US. We have family all over the country. (C12)

....

I: When they arrived here were they farmers?

R: Primarily farming, There's a few of them that might have been something like small shopkeepers. Several of them were frontiers-men — they were some of the earliest settlers in Kentucky. They were some of the earliest settlers in Tennessee, prior to the American Revolution. They were heading west with new lands … My Mitchell line came to Missouri in the early 1830s. They left eastern Tennessee and came with entire family groups. The Pattons left North Carolina and went to Georgia in the first gold rush in the United States in the early 1800s. Then they came to Missouri. So some came before the Civil War, some came after and the Civil War is what really focused a lot of people here. My family in the Civil War was split down the middle. I've heard that more Scots fought each other in the American Civil War at one time then ever fought against each other in Scotland. (C4)

For those individuals interviewed in New York, migration to the USA had generally been to the New York area and so there had been comparatively little movement away from there. This may reflect the fact that these inter-viewees were much more recent arrivals.

The experience of migration may be traumatic for many families and individuals, especially if the migration has been, to some extent, forced by political or economic circumstances. It is clear from the interview extracts above that, in many instances, the ancestors of interviewees had been forced to migrate from Scotland. Interviewees were therefore asked if they believed that their ancestors knew much of America before they moved. Clearly, many did not:

> I think they were more interested in leaving what they were leaving and going somewhere new. I don't think they had a great deal of knowledge. They may have some idea to go to Virginia because of communication between those who were here early and those who came later, but I don't know that they knew what to expect because, when they were going into the frontier, how did they know what to expect? It was a new world to them. (C4)

In some cases, some recruitment of potential migrants took place and shipping lines became important in distributing information about the New World:

> The way I understand about it from what I've been reading is that generally there is word of mouth, and agents that actually recruit people to come over as indentured servants or maybe even skilled craftsmen or ministers. It was important to people at that time to have educational leaders. So, there's a variety of possibilities there. (C8)

> ....

> I don't know. I have a greater awareness of the kind of information that was disseminated to immigrants later in the early to mid 1800s ... But I don't know as early as they came, which was before the American Revolution. So, before 1776, I don't know whether the shipping lines were distributing brochures the way they did later. (C12)

Churches were sometimes significant and this included not just the Presbyterian Church which was dominant in Scotland, but also other faiths:

> I'm making the assumption that basically what they knew was the Mormon Church. Because I know, during the middle 1800s, there was a lot of Mormon missionary work in Scotland and quite a few people emigrated from Britain to Utah and the surrounding areas. It was called the state of Deseret back then, that was before Utah was a state. (C2)

Even in the postwar era, the voyage to America could seem a trip into the unknown. Those interviewees who were actually born or brought up in Scotland also confessed to having insufficient knowledge of America before they moved in the 1950s and 1960s, and spoke of the 'culture shock' of settling in the United States:

> **R:** I married an American serviceman and then came to the United States. If you want to know what culture shock is like, I had come from the city of London to a town that you have never heard of, Rocky Ford,

Colorado, my husband's home. It's a tiny little town in south eastern Colorado.

I: Tell me a bit about the culture shock. What were the things that struck you at the time?

R: First of all, I had lived in London. In London, there was the theatre and the whole thing. I came to Rocky Ford, Colorado and there was absolutely nothing. There was one tiny little movie theatre. Apart from that, it was just the way people lived. It was a very western America type of town and still is. The majority of the people there, in my opinion, lived very poorly compared to how I had lived … The food did not agree with me at first. I've got used to it now but there was always far too much of it and far too rich for my tastes. I think most of the culture shock was from living in a big city and moving to a tiny village. However, before we even went to Rocky Ford, we spent a week in Denver, because my husband had cousins and an aunt that lived there. Denver was really not that much different. Denver was a cow town in 1954. It isn't today, but it was very different then (C17).

....

I: Did you know much about Toronto?

R: No. I never even knew the currency. Well, I knew it was the Canadian dollar but a big change from the pound. I just went there sort of blindly. I flew there from Prestwick and went to Gander, Newfoundland. And that was a big shock because it was a nice spring day or evening when I left Prestwick. Everything was so green, then we got to Gander about 4 or 5 in the morning, all you could see was snow outside the runway and it was cold as hell. So that was a big shock. We went from Gander down to Montreal and then Toronto on the plane. It was a nice warm day arriving in Toronto (C9).

The experience of this particular migrant illustrates the nature of transatlantic communication in the 1950s. Many migrants to America and Canada arrived by sea after a five- or six-day voyage. For those who arrived by air, transatlantic flights generally stopped at airports such as Gander to refuel, and they were expensive and irregular. This made it difficult for migrants to travel home to visit family and friends and to maintain their links with their homeland.

Conclusion

Previous research, population statistics and the personal accounts of those interviewed paint a consistent picture of Scottish migration to the United States. From small concentrations in the Carolinas and New England, the Scots moved along the eastern seaboard and then into the west. In doing so, some became rather isolated socially but they generally seem to have prospered. Certainly the Census paints a picture of a relatively well-established and well-educated community, albeit a rather ageing one. The interviews also confirm that many individuals had considerable knowledge of their families' histories, reflecting the growing interest in genealogical research among the diasporas.

Unlike many other immigrant groups, the Scots do not necessarily appear to have formed especially large concentrations within cities and, in many locations, there were only a small number of Scottish organisations, mostly with charitable aims. This reinforces Charlotte Erickson's (1972) point that the Scots were 'invisible immigrants'. The growth in Scottish organisations in the second half of the twentieth century has, however, been significant and reflects the growth of 'symbolic ethnicity' to which I have referred in Chapter 1. I now turn to consider the nature of these Scottish organisations.

Chapter 3

Scottish expatriate organisations

Expatriate Scots have a reputation for establishing Scottish societies, in whatever country they live in and the internet reveals a huge range of Scottish organisations across the globe. Some are focused on music, dancing and the arts; some, like Burns clubs, may have a more literary focus; some relate to the Gaelic language; while others are purely social in character. There is often a romanticism about many of them. As Finlayson (1987, p. 95) suggested:

> There is no difficulty whatsoever in assembling a room full of sentimental Australians, Canadians, North and South Americans or Africans for a Burns Supper or a St Andrew's Day dinner. Their hearts are, for that moment, in the Highlands, though their physical presence is in Sydney, Toronto, Boston, Rio or Nairobi. Their emotions, rallied by haggis, whisky, sherry trifle and a piper in full ceremonials, conjure the cry of the whaup[1] in the heather and sunsets over Arran and the Western Isles.

Such organisations may not therefore encourage a view of Scotland itself which is accurate or realistic, but that is not their purpose. They have an important social function in gathering together people with a Scottish heritage or connection and enabling them to participate in a range of events.

This chapter describes the development of such organisations within the US and the involvement of American Scots within them. I use quotations from my various interviews to show how people have become involved, the varying degrees of involvement of the organisations' members, and the size and relative health of the organisations concerned.

---

1 A 'whaup' is the Scots word for a curlew.

Scottish organisations

Origins

Like many immigrant groups, Scots in America often felt a need to band together and to share in their common heritage, and there is a long tradition within the US of Scottish organisations. The earliest Scottish society appears to have been the Scots Charitable Society of Boston, established in 1657 specifically to ease the plight of Cromwellian prisoners. Subsequently, throughout the eighteenth and early nineteenth centuries, St Andrew societies were established in Charleston (in 1729), Savannah (1737), Philadelphia (1747), New York (1756), Alexandria, Virginia (*c.*1760), Albany (1803), Baltimore (1806) and Buffalo (1843) (Ray, 2005b). The New York foundation followed an earlier society, which operated only briefly between 1744 and 1753 (Morrison, 1956). In 1768, the North British Society of Halifax was established in Nova Scotia, the oldest Scottish organisation in Canada (Hewitson, 1993; Cowan, 1999), and this was followed by a society in St John, New Brunswick, in 1798 (Ray, 2005b). Most of these societies had charitable aims, helping destitute immigrants from Scotland who found themselves stranded in eastern seaports.

As noted earlier, some Scottish societies were remarkably parochial:

> Certainly in the 1800s natives of Lewis and Skye, Caithness, Orkney and Shetland, Aberdeen, Dundee and Glasgow belonged to their own local societies in Chicago, New York and Boston. Border clubs in Boston and Philadelphia arranged the celebration of the Hawick Common Riding, and the Shetland Benevolent Association of Chicago staged their version of the Up-Helly Aa fire festival. Other events regularly marked included the births of Sir Walter Scott and James Hogg, the Ettrick shepherd-poet, and the Battle of Bannockburn. (Hewitson, 1993, p. 128)

In the interwar period, there were large numbers of emigrants to North America from the island of Lewis, many of whom sailed on specially chartered ships, such as the *Metagama* and the *Marloch* (Wilkie, 2001). The result was the establishment of vibrant Lewis Societies in American cities such as Buffalo, Cleveland, Detroit, and also Montreal (McCarthy, 2006a). There was also a Lewis Society in Duluth, established by natives of the island, and which held all its meetings in Gaelic. It survived until 1955 (Rubinstein, 1981).

There were Burns clubs in America, the first one founded in New York in 1847, and clan organisations also made an early appearance. An Order of Scottish Clans was founded in St Louis, Missouri, in 1878, although most clan organisations were actually in the east. The 'clans' were in effect lodges that adopted the names and supposed tartans of Highland families (Donaldson, 1980).

Clearly, these societies had important social as well as charitable aims and celebrated, amongst other things, particularly Scottish events such as Hogmanay. It was also common to celebrate St Andrew's Day, and Scots living abroad played an important role in developing the tradition of publicly honouring the nation's patron saint (Hanham, 1969; Buettner, 2002). Indeed:

> St Andrew's Day was observed in the US in generations when it was almost forgotten in Scotland — a curious example of the triumph of national sentiment over ecclesiastical standards which had at the Reformation renounced the observance of saints' days. (Donaldson, 1966, p. 126)

There are interesting accounts of St Andrew's Day celebrations in the anniversary books of the St Andrew's Society of New York. As these annual celebrations grew in size and scale, increasingly larger venues were sought and, in 1905, the Waldorf-Astoria Hotel was used for the first time. This year also marked the first occasion on which women were present, occupying boxes around the main ballroom, where the male diners were seated. The following year, 1906, marked the 150th anniversary of the society's foundation and the St Andrew's Day banquet was therefore a special celebration, attended by both the industrialist Andrew Carnegie and the British ambassador:

> The tables were colorful with flowers and silk flags made up of the Stars and Stripes, the Red Lion Rampant and the Saint Andrew's Cross. Each diner found at his place a tiny sprig of purple heather fresh from the moors of Perthshire, the gift of A. C. Newbigging of Edinburgh. The sweet familiar odor quickened the sense of Scotland o'er the sea, and no doubt reawakened for many in that crowded ballroom familiar scenes of their Scottish homes, or of Scottish things transported to new homes in the United States. It may even be that a few unobserved nostalgic tears fell among the tiny purple blossoms (Morrison, 1956, p. 61).

The membership the following year had reached 500, and in 1909 the guest speaker at the banquet was entertainer Harry Lauder.

Of particular significance to many of the societies was the organisation of Highland Games. Perhaps the earliest in North America was the Glengarry Highland Society Gathering in Glengarry County, Ontario in 1819 (Jarvie, 1991). Within the United States, Highland Games or Gatherings were generally referred to as 'Caledonian Games' and the first 'sportive meeting' as it was called was organised by the Highland Society of New York in 1836:

> The activities seem to have been confined to games of caman or shinty,[2] followed by dancing accompanied by the bagpipes, but it represented an expression of Scottish patriotic feeling, held with all the native pageantry the participants could muster. (Redmond, 1971, p. 37)

Probably the first traditional games were held in Boston in 1853, six years after the city had held the first Caledonian Ball. Further games were begun in Philadelphia (in 1858), in Newark (1861), Brooklyn (1867) and shortly afterwards in Milwaukee, San Francisco, Cincinnati, Chicago, Detroit, Cleveland and Pittston. They were part of a nationwide growth in sporting activities within the United States. By 1867 it was possible to hold an International Games, between the Caledonian clubs of Canada and the US, at New York. Three years later, a North American federation of Caledonian clubs was established (Redmond, 1971).

As well as the sports contained within the Highland Games, the Scots also exported sports such as curling and golf. Curling was well established in America by 1867, when about thirty constituent local clubs formed a Grand National Curling Club (Donaldson, 1980). Further north, curling was a sport at which Canada in particular excelled and 'made their own' (Cowan, 1999). Golf is said to have been introduced to the United States in 1818, and it flourished by the late nineteenth century.

Outwith the ritual of the Highland Games, there were a number of pipe bands established within America, playing at dances, concerts and balls. The first seems to have been the Gordon Highlanders in Buffalo in 1890, followed by the Pittsburgh Bagpipe Band Society in 1900 and

---

2   The game of shinty — or *camanachd* in Gaelic — is played exclusively in the Highlands of Scotland, although it has been exported to North America. It is played with a ball and sticks and, like hurling in Ireland, may be seen as being related to hockey.

the band of the Massachusetts Highland Dress Association at Boston in 1902. During the next ten years, pipe bands were established at New York (in 1905), Providence (1907), Chicago and Saint Louis (both 1908), Milwaukee (1909), Holyoke (1910), and at Yonkers and at Rockford in 1912. Berthoff (1982) suggested that the quality of both the bands and the dancers for whom they played was somewhat variable.

There were also a number of Scottish-American newspapers established during the nineteenth and early twentieth centuries, although many were quite short-lived (Berthoff, 1953). The *Scottish Patriot* ran from 1840 to 1842, the *Scottish-American Journal* from 1857 to 1919, the *Scotsman* (based in New York) from 1869 to 1886, the *Boston Scotsman* from 1906 to 1914, and the *Caledonian*, a literary monthly, from 1901 to 1923.

For many, the Scottish organisations and the Highland Games were important markers of identity:

> one may attend any Scottish Highland Games anywhere and, though the accent and milieu may differ, the spirit of Scotland and its people is pervasive. For in the boldness of the kilt, the bravado of the music, and the fierceness of the sports, this small country ... unapologetically proclaims to itself and the world that here is a spirit irrepressible and immortal. (Donaldson, 1986, p. 50)

McCarthy (2006a) has referred to the importance of Scottish societies in helping to preserve a sense of identity among immigrants, in the immediate aftermath of their arrival in America. This, she suggested, was significant in helping Scots to see themselves as different from other British migrants and to emphasise the cultural element of their ethnic identities. This was important at a time when many European immigrants to America — particularly those from southern and eastern Europe — were perceived as less skilled and less literate than the host population.

Nevertheless, the process of assimilation within American society meant increasingly that the Scots identity was being diluted and, by the 1920s, Scottish organisations and Highland Games had entered a period of significant decline. Perhaps one of the reasons for this is that, unlike some immigrant organisations, those catering for the Scots had flourished almost exclusively as social clubs and not as a focus for ethnic politics (Fry, 2003). As assimilation proceeded, many Scots simply merged into the melting pot and in some cases only their names marked them out from the general population.

Decline and revival

Increasingly therefore Scots within North America appeared to see themselves as Canadians or Americans. Cowan (1999) reported his experiences of undertaking research within the Scots communities in Canada:

> The manufacture of Scottish identifiers throughout the nineteenth century masks the decline in Scottish identity. One notable feature of emigrant letters is how quickly people called themselves Canadians ...

and:

> In personal discussions with descendants of the settlers who went to Dumfries Township [Ontario] from Hawick in the Scottish Borders, it emerged that in the 1920s or '30s they had no special awareness of their Scottish heritage and assumed that everyone celebrated Robert Burns and St Andrew, yet by the seventies or early eighties, they were flying the Atlantic in search of their roots. (Cowan, 1999, pp. 64–5)

Fry (2003) related the experiences of a researcher who went to Canada to record individual oral histories, focusing on popular memories of the Highland Clearances. He quickly discovered that many of the people he contacted regarded themselves as assimilated into Canadian society and had, for the most part, chosen to ignore or forget an uncomfortable part of their history. Indeed, the two Cape Breton writers, Hugh MacLennan and D. R. MacDonald, expressed scepticism at any continuing desire by Canadians to cling to their Scottish heritage. For these two writers, 'their people' were Canadians, rather than expatriate Scots (Hunter, 2005).

Similarly, within the United States, the children of emigrants from Britain seem to have been assimilated into American society much quicker than the children of other immigrant nationalities. As a result, there was simply no second generation of Scots to keep some societies going: 'In effect, their children were simply Americans ... they seldom thought of themselves as anything but Americans' (Berthoff, 1953, p. 210).

McCarthy (2006b) concurred that the preservation of Scottish identity tended to be generational, particularly after the 1920s, when the once thriving Scottish immigrant press had disappeared and hardly any

Highland Games remained in existence. That said, however, she acknowledged that many Scottish societies did continue to prosper.

As far as Highland Games were concerned, one problem that threatened their continuing existence lay in their rather exclusive nature. During the interwar period, there was a significant increase in the number of alternative track and field events, and other sporting occasions. Newer athletic clubs were perhaps more inclusive in that they did not have Highland dancing, bagpipes and other Scottish activities to 'remind "foreigners" of their place' (Redmond, 1971, p. 100). As a result, the novelty of Scottish games rather wore off and local athletic clubs began to push the Caledonian games into the background. The frequent meetings of the newer athletic clubs were sufficient to satisfy public demand. Highland Games were, in addition, expensive to stage and reductions in attendance led to many of them losing money.

There had been, in any case, a major reduction in immigration to the United States in the 1920s, and those Scots then living within the US were becoming very scattered. Rethford and Sawyers (1997), for example, recalled the visits to America by Scottish entertainers, which had been commonplace from the days of Harry Lauder. In the postwar period, popular entertainers such as Andy Stewart and Jimmy Shand toured America but Andy Stewart and the White Heather Club played their last Chicago concert in 1963, as the Scottish audience had become so small.

That said, during the 1950s, there was the beginning of a revival of interest in 'Scottishness' and Scottish organisations, a revival that owed much to the actions of a few individuals. There has been a significant growth in the number of Highland Games during the last fifty years and this is generally traced back to the founding of the Grandfather Mountain Highland Games, in North Carolina in 1956. The Games were essentially the brainchild of Donald F. MacDonald who, inspired by a visit to Skye, founded not only the Games but also the Clan Donald Society, the Robert Burns Society of Charlotte, and the first Scottish country dance group in North Carolina (MacDonald, 1992). At that time, MacDonald himself had never actually attended a Burns Club meeting or a Burns Supper.

The first Grandfather Mountain Games were held on a Sunday, the date chosen being 19 August 1956, the anniversary of Bonnie Prince Charlie's raising of the standard at Glenfinnan in 1745. They were sponsored by five clan societies and two St Andrew societies and were attended by 3,000 people. Today, the Games have become a four-day event, attracting crowds of more than 30,000. Other Games in North Carolina are the Flora MacDonald Highland Games at Red Springs, founded in 1977, the Waxhaw Gathering of the Clans and Scottish Games, held near Charlotte and founded in 1980 and, most recently, the Loch Norman Highland Games at Huntersville, near Charlotte, founded in 1994 and which attracted 10,000 people in their first year (Ray, 2001a).

Not everyone is comfortable with the image of the Grandfather Mountain Games. The Scottish writer Billy Kay (2006) has expressed his discomfort at its military ethos and the fact that it attracts individuals who 'stand to the right politically'. He also saw parallels between its torchlight procession of kilted clansmen and the use of the fiery cross by the Ku Klux Klan; as has already been seen, this is an organisation where Scots played a key role in its foundation. Some commentators, he claimed, dismiss participants as '$2,000 Scots', referring to the expense of buying Highland dress, which serves to exclude all but the better-off (Kay, 2006).

Nevertheless, Highland Games such as those at Grandfather Mountain sparked a renewed interest in clan background and genealogy and also had an impact in Scotland itself. Clan chiefs, for example, were increasingly invited to and became important guests of honour at American Games. So the Games, by promoting the sense of 'clan' and 'belonging' fulfilled an important need within America, at a time when the extended family could no longer provide this:

> the rush to buy kilts and join clan societies may be related to the breakup of the extended family in America. When Americans lived in rural communities with all their aunts, uncles, first and second cousins surrounding them, they had a definite sense of family and identity. Now Americans often seek this lost sense of belonging and identity in organisations and clubs. A clan society based on assumed, if distant kinship fulfils the role of the extended family for urban and suburban dwellers in America. Highland Games in America now serve as the focus for large family reunions, with clan members travelling the games circuit within their region and seeing the same fellow clansmen at all of the games. Families often centre their holidays around the Grandfather Mountain Games and take camping equipment and

caravans along to set up near the games site. Each clan also has a tent on the games field where members visit with each other, catch up on gossip, and eat, drink and make merry together — much the same things that extended families do .(MacDonald, 1992, p. 282)

Another North American example of the impact of a single individual in promoting a personal vision of 'Scottishness' is that of Angus L. Macdonald, premier of Nova Scotia in Canada from 1933 until his death in 1954. Nova Scotia, as its very name implies, had been an important area of Scottish settlement but Scots were not the only important immigrant group and there was no evidence that the Scots themselves were particularly active in promoting their identity. McKay (1992) quoted research that showed that 'the kilt was never worn in Cape Breton before the tourists came'. McKay believed that Macdonald's interest in his Scottish ancestry was fired by a visit to the Scottish Highlands during leave from the First World War. His view of Scotland was therefore a purely Highland one and he encouraged Nova Scotia to embrace a Highland Scottish identity. He encouraged Scottish societies, attempted to persuade the Canadian government to dress foresters in Cape Breton National Park in the kilt, and introduced the tradition of a piper at the border at Amherst, piping tourists into the province.

Germana (2003) discussed this further, noting the erection of monuments to Robert Burns and Sir Walter Scott in Halifax, the building of a cairn using stones from Menstrie Castle in Scotland, and the import of Glasgow City lamp posts to Point Pleasant Park. She noted that even a patch of heather in the park has been the subject of lively debate, as to whether or not the original plants were brought over from Scotland.

Of particular interest is the bequest of land to the Nova Scotia government in 1934, by Donald MacIntosh, a professor of geology. His wish was that the land, on Cape Breton Island, be used to establish a cabin similar to the 'lone shieling' on Skye.[3] This was a reference to the poem 'The Canadian Boat Song', published anonymously in 1829 and which refers in one line to 'the lone shieling of the misty island'. MacDonald, as premier, set about implementing MacIntosh's wishes, and in 1947 the

3 A 'shieling' was a temporary dwelling located on Scottish moorlands, usually constructed of stone with a turf roof, and used by families while supervising livestock on high ground. They tended only to be used in summer.

newly constructed 'lone shieling' was opened by Dame Flora MacLeod, the chief of Clan MacLeod, based at Dunvegan Castle on Skye:

> This was the crowning moment of tartanism in Nova Scotia. It repre-
> sented the full naturalisation of the new truth of the province's inher-
> ently Scottish nature. The shieling quickly became a prominent, if for
> some uninformed visitors rather mysterious, part of the province's
> tourism repertoire. (McKay, 1992, p. 34)

The whole episode represents an invention of tradition. The 'Canadian Boat Song' is not merely a poem of reminiscence but has a bitter quality too, in its references to the Highland Clearances. But these verses were conveniently ignored, so that the Lone Shieling episode owes more to *Brigadoon* than to *The Grapes of Wrath*.

Thus many of the 'Scottish' traditions that have emerged in North America are, in fact, relatively recent in origin and owe much to individual effort and to individual perceptions of what constitutes 'Scottishness'. They represent a kind of 'staged authenticity' (Chhabra *et al.*, 2003), although that does not invalidate them and Highland Games in particular continue to be important — both as occasions for celebrating heritage and also as major generators of tourist revenue.

In line with the renewed interest in Highland Games came a renewal of the clan societies within America. There were a few clan societies in the United States before the Second World War, including the MacLeans, the MacBeans and the MacNeills. But other societies date from only the 1950s onwards. The Clan MacLeod Society USA was founded in 1954, as was the Clan Donald Society; other clans followed.

The bicentennial of the United States in 1776 appears to have spurred some Scottish Americans into celebrating their own heritage simultane-ously with the 200th birthday of their adopted country. Thus, in Duluth, the local Scottish organisation had disbanded after seventy-four years, because younger generations appeared no longer to be interested. Then, in 1976:

> Duluth Scots organised the Scottish Heritage Committee, which
> sponsored a festival, exhibit and a publication on the Scottish legacy to
> the United States and to the Duluth area. Children of Scottish immi-
> grants made many of the arrangements. This renewed interest contin-
> ued through St Andrew's Day 1980, with a Kirkin' o' the Tartan at St

Paul's Episcopal Church. About thirty tartans were presented before
a congregation of nearly 300; a Scottish tea, dancing and piping followed. (Rubinstein, 1981, p. 125)

What is interesting in this revival of interest in things Scottish is the almost
complete focus on the Highland tradition (Buettner, 2002). Enthusiasts
for Scottish roots therefore tend to look towards the nation's earlier past,
including the Wars of Independence, and the heroics of Wallace and
Bruce. There tends to be a neglect of Scotland's lowland culture, and a very
limited focus on the impact of Scotland on the world in the eighteenth
and nineteenth century. The Scottish Enlightenment produced David
Hume, Adam Smith and inventors such as James Watt, but they are all
but ignored. Herman (2001) argued that this period of Scotland's history
should receive more attention, pointing out that, among other things, it
was the Victorians who made the nationalist revival possible. It was the
Victorian Scots who built the Wallace Monument and enshrined Burns as
the national poet:

> It was Sir Walter Scott who blazed the trail for all future folklorists and
> preservers of vanishing cultural heritages, just as it was the Scottish
> Enlightenment which revealed how to relate these artefacts to the
> history of society, and the history of man. (Herman, 2001, p. viii)

Finally, the interest in the Scottish tradition must be seen against a growth
of interest within the United States in genealogy. As was discussed in
Chapter 1, the publication of Alex Haley's book *Roots* in 1976 and the
enormous popularity of the resultant television adaptation led to a massive
interest in family origins. It made it even more important for Americans to
explore their past and to celebrate their ancestry.

Scottish organisations today

There is no doubt that Scottish organisations and events in America have
taken on a new lease of life in recent years, with a huge expansion both in
the number of organisations and the number of individuals participating.
A clear example of this is the growth in the number of Highland Games
across the country. Hague (2001) has identified the number of Highland
Games and Scottish festivals in each US state and, using information from
Donaldson (1986), he identified seventy-five such events taking place in
the mid 1980s. But by 2000 the number had grown to 205. Only Wyoming,

North Dakota and Delaware remained as states where Scottish heritage events were not taking place. Hague (2001) suggested that, as well as the increasing interest in genealogy and heritage which occurred throughout the country during this period, the release of the film *Braveheart* in 1995 also acted as an important spur to the growth of Scottish heritage organisations in particular. What is perhaps surprising is that many of these newly established events are taking place in areas, such as the Plains states, where there have been few Scottish organisations in the past and which were not regarded as significant areas of Scottish immigration.

The situation is mirrored in Canada, where there has been a similar growth in the numbers of Scottish heritage events. Hence the foundation of the North Lanark Highland Games in Almonte (Ontario), 'where no Highlanders had ever settled' (Lockwood, 1991). But Highland Games and gatherings of this sort have become an important symbol in the lives of many people who identify with North American Scottish culture. They seem to be playing a vital role in the regeneration and sustaining of the expatriate Scottish communities (Jarvie, 2005).

One explanation for the success of many of these newly established organisations is in their ability to reach individuals whose Scottish ancestry was not necessarily key to their identity. Scottish societies have therefore adopted a very broad definition of 'Scottishness' in order to be open and welcoming, as revealed by many of their internet sites. The St Andrew's Society of Connecticut, for example, welcomes 'all who wish to share their love of Scotland, Scottish heritage and culture. Membership is open to all; you don't have to be Scottish to belong'. The St Andrew Society of Tallahassee claims it is open to persons who are Scots by birth or by marriage or simply have an 'interest in Scottish tradition'. The Central New York Society is open to 'anyone who is interested and supports the objectives of the Society'. In one of my New York interviews, an officer of one of the societies stated:

> Here in New York, there are many organisations that trace their origins back to a colonial past, but I don't believe we're like that. For one thing, most of them don't admit anybody who can't trace their ancestry back. For instance, the Holland Society, which is for people of Dutch ancestry — but only if you belonged to New York City some 200 years ago. Whereas we take Scottish immigrants into this society every day. We're

> not a genealogical society like these other ones are. We have a lot of
> people who I would put in the 'Americans of Scottish descent' cat-
> egory. Our constitution says that anybody who has Scottish ancestry
> and whom we like can become a member. (N6)

This increasing interest in Scottish heritage has had a range of other
impacts. There has been an increase in the number of individuals adopting
Scottish dress, and research has shown the way in which individuals use
the kilt as a means by which they construct themselves as American Scots.
The wearing of Scottish dress therefore expresses an individual's identity in
an immediately observable way (Crane *et al.*, 2004).

A number of other people have immersed themselves in the study of
Scottish culture and language and there has been a measurable growth
in numbers studying the ancient Scottish language of Gaelic, in both the
United States and in Canada. Many of these are mature students, seeking
to enrich their lives and answer questions about their roots. They identify
with Highland culture and are apparently seeking a more authentic understanding of it (Newton, 2004). Thus, although Gaelic may have been dying
out in Scotland — albeit there are now signs of a revival:

> some people of Scottish ancestry, totally Canadian and desirous of
> renewing contact with their roots of origin will undoubtedly turn to
> Gaelic as a vindication of their sincerity, while they fill their homes
> with the memorabilia of an idealised past. (Campbell and MacLean,
> 1974, pp. 180–1)

An increasing number of universities and colleges in North America are
now offering courses and qualifications in Scottish Gaelic.

The growth in Scottish organisations from the 1960s onwards is
reflected in the establishment of the Council for Scottish Clans and
Associations (COSCA) in 1974. Its stated aim is the 'preservation and
promotion of the customs, traditions and heritage of the Scottish people
through support of Scottish-oriented organisations' and it has become the
main co-ordinating body for Scottish groups throughout the United States
(Calder, 2006). It is also one of seven organisations that currently form
the 'Scottish Coalition' in America, the others being the Association of
St Andrew Societies, the American-Scottish Foundation, the Caledonian
Foundation USA, the Association of Scottish Games and Festivals,
Scottish Heritage USA (which supports the conservation body the

National Trust for Scotland) and the 'Living Legacy of Scotland' (founded as recently as 2000, to promote education and research into Scottish subjects). Previously, the Tartan Educational and Cultural Association and the Scottish-American Military Society were also Coalition members.

Finally, it is important to recognise that, for Scots who have emigrated from Scotland to the United States in the last twenty years, their ties remain largely with Scotland and they have tended not to join heritage organisations of the kind within the Scottish Coalition. Many, however, are followers of football (soccer) and so, particularly in the eastern United States, several Scottish football supporting clubs have been established. One of the largest is the New York City Tartan Army, which organises viewings of Scottish international football matches in certain New York pubs (MacAskill and McLeish, 2006). There are also branches of supporters clubs linked to the main Scottish football clubs of Rangers and Celtic. For individuals involved in these clubs, their Scottish identity is paramount, and research (Giulanotti and Robertson, 2006) showed that they have not embraced at all a hyphenated Scottish-American identity.

Scottish organisations in Colorado and New York

In order to illustrate the sheer range of Scottish organisations that exist in the United States, I now look further at those that currently operate within the two study areas of Colorado and New York City. This perhaps provides a flavour of their various activities.

Within Colorado, there are a number of Scottish organisations, some of which have already been referred to. The largest of these is the St Andrew Society of Colorado, based in Denver but with membership widely spread across the state. The society holds a large number of events during the year, including a Burns Supper, Kirkin' o' the Tartan,[4] St Andrew Ball and Banquet, a summer picnic and other smaller events such as whisky tastings. One of the key events is the Colorado Scottish Festival and Rocky Mountain Highland Games, held in Highlands Ranch, south of Denver, over two days in August of each year. The centrepiece of the Games is competition in the three major areas of Highland dancing, piping and drumming, and traditional Scottish athletics. In addition, there are a range of

---

4 This is a particularly Scottish-American tradition and is described more fully in Chapter 6.

musical events, country dancing, clan tents, a Scots Heritage Centre and a 'market square' of stalls selling Scottish food and other wares.

The society's activities do not include running dances or concerts; arrangements for these are left to its 'subsidiary' organisations, which are supported by the society. These include the Colorado Isle of Mull Pipe Band, so named because its first pipe-major was a native of the island, the Rocky Mountain Highland Dancers and the St Andrew Scottish Country Dancers. This last grouping runs a number of Scottish country dance classes in Denver, Boulder, Parker, Fort Collins, Colorado Springs and Pueblo, in conjunction with the Scottish Country Dancers of Colorado; the memberships of these groups generally overlap. In addition, the country dancers organise regular, usually monthly, dances across the Front Range, in Denver, Golden, Fort Collins, Colorado Springs and elsewhere. There have also been occasional, less formal, ceilidhs, although their relative rarity is a source of complaint among Scots-born interviewees and is discussed later.

Although the St Andrew Society is the largest Scottish organisation in the state, there are also smaller societies elsewhere: for example, the Scottish Society of Northern Colorado, based at Fort Collins; and the Scottish Society of the Pikes Peak Region, based at Colorado Springs. There are also a number of independent pipe bands, including: the City of Denver Pipe Band; the Colorado Skye Pipes and Drums, founded as recently as 1999 and based in Colorado Springs; and the Pikes Peak Highlanders, also from Colorado Springs.

Within New York City, there are likewise a number of Scottish organisations. The oldest is the St Andrew's Society of the State of New York, founded in 1756. The society is rather traditional in outlook and women were admitted as members only in November 2010, although they had previously been able to attend various events. The society organises an annual banquet in November, to celebrate St Andrew's Day, and a range of events, from the Kirkin' o' the Tartan in April, to social events such as clay pigeon shoots, golf and whisky tastings. The society also supports local Highland Games and, importantly, runs a scholarship scheme, which allows Scottish-American graduate students to study in Scotland, and vice versa.

Exactly a century younger than the St Andrew's Society is the New York Caledonian Club, founded in 1856. The club hosts a number of cultural and social events, including an annual Burns Supper, a Saint Andrew's Day Kirkin' o' the Tartan, Hogmanay celebrations and ceilidhs. The club also has an educational mission, with a Scottish Studies Programme providing classes on subjects including bagpiping, speaking Gaelic, and various styles of dance.

The American-Scottish Foundation, founded in 1956, is rather different in its purpose. It aims to advance contemporary Scottish interests and meet contemporary Scottish needs in America and it is commercial as well as cultural in orientation. It conducts various activities, including fundraising, education, social interaction, facilitation, consultation and promotion of inward travel to Scotland; it collaborates with and supports Scottish cultural and commercial organisations.

Importantly, the above three New York organisations have acted as the core members of the National Tartan Day New York Committee, taking responsibility for the organisation of the annual Tartan Day events.

In addition, in New York, as in Colorado, there are a number of Scottish dance organisations, including the Royal Scottish Country Dance Society's New York branch, and the Scotia Dancers of New York. There are also various pipe bands, such as the New York Scottish Pipes and Drums, and specialist heritage bodies such as Scottish Heritage USA, which supports the work of the National Trust for Scotland.

One important difference between Colorado and New York City is the presence within New York of a significant number of individuals who were actually born in Scotland and who have emigrated to the United States relatively recently. Many of these individuals have shown relatively little interest in Scottish-American heritage societies but have set up their own organisations, most notably in relation to football (soccer). Thus, as noted earlier, there is a large New York City Tartan Army and branches of Rangers and Celtic football supporters clubs.

Across the United States, Highland Games have been important events on the Scottish-American social calendar. Arguably the largest Scottish event in Colorado is unrelated to the local St Andrew Society and is the Longs Peak Scottish-Irish Festival and Highland Games, held in Estes Park in September each year since 1976. There is a large festival committee to organise an extensive programme of events over four days. As well as traditional athletic events, pipes and drums, and dancing and music competitions, there are usually a number of visiting performers ranging from solo singers to military bands. There are tattoo performances on two nights and some of the bands visit Estes Park as part of national tours. Thus the Longs Peak Festival has a place in a national calendar of Scottish and Irish events and is not restricted to Colorado. Within the New York area, there are Highland Games in Long Island and also in New Jersey. In the past, Games have been held in Central Park but they were apparently thought to be too damaging to the park.

Another significant group of Scottish organisations are the various clan societies. Most clans appear to have organisations that operate across America, with representatives in most states. Some local groups are quite small but have a presence at the various Highland Games, produce newsletters and have websites to keep in touch with members. In New York, the local clan organisations are quite significant and the Clan Campbell Society is a member of the New York Tartan Day Committee. The Clan Currie Society organises an annual event on Ellis Island during Tartan Week, to celebrate and remember the Scots who migrated to America.

There is also a small but significant grouping of people involved in Gaelic language and culture and An Comunn Gàidhealach America (ACGA) has representation across the United States and there are a number of local Gaelic learner groups. However, despite the existence of ACGA and an apparently growing interest in Scottish heritage (including Gaelic learning), the numbers of learners appears to be rather static. One reason, according to a New York interviewee, might be the style of teaching, as the learning of any language will be difficult unless learners can immerse themselves in it and practise day-to-day conversation:

> ACGA itself is not very big. At the moment we have about 230 paid members. We're always hovering between 100 and 300. We don't seem able to break out of that. There is a smaller but more concentrated group in the north west in the Seattle area, who do a lot with people in Vancouver. As far as classes here, I have about twenty people each semester. You start off with more in the fall and then they drop off in the spring. (C21)

....

> **I:** And how big is the Gaelic-learning community in this area, in the north east United States?

R: In the north east, it's a lot smaller than it should be, given the interest that could be generated. The teacher for the club, a wonderful man named D_____, teaches from a book that's been out of print for over twenty years, Roderick McKinnon's *Teach Yourself Gaelic*, which is very dry, very grammatical and it's a hell of a bad way to learn a language as a living language. I recently got a more colloquial Gaelic language book by Kathleen Spadaro, with the accompanying CDs and that's much more of Gaelic as the living language. I'm still taking the class with D_____ because I still think the grammar is important, although not easy. I've studied other languages and, having said that, Gaelic is not amongst the easiest. (N4)

With such a significant number of Scottish organisations, it is to be expected that there will be some overlap in membership, with individuals being members of, for example, the local St Andrew Society, a clan organisation and a dance group. This membership overlap did not appear, however, to lead to much co-operation between organisations. Some people made reference to the links that existed between St Andrew societies and the various dance groups, with the societies supporting dance teachers to obtain qualifications. There was also reference to the links with clan organisations which were such an important part of the Highland Games.

But others felt that organisations operated in a rather independent way:

Well, I don't see us doing things jointly. We certainly don't plan things together that much but we also do things together. For instance, we had a ceilidh last month. Big Scottish Games up in Estes Park and we had some of the Isle of Mull Pipe Band there. A few Highland dancers came and performed at the ceilidh. [The dance group] is associated with the St Andrew Society, so there is a link there. But I'd say for the most part that our group functions pretty much on its own but we do communicate with the other groups. I don't see them being that closely tied. I think the Highland dancers are closer to the St Andrew Society than the country dancers are. (C2)

The Irish are much more collegiate. They're much better at getting together. The Scots still have this sort of self-reliance, so there's lots of

very successful Scots who recognise their Scottishness but don't necessarily feel the need to go down the pub together with a lot of other
people of Scottish heritage. The incredible thing is that there are four
major Scottish organisations in New York alone — the Caledonian
Club, St Andrew's, the American-Scottish and Geoffrey Scott-Carroll's
group — and they don't get along! You'd think that here was an opportunity but, with the exception of Tartan Day, where they have a sort
of joint committee that organises it, there is very little interaction
between those groups. (N11)

Sometimes, however, organisations came together, a particular example
being the Kirkin' o' the Tartan ceremony:

Occasionally the bands compete against each other because they're
in competitions. But when they're not, they occasionally do performances together. The Kirkin' o' the Tartan at St John's Episcopal
Cathedral is one. The City of Denver Pipe Band and the Isle of Mull
[Pipe Band] were together and did this beautiful Kirkin'. It is a huge
cathedral and the pipes just fill it of course, it's fantastic. (C7)

Although the various organisations appear on the surface to be very active
and organise a range of events, my own observations would suggest that
attendance at some of the events was a little sparse. This raises the issue
of exactly how healthy the various groups actually are. On the one hand,
membership figures suggest thriving organisations:

We have approximately 600 families that are members. We don't count
individual members; there are as many as five or six in one family. We
have some groups within St Andrew Society. We have the Rocky
Mountain Highland Dancers who are very active, mostly youths, but
some are not. We have the Colorado Isle of Mull Pipes and Drums,
which is a pipe band. Last year, I believe they finished first in the South
Western Pipe Band Association competitions in all the western US.
We have the Colorado Scottish Country Dancers. They do very good
work and have lots of fun. The St Andrew Society puts on almost an
event a month through the year. Our biggest event is we just held
our 40th Highland Games in Highlands Ranch, Colorado this year.
A very successful event, we draw around 8,000–10,000 people over
the weekend. We have fifty clans and we have dancing. The year before
last we had the North American and US National Highland Dance

Championships in our Games. This was a very big event. We had dancers from all over Canada and the US. We brought judges from Scotland in and it was a very, very successful event. They have it about every eight years when we hold the championships here at our Games, they rotate them around the country. (C4)

On the other hand, it became clear during interviews that a large part of the membership was essentially passive and, while attendance at the bigger events such as the Highland Games was good, attendance at monthly events was not. It was also suggested by interviewees that the active membership was rather middle-aged and this could pose long-term problems for the health of Scottish groups:

> **I:** How healthy do you think these organisations are in Colorado?
>
> **R:** As good as any probably. We aren't blessed with a lot of funds to do what Illinois and New York do. Those organisations were formed to help destitute Scots. That's in the opening part of our constitution but it's not something we have the money to do. What money we do have to share goes to help Highland Dancers and Scottish Country Dancers to go to regional or national competitions. The band is pretty self-sufficient. Those are three organisations under our umbrella. Those are the ones I know about. I did help organise one in Colorado Springs and it's kind of on shaky grounds; I am not real sure because I have not had much contact with them lately. (C16)
>
> ....
>
> There is only a small active nucleus out of about 700 members. There's maybe twenty to fifty that congregate to these events that they have. It is very small participation other than the St Andrew's Ball, the Burns Supper, the Kirkin' o' the Tartan and the Games. Other than that, the other 500 people probably read the newsletter and put it away. That's my opinion. They have only about thirty people attend the General Meeting. Luckily they have a by-law that says whoever is present is a quorum. If they had to have a quorum they would be in a lot of trouble. (C17)

This rather 'elderly' feel which some organisations have was captured in an interview in New York with the wife of a St Andrew Society member:

> **I:** Have you joined any organisations yourself?
>
> **R:** I haven't, but my husband has joined the St Andrew Society and

I've gone along with him to a couple of their functions, an annual dance or whatever it was.

I: Why did he join them?

R: Through the years, he met up with some other Scottish guys who live here. One of them was a member of the Society, he said 'Do you want to join?' And it was an opportunity for him to wear his kilt sometimes, you know. And I don't know if it's maybe advantageous business-wise as well, to be in that community, make connections, networking, that kind of thing.

I: How do you feel about the St Andrew Society, when you go along? How does it seem to you?

R: Archaic! In fact, I've only been to two of their annual dinners. I think the first one I went to was a few years ago and there must have been a good few hundred people there. It was in the Waldorf Hotel, a huge, huge function. And to me it looked like about 70, 80% of the people who were there were men over the age of seventy. And I think it's only recently, in the last decade or so, that they've started to let women in. So I think they're kind of stuck in their ways. And, in fact, I think one of the guys who wanted my husband to join, he was a younger guy in his thirties, and he's one of these guys trying to get them to be more modern, and get younger members into it. I think that's why he wanted my husband to join as well.

I: You don't feel very comfortable there?

R: Not really. It's not really my cup of tea. It's quite an old-fashioned organisation. And I know that any activities that they have that they've invited my husband to, it's things like hunting and golfing, whisky-tasting, things like that. So it's not my thing. (N13)

All interviewees agreed that the Highland Games were the most successful of the various Scottish events. In the Denver area, the Rocky Mountain Games, run by the St Andrew Society and located at Highlands Ranch, were dwarfed by the Longs Peak Festival at Estes Park, which has become one of the larger Games in America. The Highlands Ranch Games were seen by many as being relatively local in nature and, because they were run by the St Andrew Society, had a direct link to the society's membership. The Estes Park Games was a freestanding event, supported by local volunteers, and was not linked to a particular society or a membership. The responses by the various interviewees provide a good flavour of the range of activities that are involved:

> The Estes Park games are quite a separate entity. It's a major, major event and it's something that has been going on, I think, for the last twenty-five years. It keeps getting bigger and bigger. But my understanding of that event is not so much that it's a membership event, it's not related to any membership. Estes Park tends to ride on the coat-tails of other major Scottish festivals, for example in California. So that last year, for example, the Royal Scots Guards came to the US. And they were performing in California and then they came here to Colorado and then they went on to New York. And so they are able to ride on the coat-tails of other events, whereas it strikes me that the Highlands Ranch Games are more independent, smaller and more specifically for Colorado. [Estes Park] are much more international. They have brought in a Canadian gun-run team. A New Zealand pipe band. A Canadian Air Force pipe band. They always have the US Marine Corps there. And as I said, last year they had the Royal Scots Guards. (C6)

....

R: [Estes Park] started with four families and a picnic twenty-seven years ago and Dr Durward and some of his friends started it. Because they all had a love of the Scottish history and Irish history and they wanted to preserve that, so their children and grandchildren could have an active part in remembering that. As well, Dr Durward was president of the Chamber of Commerce in Estes Park; so one of his main purposes was to extend the tourist season, so that it would help the people of Estes Park with their season. Of course, it's more than done that now. It started out with four families and a picnic and this last year we had over 70,000 people over four days.

I: What's involved with the festival?

R: It starts out on Thursday, Dr Durward takes a few of the guest band members down to Denver and they do a wreath laying at the war memorial at the Capitol grounds. Then Thursday night in Estes Park is the first tattoo performance. That involves all the guest bands and the jousters and the Dogs of the British Isles. Then Friday there is a seminar and Scotch tasting that goes on all day over at the Holiday Inn. Then Friday night is another tattoo as well as two other concerts that start up and go Friday and Saturday night. One is a folk concert and the other is the Colorado Celtic New Year concert. Then there's a ceilidh after the tattoos and the concerts Friday and Saturday nights. The Field opens on Friday at noon, goes until 5 p.m. Then Saturday morning we have a parade down our main street with all our guest bands and the clans and the dogs and everybody. The Field is open after that, it is open all day — 9 a.m.–5 p.m. — that's where all the competition takes place. There's competition in Highland Dance and Irish Dance and of course piping and pipe bands and drum salutes. Jousters have their own competitions, as well as the Scottish athletics and the Dogs of the British Isles. On top of all that there are merchants and crafters and fruit vendors and all kinds of things to see and do. So, it is a lot of fun (C5).

....

R1: A typical day at the [Long Island] Games is we'll have several pipe bands, and they'll march up and down every half hour or so. We'll have entertainment by all kinds of singers, we have the athletic games going on over in a different field, a children's games, we have antique British cars, we have the Scottish Military[5] there and guys making suits of armour. We have a group called the Champions of the Cross, which is a society for creative anachronisms — they teach people how to sword-fight. We have dogs doing obedience. And all kinds of food.

R2: We did have sheepdog trials. It was just one dog and a couple of sheep. Then I don't know if the sheep died, it was the dog and a couple of ducks. And they ran around. We haven't had that for some time now. We try to put an emphasis on children — the children's games, the children's entertainment. Probably all of the morning is children's events. (N14)

The scale of these events mirrors that elsewhere in the United States. They are much bigger events than those in Scotland itself, with many more participants, and yet clearly some of those involved had a concern that membership of supporting organisations was often rather passive. This suggests that such events rely to an enormous extent for their success on the efforts of a few committed individuals. It is not obvious therefore just how much the Scottish-American communities as a whole are actually involved.

5   The Scottish-American Military Society.

Becoming involved

Despite the relatively small number of really active individuals in these various Scottish organisations, clearly the overall levels of membership are significant. Most of the individuals interviewed were members of one or more Scottish-American organisations and most participated in a range of events. Mention has already been made of the rather middle-aged nature of the sample and this echoes the work of Novak (1971) with his reference to 'Saturday ethnics'. It has tended to be the middle class and middle aged who have the time and money to indulge in the voluntary, leisure-time activity of pursuing their ethnic roots.

Certainly, initial contact with potential interviewees had been through websites and, as a result, the first list of people agreeing to be interviewed consisted of those who were members of a Scottish-American organisation. These people in turn suggested others for interview but, presumably because of the social networks that exist between Scottish expatriates, they too were often organisation members, although they were not necessarily active. One of the difficulties faced in undertaking this research was that it proved well nigh impossible to identify Scots who were not so involved, although the US Census showed that there is clearly a large number of people across the country who are either Scots-born or who claim Scottish ancestry. It was believed that such individuals had perhaps made a conscious decision not to become involved with other Scots:

> **R:** There are an awful lot more Scottish born in this area than we know anything about. They have been coming in business-wise for the past ten or fifteen years, maybe more. Some will contact us and want information but we don't get that many members. Here's what several have told me is that when they come to another country, if they are going to be here — as they think permanently — they want to meld in with the population here. Their way of speaking will have them stand out, so many of them are not interested in continuing to do Scottish things in this country. I guess it's that 'when in Rome' kind of thing.
>
> **I:** So they want to become Americans?
>
> **R:** Right. (C16)

This suggestion that migrants to America who were actually born in Scotland may not wish to participate in Scottish expatriate societies is interesting. It echoes, to some extent, the views of the Scots-born in the sample, in regard to the St Andrew societies and the way they operate, discussed later in the book. It certainly appeared to be the case within the New York group of interviewees where a shared love of Scottish football or business connections tended to be the main reasons for some recent Scottish immigrants to get together. It also suggests that the bulk of those who are actively involved in Scottish-American organisations are more likely to be Americans by birth.

We have already seen in the individual family histories described in Chapter 2 that many interviewees had to look back over several generations to identify the initial arrival in the United States of their Scottish ancestors. Indeed, an awareness of these ancestors and of their 'Scottishness' had sometimes only occurred after detailed genealogical research. Given that many interviewees had therefore had only limited exposure to a Scottish family identity, what then had encouraged them to become involved in Scottish organisations?

Several people spoke of 'discovering' their ancestry or of hearing and identifying with Celtic music or Gaelic as a kind of epiphanic moment:

> I didn't even know that my ancestry was Scottish and I was in a music store or some place where I heard Gaelic singing. I had never heard it before and I didn't even know what language it was and it just immediately hit me and my first thought was: 'I have to learn that language'. It was so bizarre and I didn't even know what it was. And then I found out that it was Gaelic and then started looking around to find an organisation. And at about that point I think my mother came to visit and I said something and then she said: 'Oh you know our ancestors are from Scotland.' I always thought they were from England and I didn't want to be from England and so I just kind of buried that all these years and so it was kind of funny. So then I just started looking around for a teacher and then I found the teacher in Denver. (C3)

> I had a vague awareness of Scottish ancestry before I did any genealogical research and I think that was one of the reasons that my wife and I went on a trip to Scotland. We gave ourselves a trip for our twenty-fifth anniversary. We went in 1992. I absolutely fell in love with Celtic music. I came back and sang in the shower for a few years and I decided I wanted to get serious about it. So my way into all of this was

an interest in Celtic music. In order to be serious about it, I realised that I wanted to be able to sing in Gaelic as well as in Scots, which I could handle in English. So at the very time that I started taking guitar lessons again and working seriously on Celtic singing, I started lessons in Gaelic. That was five years ago. At this point, Gaelic is probably at the top of the list with respect to my Scottish activities, but it wasn't Gaelic that got me first interested. I'm very active in Scottish Gaelic here. We have a very active community of Gaelic speakers. I'm the keeper of an email list and I have more than fifty names of currently active Gaelic learners in Colorado. (C12)

One woman referred to her son's experiences while on holiday, walking in Skye. From her description, he had clearly been attempting to negotiate a difficult rock traverse known as 'The Bad Step' on the footpath from Elgol to Loch Coruisk:

When Degan went to Scotland, he was climbing in the Cuillins and nearly lost his life in one place. He could have. It was raining and it was sheeting and they had to pass a high cliff area to continue down to the sea rocks or you could slide by there and they had to be very, very careful. Degan came back and started talking about that oddly. The way he talked about it was, 'after that I felt like I was at home. That I went through some kind of entry or something.' What I'm speaking to here is not hard facts that would be useful to you but more a sense of feeling connections to landscapes, a sense of familiarity. (C11)

Another woman had participated in a house exchange and had been astounded at the similarities that she found between the two households:

Going to Scotland in 1993 and staying in someone's home, it just felt incredibly familiar and meeting the people felt very comfortable. The Munros and us were raising our daughters the same way. We had the same values. We parented the same way. The house I stayed in was freaky. They had wallpaper that was the same that my mother had picked out like twenty years ago for our house. Their towels were the same. I was always raised to have tea and to never have coffee. I just felt at home. That was the basis for making a lot of friends over there. (C18)

Interestingly, it seems to have been the Gaelic language, or more specifically Gaelic singing, which made a particular impact on a number of individuals. Indeed, some potential interviewees began to include Gaelic greetings and other phrases in their emails, when they were communicating with me:

> In my trips to Scotland, I was in Tobermory on Mull. I was standing in the front of a shop and I heard Gaelic being spoken. It sounded kind of fun and then I saw the Gaelic signs in the area. My first thought was: 'How do they make a word out of all of these consonants and one vowel?' So I decided that would be interesting if I ever had the chance. In our Highland Games one of our entertainers is named Donnie McDonald, who is a part of Men of Worth [a local folk band] and out of California, raised in Lewis. He's a native speaker. There was an announcement in our *Celtic Connection* publication, here in town, that he was going to put on a Gaelic song day at this small church in the south part of Denver. I thought that would be really neat because I helped Donnie set up and he'd given me a CD and he was a very nice man. So, I decided to go and see what it was like. So I went. My Gaelic teacher, who I didn't know then but who was to become my Gaelic teacher, was co-sponsoring this with Donnie. It was a day of Gaelic music with Donnie talking about the Gaelic language and the subtleties of it and singing songs in Gaelic and talking about how to pronounce the words. My teacher said after the class that the new classes were starting up in a week and does anybody like to sign up? So I signed up. I've been at it now starting my fifth year. (C4)

R: I think I was attracted to the pipes and Highland dancing and all that stuff. I knew about Gaelic but at that time I was a teenager and it was virtually impossible to try and learn it. There weren't materials or anything available. But the one thing that did happen to me back then was I bought a record called *Heather and Glen*. Have you heard of it?
I: No.
R: Well, you've heard of Hamish Henderson?
I: Yes.
R: He and the American Alan Lomax did a lot of field recordings in the early 1950s. I don't know if it was released in Scotland but in this country they released it. It is music of the Lowlands and the north east and people like Jeannie Robertson were on it and John Burgess the piper. The second side was Gaelic singing and people like Flora

MacNeil, who was just a teenager herself then. So that had a strong effect on me.

I: You began to learn as a teenager?

R: No. I liked the music but you really couldn't learn it. It wasn't until years after that I was at the Highlands Ranch Games, that were held in Golden at the time, and I stumbled upon a book called *Gaelic Without Groans*. That started me off in a practical way but the seed had been planted with Alan Lomax and the field recordings thirty years before. (C21)

Other people had become involved in a more gradual way, attending society meetings and Highland Games over a period, before becoming involved in their organisation. One couple had started to attend the Estes Park Games, because their parents were office-bearers in the local branch of their clan society and needed help to run the clan tent at the Games. They had volunteered to help and had gradually become key members of the festival committee:

I: How did you end up being part of the organisation?

R1: It was one of those weak moments. When my father passed away in 1996, I assumed the position of Colorado commissioner because we were having our Annual General Meeting for Clan Pollock in Estes Park. So I was commissioner for about three years. I was attending, at that time, five different Games in Colorado. Using up too much vacation days to do Games and also feeling after that many years that it was time for new ideas to be injected into the clan. So I resigned and nobody took over that year. So we went up to the festival just to see what the festival was about. Most of the time you really don't even get to see the festival while you are manning the tent. As we were walking around we kept hearing different spectators going: 'Where's this? When's that?' So we talked to Dr Durward [committee president] after that year's festival and volunteered to be what we called 'roving hosts'. We would take programmes, wearing nametags that said 'Information'. We were roving hosts for three years. In July or August of 2002, Dr Durward called us and said that the folks that had been in charge of the clans for fifteen years wanted to retire and asked us to assume the chairmanship.

I: What does that involve?

R1: The pay for the tent spaces is set by the festival to recover the costs.

A lot of this I will refer to Peggy because she does most of the behind-the-scenes work.

R2: I'm the paperwork and he's the public relations. They send in their registration and their money. We have two separate tents only because as many clans as we have require it. We try to put them in the tent so that they're happy. So that one clan is not next to a clan they don't need to be by, because they do hold grudges. They do opening ceremonies. They have Tartan Parades. On Sunday we have Kirkin' o' the Tartan. We have to get them all lined up. (C15)

Finally, for some the Scottish societies provided an important opportunity to meet people with similar interests and a shared ancestry. Some people spoke of making contact with their local Scottish society as soon as they moved into an area:

R: St Andrew Society — I belong to that. And the Colorado Dance Society. I started dancing in Arkansas several years ago. Moved to Little Rock and lived there a year and didn't know anybody and I had been going to the Scottish Games and going to Scotland for years and I thought well, you know, since I don't know anybody, I'll just throw in with the Scots and dance with them. That's when I started dancing.

I: So you just took a notion to become involved?

R: That's a nice way to meet people with the same interests, same background and they're nice people. Nice people and that's how I got involved into dancing. But I probably had already been going to Scotland for ten years before that though, for fun. (C1)

The nature of involvement

Interviewees were involved in a wide range of activities, reflecting the range of Scottish organisations within the two study areas. As noted earlier, although many people were members of different societies, the level of commitment to them varied considerably and some people were active only in one element, such as dancing or the pipe band. However, the events that were the largest and most complicated to organise were the Highland Games and a number of interviewees spoke of attending several of the Games, in some cases as performers.

Others, who had an involvement in clan societies, spoke of having a clan presence at a number of different Highland Games. It was also clear that new Games were being established in new locations and the comments by the following interviewee echo the research by Hague (2001) into the expansion of Highland Games across the country. There were thus a number of additions to the 'circuit' of Games that people attended:

I: Tell me a bit about the Games. Is it just Estes Park you have been involved with?

R: No. It is scheduled real well. The Games are scheduled so that there's probably one to two a month so that you are capable of going to all of them. Some of them are small and delightful, because you get to make closer contacts with people and friends. We have our tent and set up all of our supplies.

I: This is the clan tent for the Pollocks?

R: Yes. Then Estes Park furnishes tents. The Denver Highlands Ranch Games, the Rocky Mountain Games, they're the oldest in Colorado. They started up in Golden. Colorado Springs Games have disbanded due to necessity of the location. They held them a number of places over the years and then they moved them out to the Air Force Academy grounds and then that's been discontinued. They could no longer go out there. Then there's Kiowa out in eastern Colorado. Sterling has just started new Games.

I: Is there such an interest that they would start new Games?

R: Scottish organisations are really strong in Colorado. We've seen it develop more and more. When we first started going to Estes, we had twenty-five or thirty clans. This year they had more than sixty. The AGMs are often held up there because it's such a beautiful place and everybody says it recalls their Scottish homeland. (C14)

Many interviewees — or their families — were not actively involved in the organisation of either Scottish societies or the Highland Games but performed in music or dance at various of the events. One couple had a daughter who was involved in teaching the Highland Dancing group and a son who had started as a dancer, before moving on to learn the bagpipes. This particular couple visited Scotland regularly and imported tartan cloth for kiltmaking. They had been responsible for providing the Colorado Isle of Mull Pipe Band with their kilts:

R1: He first started out as a dancer and progressed up the ranks until he was about eleven or twelve and he came to his mother and said: 'I am not going to dance any more.' After long, he played the pipes.

R2: He was wanting to do it.

R1: He picked up the pipes through the Colorado Youth Band and he's gone with it after that, he just took off. It was two years ago that he won the overall piping at Highlands Ranch.

R2: Oh, the Silver Champion. The interesting thing was that he was competing against two of his students for that same championship. He started piping at about twelve. He continued dancing until about thirteen. He said: 'I can't do both.' The beauty was that dancing forced him to practise, but his heart really wasn't in it and the piping called him. So he took off and didn't look back.

I: Was he a member of some of the local bands like Isle of Mull?

R2: He was. He was the pipe-major for Isle of Mull for two years there. He started out with the Youth Pipe Band, that's where he started learning. But then he soon went way beyond that and then he joined the City of Denver Pipe Band for a while. Then he went away to college and came back. He got a college piping scholarship and that's his first love. If he could earn a living piping he would.

I: He's never thought about trying to teach it full-time?

R2: He would love to. But financially he couldn't survive that and mom's not going to continue supporting him!

R1: There were some students who he taught. When he was here he had lessons almost every night.

R2: The problem was that he was having it at our kitchen table and we can't live that way either. We're trying to hide in the basement. I love piping music but not inside my house every night. (C7)

Most interviewees had developed an interest in Scottish music linked to dancing and piping. But there was also a significant number who were involved in learning or teaching Gaelic and who had been involved in playing in or listening to sessions of Celtic folk music. This in turn sometimes led to a wider interest in Celtic history and folklore:

I: You were saying how healthy the Gaelic group was. Are you involved in any music groups that are linked to that? For example, are there groupings of Celtic musicians?

R: No, no there's not. There are a couple of Celtic sessions in the area.

One in a coffee house in downtown, for example. They were very active a while back. By the time I learned about them, there wasn't much left of them. Hopefully they will regenerate. The musicians tend to know one another some way. There are a number of professional groups around but I don't go up to that level. (C12)

We have already seen the importance of clan organisations in America. Membership of individual branches of clan societies varied, with branches in the eastern United States tending to be much larger. But, even where numbers locally were relatively small, individuals clearly valued being part of a larger and long-standing ancestral grouping. Across North America as a whole (including Canada), memberships were often very large. Thus for the Clan McDougall, there appeared to be thirty or forty families in Colorado who were members, together with three or four in Utah, ten in Wyoming and about fifteen in Montana. The Clan McLeod Society had about thirty or forty members in Colorado at any one time. But this was only part of a much wider North American picture:

It's very thriving. We have a website of Clan McIntosh in North America. It also represents Canada. I, of course, respond to all these folks. I don't know what our count is but it's a few thousand people. We are in direct contact with John McIntosh who is the Chieftain. He supports us and writes articles for our newsletter. So we are authorised by Clan McIntosh in Scotland. They have recognised us. We look to them for authorisation for things. (C8)

Because of previous intermarriage within Scottish expatriate society, individuals tended to have links to several clans. They then made choices about the clan on which they would focus. This process mirrors that in which white Americans make choices regarding the particular ethnic grouping to which they wish to belong (Waters, 1998). One interviewee stated that he did not 'have a clan affiliation yet'. He was concerned because two ancestral lines which he had been following had come to what he described as 'dead end clans that aren't represented really by active clans today'. Some clans appeared to be more 'popular' than others and some individuals made choices to belong to a particular clan simply so that they could participate in parades at the Highland Games:

R1: I would love to meet some McDougalls or some Johnstones because I have a Johnstone on my mom's side too. That's how we met actually, at the Scottish Games and I went over to say 'Hi' to the Johnstones with my mom and there he was. Came over from the McDougall tent to say hello to the neighbours.

R2: We can't trace back our heritage too far because they're going to go like this ...

R1: They're going to connect.

R2: I have Johnstone, Buchanan, Ferguson and McLean in mine.

R1: I have Johnstone, Ferguson and McDougall, so we have two clans in common. It's funny how that happens even in a country as big as America. (C13)

Although this particular couple also had the Ferguson name as a common ancestry, they appeared to have opted not to pursue it, focusing instead on the McDougall and Johnstone lines. In another case, a woman had decided to ignore her ancestry on the male side, because their name (Steele) was not linked to a clan; instead she had decided to follow the female line, whose surname was Clark, as this would allow her to join a clan and participate in clan parades and other activities:

R: About one year ago. I joined the St Andrew Society and I also joined Clan Cameron. My Steele relatives would probably turn in their grave if [they knew] I did that. I don't think they were involved with the Camerons at all.

I: Is Steele linked to any clan?

R: No, I was going after the Clarks. The Clarks are linked with the Camerons. If I want to be in the parade that is the only way I can get in. (C18)

The most important activity for clan organisations appeared to be their presence at the Highland Games. This represented an opportunity to parade, to meet other clan members and to recruit new ones, to provide information on clan histories and advice on genealogical research, and to sell crafts, books, CDs and the like. At the 2003 Games at Estes Park, a total of sixty-three clans were represented, an increase of six on the previous year. The chair of the Clan committee for the Games estimated that the database of clans who had previously attended the Games, or had expressed an interest in attending, stood at ninety-six, so there was thought to be considerable opportunity for expansion:

R1: [There's] a feeling of belonging to a certain clan. The one thing

I see is that they are ecstatic when they find out they can belong to a certain clan.

R2: That they actually belong somewhere. It took probably 75% of our day looking up at rows and rows of people standing there, saying 'OK, you belong here', 'Go over here', etc., directing them to where they needed to go and they were like, 'All right, where can I buy stuff?'

I: It's such a big deal for people?

R2: Oh, they just love it.

R1: We do not get into depth at all, other than which clan they would be eligible to belong to. Beyond that, the festival also has the Tartan Society, which does a lot more in-depth genealogy than we do. We would not have time to do that and continue to do the things we need to with the clans (C15).

....

R: Rex and I are very active in setting up the Clan McLeod stand at all of the Games in the state. That means four or five different times during the summer.

I: When you take the Clan McLeod tent around to the various Games, what sort of people will come to you? Will people with the McLeod name come and join?

R: McLeod or one of the sept[6] names associated with the clan.

I: Do you recruit a lot of new members that way?

R: We usually have about 30 or 40 members in Colorado in one year. It takes an awful lot of recruiting to get that many. Although there are a few that just continue their membership here year after year.

I: Do you sell stuff?

R: Yes, we do that. The Games in Estes Park cost about $250 just to set up there. So we try and recoup some of that money. Highlands Ranch usually costs about $100 to set up at. We're just trying to pay for that so we can break even. I make a lot of crafts and sell a lot of things just to try to do that (C7).

Although interviewees stressed their enjoyment at being at the Highland Games and the friendships that had developed, there is also a

6 In Scotland, a sept is a family that is absorbed into a larger clan. Each Scottish clan typically has a number of septs, each with its own surname. Septs have the right to wear clan tartans although they may have tartans of their own.

competitive edge to the clan presence. For example, the various Highland Games committees judge the clans on a range of criteria and prizes are awarded to the 'best' clan. The various criteria include appearance on parade, the wearing of clan tartans, the carrying of clan colours and flags, the overall appearance of clan booths or tents, knowledge of clan histories and genealogies at the booths, and courtesy of clan members towards visitors. There is a particularly strong emphasis on the wearing of tartan, both in the booths and on parade. It should be pointed out, however, that this idea of judging a particular clan as being the 'best' is an American tradition and is completely unknown at Highland Games within Scotland:

> **R1:** When they announce your clan and you pass the colours, you have to dip your standards. Our clan used to have quivering salutes. Some things that our former leader, before he retired, did to juice things up a little.
>
> **R2:** He was a navy officer.
>
> **R1:** To just juice things up a bit. You can actually win separate events. You can win just parade. You can just win booth without winning the overall. If you score high enough in parade and tent then you win the overall (C13).

In addition to the Games, clan convenors frequently send out newsletters to members or organise social events. The Clan McLeod representative for Colorado put out a newsletter two or three times a year and during the winter organised a social gathering, which she described as 'a potluck dinner'. Across the United States, there was a nationwide newsletter and magazine, as well as an annual meeting, at which they tried to be represented. Clan McDougall produced a newsletter about six times a year, called *The Tartan*. The local convenor similarly tried to arrange social events, such as parties and summer picnics.

Finally, a number of interviewees were active in the learning and teaching of Gaelic. They too often used the Highland Games as opportunities to encourage more people to become involved and possibly also to recruit them to membership of An Comunn Gàidhealach America:

> **R:** I've had at times a Gaelic tent at the Highlands Ranch Games. I take out a membership as a political thing. I'm mostly involved with ACGA.
>
> **I:** Do you go to Estes Park as well with your tent?

R: Some of the other students do, especially people in Boulder since it is a lot closer. Other times I am conveniently out of the area at that time or just getting back from Nova Scotia and I need a weekend to catch up and clean up after the dogs. They are bigger games in Estes Park. I don't know if they do any more good.

I: What do you do at the tent? Do you recruit people for classes? Are people exploring their family backgrounds? What sort of business do you get?

R: The ones interested in their family will go to different clan tents. Some are just looking around in general and seeing what is interesting. Others have varying degrees in the language and they may or may not come to classes or join ACGA. We get a few people who are from Scotland who have a Gaelic background. That's a good way to try and identify those people, because how else would you do it? (C21)

The nature of the membership

I have already explored the revival of interest in Scottish organisations during the 1980s and 1990s and the growth in the number and scale of Highland Games in America (MacDonald, 1992; Hague, 2001; Ray, 2001a). Given that this revival has taken place at a time when immigration from Scotland to America has generally declined, it is reasonable to assume that it is linked to a growing sense of identity and ethnicity within America's white population, rather than being linked to a fresh influx of expatriate Scots. Thus one might expect that the majority of those who are currently involved in Scottish organisations in America are American born, rather than Scots born, and this appeared to be the case. Most interviewees took the view that American-born Scots were the most heavily involved in heritage organisations:

It's more of an awareness of where we're from and our culture and all of that and I can only speak for more myself but it's mostly descendants. Because of the media and the TV and the Games themselves and you know most people, when I would go out in my kilt years ago, almost everybody that would come up and talk to me would have a Scottish ancestry somewhere in their history. And if you looked far enough back there is a Scot back there somewhere and then that develops their interest in the Games and the dancing and the music and so forth. (C1)

> In our festival, most people are not from the old country, they're Americans that have been born and raised here, but they've grown to love that heritage. (C5)

A particular focus for some interviewees was the development of business links between Scotland and America and they saw the involvement of Scottish expatriate organisations as a part of that process. In one case, the view was taken that native-born Scots would be more attracted to business organisations than to Scottish social societies and so this helped to explain their limited involvement in the latter. In another case, the involvement of social societies like the St Andrew Society provided a useful bridge to the American-born expatriate Scottish community:

> We've got some native-born Scots but they have been in the country for a long time. As you probably know, you can hardly get into the country now from Scotland if you want to live and work here. It is almost impossible unless you are a scientist. I think there are probably native-born Scots that we don't know about. I am not sure of the reason. Sometimes I think it's just that Scots are just not joiners. They're very selective in who they join. We established several years ago a Scottish Business Forum in the hope that we could increase traffic between Chicago and Scotland. That has turned out to be our native-born Scottish organisation. It's run by a native-born Scot and it seems as they have migrated to that group. (C16)

....

> The British-American Business Council's events tend to be more social than anything else. They're not big enough — I think their membership is only seventy. If the ambassador came from Washington, I would not go to the British-American Business Council to ask them to be the vehicle for a lunch or a dinner because frankly they're not big enough. There are much bigger business organisations that would be a better vehicle. But the British-American Council is more socially organised. Therefore, what we're trying to do, and it's mutually beneficial, is to bring in the St Andrew Society and allow the members of the St Andrew Society to have access and participate in the BABC events, as members. And it's both aimed at Americans that might be interested in their British heritage, and sometimes not necessarily new arrivals but people that have lost touch with their roots and they find out that

there's a St Andrew Society, a BABC and might have an interest in getting involved. (C6)

It is undoubtedly the case that some of those involved in organisations are native-born Scots. For example, at the time when the Colorado research was undertaken, two of the seven elected council members of the St Andrew Society of Colorado were Scots born. When researching in New York, several of the key figures within the Royal Scottish Country Dance Society's New York branch were also born and raised in Scotland. But, as noted earlier, it may also be the case that some Scots may actually choose not to join expatriate societies. Some may see them as too dominated by Scottish Americans with an interest in heritage issues and may not therefore see them as particularly relevant. Other individuals may feel that they want to become more integrated into American society and see no need to cling to their past. This was a particular issue raised in relation to the Gaelic learning groups, where native Gaelic speakers did not get involved, perhaps because they viewed the language as having little value in an American context:

> **I:** To what extent are the people involved with the Gaelic classes Americans versus Scots born? Do you have some native Gaelic speakers?
>
> **R:** Well, we've identified at the Games, people that come up and say, 'Ciamar a tha sibh?'[7] and that type of stuff. But one of the problems with the Scottish community as opposed to the Irish community is that the native speakers for the most part are not involved.
>
> **I:** Why do you think that is?
>
> **R:** They don't join into the Gaelic-Scottish organisations. They might join the St Andrew Society or other groups, Caledonian clubs. The theories that have gone around are, one, the treatment of Gaelic itself in Scotland. It would be kind of like if an American were to go to Australia and find an Appalachian club. So even if you are from Appalachia you would be a little leery of why are these people interested in something from Appalachia. Also a lot may not write or read Gaelic. And they may not have spoken it in a while so they may be rusty themselves and a little scared. And unless they feel a strong identity ... There are a few

7 'How are you?'

native speakers here who teach and have a strong identity, that it's part of their mission. But apart from those very few people, speaking Gaelic is no different than speaking anything else, so what's the attraction other than you can hold a conversation in it? (C21)

This evidence, that some native-born Scots are possibly reluctant to participate in expatriate Scottish organisations, highlights differences in attitudes towards Scottish identity between native Scots and Scottish Americans. It emerged in a number of the interviews, especially in relation to the activities of the more traditional bodies such as the St Andrew societies and it is of interest to explore further.

The views of the Scots-born

Those interviewees who had been born or brought up in Scotland had a significantly different approach to social activity than the American Scots who were generally the most active in Scottish societies. Many St Andrew Society activities tend generally to be limited to key occasions such as Burns Supper, St Andrew Dinner and Ball, Tartan Day and the like and societies themselves do not often become directly involved in organising regular Scottish dances; rather these are the responsibility of local dance groups, such as the various branches of the Royal Scottish Country Dance Society (RSCDS). A number of those interviewed, who had been born in Scotland stated that they would have liked to see a wider range of activities, including ceilidhs, and there was a particular concern that most dances tended to be rather formal affairs.

At this point, it is worth saying a word about the different forms of Scottish dancing. Highland dancing is very formal, performed by individual dancers and is most commonly seen at Highland Games, dancing displays and competitions. Dancers compete for awards, which are made on the basis of skill, style and footwork. The most common dances are the Highland Fling, the Sword Dance and the Sean Triubhas.

Scottish country dancing is social dancing, in which couples usually line up in sets of three, four or five couples and perform a wide range of dances, using various steps and movements. Dances tend to be divided into reels (the fastest dances), hornpipes, jigs and strathspeys (the slowest). The revival of Scottish country dancing from the 1920s onwards owes much to the efforts of Jean Milligan and Ysobel Stewart, who collected and published the older dances and helped to popularise them again. Today, the RSCDS, which they founded, has branches across the world.

Finally, the most informal form of Scottish dancing is ceilidh dancing. This is the dancing that is most common in Scotland itself, with dances such as the Gay Gordons, Dashing White Sergeant, Eightsome Reel and Strip the Willow being the mainstay of many social events. Many Scottish children are taught the basic steps of these dances at school and, while individuals may not be proficient at such dances, most people are probably able to make a passable attempt at doing them. From the 1970s onwards, there was a significant growth in interest in ceilidh dancing, helped by clubs such as the Riverside Club in Glasgow, which ran regular ceilidh sessions (Morrison, 2003).

Interviewees who had been born in Scotland therefore tended to have a knowledge of and a background in ceilidh dancing and wished to have the opportunity of attending ceilidhs. They also appeared to approach such dancing in a fairly casual and relaxed way, as they thought this would lead to greater enjoyment. American Scots, however, appeared to be more interested in the more formal country dancing and adopted a very 'correct' way of dancing, with great attention being paid to footwork:

> **R:** When I lived in Virginia Beach for seventeen years, I was the president for four years of the Tidewater Scottish Society. We used to run a lot of dances there and all that. But since I came to Colorado, I haven't met too many Scots here. There's a St Andrew Society here, but I wasn't that impressed with them the couple of times I have been.
>
> **I:** You've been along to a couple of their functions?
>
> **R:** Well, they've got Scottish country dancing. It just wasn't my cup of tea so to speak. It's different from the Scottish dancing at home. Here it's all groups of eight or six, and no hooching[8] or anything like that. Very sedate. Whereas you used to do the Gay Gordons and Eightsome Reels in Glasgow and whatnot at the Highlanders Institute and you're hooching away there. You'd a wee dram before you went, mind. (C9)

8   At a ceilidh in Scotland it is common for individuals to yell out during the dancing, and this is what is being referred to as 'hooching' — the point being to add noise, excitement and possibly ribaldry to the occasion. The Highlanders Institute referred to was a social club in Glasgow for migrants from the Highlands and Islands, which ran regular weekend ceilidh dances in its day. It closed in the late 1970s.

When I first came here in 1972, the St Andrew Society was very small. It started around 1969, I think, but it was a very small group. The dancers were mostly from home, with a few Americans. The dances were fun. We had them as they do now, in church halls or wherever we could get free space. There were a couple of couples that led it. We had music and that was it. We did the Eightsome Reel, the Dashing White Sergeant, the Military Two-Step, the Highland Scottische, we did all those kinds of dances and it was a lot of fun. I can't tell you why I dropped out of the dancing, perhaps because of my career, I was travelling and life gets in the way. A couple of years ago I got lonely to do Scottish dancing. I love dancing. I called up one day and got some information. I actually probably got it out of the newsletter. I went to the dancing. I only went for two months and I stopped going because I found it very staid, very much more formal — not in sense of dress, but you couldn't hooch or anything like that. (C17)

I don't like going to the RSCDS because there's so many new dances and my memory's not what it was. But I go to the Highland Balls and ceilidhs and do the older dances. (N15)

R: In Inverness, they taught us Highland dancing in the Boy Scouts and things. I could do an Eightsome and a Foursome and all these dances with the best of them. I got into country dancing over here and I didn't know any of the dances.
I: Because they're set dances?
R: I know the Eightsome Reel, but they don't do them the same way. They have developed their own patterns and some of them are quite local. That was disconcerting.
I: They didn't have ceilidhs where you would do the Dashing White Sergeant and the Gay Gordons?
R: I ended up teaching the Gay Gordons at one stage because they were all doing different dances. I think that's what happens. The third-generation Scots go and read a book and become dancers. The dances aren't the same as we used to do then.
I: You found it hard to get into that?
R: I didn't want to change what I knew was the right way to do it.

That and not too many of them were actually Scottish. They are Americans. (C20)

Personal observation would suggest that there is indeed a relatively poor knowledge of ceilidh dances within the Scottish-American community. While in Colorado, I attended one ceilidh in Denver where the opening dance was a Gay Gordons. As described above, this is a dance that is a mainstay of almost any Scottish social event and is relatively straightforward. Within Scotland, the dance would simply be announced and, as the band played the opening bars of the music, couples would move on to the floor with little further thought. In Denver, however, those present required four 'walk throughs' before they appeared confident enough to dance it. This was also the case with other ceilidh dances and this experience bears out the views of interviewees described above.

What is also interesting within America is the fact that some of those who are members of Scottish dance societies actually have no Scottish connection whatsoever. Their interest is in the dances themselves rather than in their origins and their wider significance. As a result, they perhaps have a more 'intellectual' approach to dancing, rather than the relaxed and informal approach adopted by those who are Scottish born and who grew up with the dances concerned. In New York, for example, the local branch of the RSCDS appears to have had a non-Scottish origin:

> The branch was actually started by a Jewish folk dancing group who were exposed to Scottish country dancing and they liked the discipline of it. There is a discipline you don't get in some other types of folk dancing. They imported a teacher of Scottish country dance from Boston and she willingly came down to Manhattan and taught Scottish country dancing to this group of folk dancers. Eventually they got enough people together and they had Jeannie Carmichael, the lady I'm talking about from Boston, a dance teacher and a Glasgow woman and they finally got enough experience that they sent people to St Andrews in Scotland to go in for a teacher's examination. And they formed their own class and then they applied to Scotland to form their own branch, because they had the numbers. This happened in 1953, they became a branch of the RSCDS. (N9)

The apparent formality towards dancing exhibited by the American Scots was also believed by many interviewees to extend to Scottish dress. It was observed that the approach of Americans towards aspects of Scottish dress may be historically accurate but would not perhaps be recognised by most modern Scots. Some American Scots talked to me informally about the need to wear the 'correct' clan tartan and had been careful to order the appropriate garments from Scottish dress suppliers. There was occasional surprise when I confessed that my own kilt was an invented tartan called 'Flower of Scotland' and that it had been bought cheaply in an ex-hire sale. This, however, is the way many individuals in Scotland acquire kilts.

Indeed, many American Scots appeared to view the kilt as being formal dress wear, rather than a more casual item of clothing. Hence:

> **R:** Some Scots that have observed the Games say there are more kilts here then you will ever see in Scotland. That has to do with the notion that the Scottish culture is frozen, in a sense — for some people certainly.
>
> **I:** The Scottish culture here, in America?
>
> **R:** Yes, exactly. So you will have a picture of a great-great-grandfather and he is dressed in Scottish clothing, and you will match that — as opposed to thinking 'I will get a different kind of tie' — because it was what you wore every day. But it is not what you wear every day and it gets kind of settled in and you get critiqued if you don't wear quite the right set of things.
>
> **I:** So, when people are thinking about their identity, you think people have a very historical view of what it means?
>
> **R:** That's one possibility. (C11)

> **R:** Do you wear a kilt?
>
> **I:** Yes.
>
> **R:** Then you know a kilt is a natural thing. I mean, it doesn't hang with straight sides and the pleats look as though they were ironed with starch. It's a casual thing. These aren't casual things. They hang like the Scots Guards on parade. They don't look natural.
>
> **I:** Is that because you think people are wearing kilts at only very limited times and so they don't get used to it?
>
> **R:** Yes. (C20)

Native-born Scots appeared slightly bemused at the way in which American Scots dressed, particularly for the Highland Games. While impressed at the scale of the organisation, they were nevertheless taken aback at the swords and other accessories which were carried:

> What I find amusing at the Games is the degree of 'authenticity' that many of the attendees bring to the event. Many of them are armed to the teeth with claymores, spears, swords etc. — and all in kilts — so much so that you'd have sworn they'd just walked off the battlefield at Culloden! (C6)

....

> The biggest Games I have been to was when *Braveheart* came out. I believe it was wrong for the Scots, because this movie got their blood boiling. They all got dressed up there. Some of the sights you see are not Scottish. I've even seen guys with different tartan socks on, you know, on each leg. And kilts, it's unbelievable, the length of them. They're mini-kilts! The biggest Scottish games were when *Braveheart* was popular years ago. (C9)

There did appear to be a concern amongst native-born Scots that the 'Scottish' societies were gradually becoming less 'Scottish' and that their activities were becoming less 'authentic'. This appeared to reflect a reduced immigration from Scotland, so that the traditions being developed by some organisations were increasingly 'Scottish American', rather than purely Scottish ones:

> Every time we moved the first thing I did, I would go and look for a house, and the next thing I would look for a Scottish society, because that was our roots. In New Orleans it wasn't too active, but it was fairly active. Pennsylvania had a bigger one. Seattle had a good one. When we came here, we went to a St Andrew's Dance one night and there were hardly any true Scots to run it. A lot of people died off and there's not too many young people to replenish them ... But there's a lot of stuff that they do that just isn't authentic, which would put you off. (C10)

On a more personal level, one interviewee, in reflecting on what he saw as the formality and seriousness of American Scots in their approach to their 'Scottishness', suggested that there were significant differences in personality traits between the two groups:

> It's a different sense of humour. Since I have been here in Colorado, I've sort of clung to any Scots guys. There aren't many Scotsmen here.

> There's a few Scottish women around here that married American men from the Second World War. Maybe it's me but I don't see them having the same humour. I don't see that it's the same conversation in American men that we have with ourselves. Maybe I'm clannish, but a different upbringing. (C9)

And in New York recent migrants noted that native-born Scots were likely to attend concerts by Scottish entertainers and musicians but were probably not interested in Scottish-American heritage societies. There was therefore a clear divide in relation to social activities and tastes:

> Sometimes you see something that crosses over, like a Billy Connolly gig or the Proclaimers and all these Scots come out of the woodwork. It's amazing because they don't come out for Scottish-themed things. Which I think is fine because of the sense of identity, the Scottish cringe, that sort of thing. I think the longer you're here, you feel a bit more remote and you get over that sort of thing. (N5)

Conclusions

This chapter has described the range of Scottish organisations existing in America and the ways in which their activities have changed over the years. It is clear that they have played an important role within the diaspora but that role has altered significantly. Initially, they were agencies of support, to help newly arrived Scots migrants find their feet in America as well as having a social role in facilitating Scots families to remain in contact. But as emigration from Scotland slowed during the Great Depression, and as Scots within the United States became more scattered as they moved around the country, such organisations appear to have become less significant.

The major change seems to have come in the 1950s with the growing interest in heritage and family history, and the activities of individuals such as Donald F. MacDonald, the founder of the Grandfather Mountain Highland Games, and Angus L. Macdonald in Nova Scotia. The expansion in both the number and the scale of North American Highland Games has been remarkable and demonstrates very clearly Gans' (1979) 'symbolic ethnicity' in relation to the Scots and the growth in heritage as a leisure pursuit. North American Highland Games are clearly very different to those that take place in Scotland itself and demonstrate an invention of tradition within the diaspora community.

What might one make of this? Scottish organisations now appear to be increasingly middle-class affairs. Participation in their activities often involves considerable expenditure — particularly on Scottish dress — and this can be costly. It is also a leisure time activity (Novak, 1971), and so participation may end up being rather limited to those with enough time and money to play a part.

The purpose of symbolic ethnicity is, in part, to distinguish one's own ethnic group from others. To that extent, the growth of Scottish organisations, and particularly their highly visible events such as Highland Games, have raised the profile of Scots in America. Waters (1990) was able to suggest that the Scots were less popular as an ethnicity than many others but this appears to have changed, as Scottish diaspora traditions are invented and spread.

One interesting issue that has emerged from the research is the increasing 'disconnect' between American Scots and native-born Scots within the USA and this has manifested itself in a number of ways. Those individuals born and/or brought up in Scotland appeared to be less interested in joining heritage organisations than American Scots for whom heritage and ancestry are important. Native-born Scots were less concerned about their identity or ethnicity, as they rarely had to think about it; it was, in Billig's (1995) phrase, 'banal'.

As well as differences in their attitudes to Scottish organisations, attitudes to dance, Scottish dress and tradition also varied and native-born Scots clearly were less concerned about the 'correct' way to dance, to wear a kilt or having the 'correct' clan tartan. They were far more relaxed about these things and perhaps a little bemused about how significant they seemed to be to the American diaspora Scots.

These differences are most clearly illustrated by the emergence of quite distinct American Scottish traditions which are rooted entirely in America and which have little to do with the Scottish 'homeland'. One of the best examples of this invention of tradition is Tartan Day, and it is to this that I now turn.

Chapter 4

Tartan Day

Countries usually have a national day of celebration and so too do many national diasporic groups. Some nations and national groups celebrate an agreed national day such as the day of their independence, while others (like the Irish) celebrate the day of their patron saint, Saint Patrick. Scotland is slightly unusual in that it is not an independent country — a 'stateless nation' in McCrone's (2001b) phrase — and so has no obvious national day. Within Scotland itself, the most significant celebrations tend to be on 25 January (the birthday of Robert Burns, the national poet) and on 31 December (Hogmanay). The diaspora may have celebrated the patron saint St Andrew's Day (30 November) when it was more or less ignored at home. But the St Andrew's Day Holiday (Scotland) Act, passed by the Scottish Parliament in 2006, gave encouragement to employers to recognise the day and potentially award it as a holiday to their employees. Since then, there has been a noticeable increase in the number of celebrations in Scotland taking place on that day.

For years, Scottish organisations elsewhere celebrated these days — including St Andrew's Day — but in the last twenty years or so North America has seen the emergence of another distinctive day on which expatriate Scots celebrate their heritage. This is Tartan Day, held each year on or around 6 April.

This chapter describes the origins of Tartan Day, its growing significance and how it might develop in the future. I also discuss the occasional tensions between Scottish Americans and 'homeland' Scots in regard to the celebrations, and not least to the use of 'tartan' as the means whereby Scotland is identified.

Origins of Tartan Day

The idea of celebrating a Scottish national day overseas appears to have had its origins in Canada and, more specifically, within the province of Nova

Scotia. In 1986, the Federation of Scottish Clans in Nova Scotia discussed the issue and subsequently they wrote to each provincial legislature within the country to urge the establishment of a day that they proposed be called Tartan Day. There was a suggestion that 6 April might be the appropriate date, as it was the anniversary of the signing of the Declaration of Arbroath in 1320, asserting Scottish nationhood. After Nova Scotia in 1987, other provinces passed Tartan Day Acts; the first Tartan Days were celebrated in Ontario and Saskatchewan in 1992, New Brunswick in 1993 and eventually in all Canadian provinces with the exception of Quebec and Newfoundland (Fraser, n.d.).

Within the United States a number of Scottish organisations began discussions as to how to follow suit, and an interesting personal account of these early negotiations was given in interview by Alan Bain, president of the American-Scottish Foundation. The foundation is a membership organisation based in New York, which aims to strengthen the individual, institutional and business links between Scotland and America through a range of social, cultural, educational and economic activities. It is perhaps more business-focused than most Scottish organisations within the USA and every year holds a Leadership Conference involving Scottish organisations, businesses, philanthropists and the like, with a view to enhancing links, collaborations and fundraising. The foundation has been very active in Tartan Day:

> I'll give you the history. In 1994, the Caledonian Foundation based in Sarasota, Florida, set up initially to support Scottish Opera but now supporting Scottish culture and arts generally, was celebrating its twenty-fifth anniversary and this formidable lady, Miss Duncan Macdonald — the vice-president I think at the time — suggested that it would be a very good idea to invite representatives of all national Scottish organisations to come down to Sarasota to help in the celebrations and to meet each other, to network. I was invited to go down, representing the American-Scottish Foundation, which is not localised as a lot of societies are.

> I went down there and I met the gentleman who represented the Council of Scottish Clans and Associations, the head of the Scottish Games Association, the Scottish Heritage Society, the Caledonian Foundation and maybe one other. We've subsequently added the Scottish-American Military Society to our group. And Duncan invited

down a gentleman from Canada, from Toronto, who was the convener of Clan Fraser in that area. And they'd come up with the idea of Tartan Day in Canada. And he explained why and why the date was chosen, its significance, and we thought this was an excellent idea for us as a group. It was not competitive with anything that anybody was doing. So we were each given a remit and my remit was to take Tartan Day on as a project in New York City, which we did. Then, by happenstance, I was approached by a group that wanted to put Tartan Day on in Washington DC. Now one of the outgrowths of that is that, in order to put on the best possible event in the city and to make sure that the event would be perpetuated, we formed the National Tartan Day New York committee, which encompasses the St Andrew's Society, the New York Caledonian Club, now the Tartan Army. And we meet regularly, and our remit is basically the parade and events surrounding the parade to provide social activity and fun for people who come to our city to support the event.

The whole premise of Tartan Day, which I have to point out is an American idea borrowed from the Canadians, and I should explain our issue when we were meeting and discussing its merits and what we were hoping to achieve out of it. Our issue is that the Scottish involvement in this country is so essential — it goes to the very foundation of this country — but Americans at large do not understand that many of the Founding Fathers were Scots or of immediate Scottish descent. So our point in Tartan Day was to get the message out about Scotland's historic influence on the formation and creation and building of this country. (N10)

The idea for Tartan Day was subsequently taken up by Trent Lott, the Republican leader in the US Senate who 'invented for the Senate's benefit a remarkable interpretation of history' (Ascherson, 2002). He proposed Senate Resolution 155, which was passed unanimously on 20 March 1998. Together with its preamble, it read as follows:

Whereas April 6 has a special significance for all Americans, and especially those Americans of Scottish descent, because the Declaration of Arbroath, the Scottish Declaration of Independence, was signed on April 6, 1320 and the American Declaration of Independence was modelled on that inspirational document;

Whereas this resolution honors the major role that Scottish Americans played in the founding of this Nation, such as the fact that almost half of the signers of the Declaration of Independence were of Scottish descent, the Governors in nine of the original thirteen States were of Scottish ancestry, Scottish Americans successfully helped shape this country in its formative years and guide this Nation through its most troubled times;

Whereas this resolution recognises the monumental achievements and invaluable contributions made by Scottish Americans that have led to America's pre-eminence in the fields of science, technology, medicine, government, politics, economics, architecture, literature, media, and visual and performing arts;

Whereas this resolution commends the more than 200 organisations throughout the United States that honor Scottish heritage, tradition and culture, representing the hundreds of thousands of Americans of Scottish descent, residing in every State, who already have made the observance of Tartan Day on April 6 a success;

Whereas these numerous individuals, clans, societies, clubs and fraternal organisations do not let the great contributions of the Scottish people go unnoticed:

Now therefore be it Resolved, That the Senate designates April 6 of each year as 'National Tartan Day'.

It is perhaps worth taking a moment to discuss the significance of the Declaration of Arbroath. The declaration followed the Scottish Wars of Independence in which first William Wallace and then Robert the Bruce fought for Scottish independence and nationhood, defeating invading English armies at the battles of Stirling Bridge in 1297 and Bannockburn in 1314. The Declaration of Arbroath was in the form of a letter sent to Pope John XXII and dated 6 April 1320. It asserted Scotland's status as an independent sovereign state. Its significance for the United States lies in the fact that it has been seen by some as a model for the American Declaration of Independence. Duncan Bruce, president of the St Andrew's Society of the State of New York, has analysed the two documents and pointed out the similarities:

By the way, I should tell you and I hope I don't sound immodest but Tartan Day in the United States started when a friend of mine took my first book [*The Mark of the Scots*] to Senator Trent Lott, who at that time was the Senate majority leader, and he's part-Scottish. He proposed that National Tartan Day be created and be a holiday, even used some of my words. And then finally, when the declaration was signed, he used my stuff again. So my book was the first one, as far as I know, and the only one so far to detail a line by line comparison of the Declaration of Arbroath versus the Declaration of Independence. I think anybody who looks at my line-by-line comparison would say, 'Well, that's certain, that one is derived from the other.' Most importantly [are] the two concepts. The one concept is that in both documents the people are being governed with their consent which is necessary. Now going back to mediaeval times, well that's a pretty advanced document. And the other [concept] is that even though they loved King Robert and he was doing a great job, if he ever turned around and put them back under English control they had the right to get rid of him. (N6)

There has been considerable debate about the connection between the Declaration of Arbroath and the American Declaration of Independence. Although Duncan Bruce is in little doubt that the one influenced the other, academic historians have exercised a great deal more caution. Fry (2003), for example, pointed out that the language of the two declarations could not possibly be similar because one was written in English, the other in Latin. He went on:

Not a single reputable historian sees parallels between the concepts enshrined in the two declarations, because parallels do not exist. In reality, and with apologies to Senator Lott, there are no grounds for thinking that any American gathered on that steamy day in Pennsylvania gave a moment's thought to the Declaration of Arbroath; with the possible exception of John Witherspoon, none had probably heard of it. Even if they had, it would have been hard to imagine a place or time less relevant to the aspirations of the Thirteen Colonies in 1776 than the Scotland of the fourteenth century. (Fry, 2003, p. 227)

There has also been an interesting debate in the journal *Scottish Affairs*, in which Euan Hague (2002b), a Scottish academic now resident in the USA, has questioned the authenticity of Tartan Day and its apparent rewriting of Scottish history. His article prompted a response from Duncan Bruce (2002) himself, in turn critical of Hague, followed in turn by a final rejoinder from Hague (2002c).

What is not in doubt is that, as with other events such as the Kirkin' o' the Tartan, the US Senate, in passing the Tartan Day resolution, promptly invented a tradition, one specifically developed outwith Scotland to serve a diaspora community (Hague, 2002b). Cowan (2005) noted that much of Trent Lott's history is sheer invention. Apparently, Lott made known when accepting the Wallace Prize in Washington in 2000 (described below) that a major influence in his thinking was Mel Gibson's blockbuster film *Braveheart*, released in 1995 and both directed by and starring Gibson as William Wallace. The film was hugely successful on both sides of the Atlantic and won five Academy Awards, including those for Best Film and Best Director (MacArthur, 2003).

Yet, although the history portrayed in *Braveheart* may be as questionable as that portrayed by Tartan Day, both have undoubtedly struck a chord with many people in both Scotland and in America. American Scots, while not necessarily identifying with Lott's politics, were prepared to exploit his interest in order to have Tartan Day officially recognised. It is, of course, much more about America than about Scotland. Fry (2003) described the discomfort of Scottish politicians who attend Tartan Day and experience significant culture shock. Most are unused to being required to shout 'Tartan!' and 'Freedom!' at the tops of their voices. As he pointed out:

> The source of embarrassment lay in the fact that this ceremony, just like those Highland Games in the Old South, was not really about Scotland but about America. It did not convey what Scots think about themselves, but what Americans think about them: and in both cases the thoughts may be a little confused, which does not help. (Fry, 2003, p. 225)

Indeed, there seems to be a widespread recognition that, while the idea of Tartan Day has been embraced relatively enthusiastically within the US, many people in Scotland are ambivalent about it. There are concerns about its name for one thing, with many Scots believing that the use of the word 'tartan' to identify Scotland is serving to perpetuate an outdated 'shortbread tin' image of the country. As Hague (2002b) has pointed out, the development of Tartan Day will inevitably influence how Scotland is represented and perceived in the United States and he noted that there have been three main reactions to the Senate decision. One highly critical group argued that Tartan Day will promote an 'out-dated stereotype of Scotland that perpetuates images of haggis, tartan, caber tossing, shortbread and the Loch Ness Monster'. A second group, comprising the Scottish business and political communities, has been broadly welcoming. The third group, as discussed above, has questioned the underlying historical basis of the Tartan Day resolution, particularly the influence of the Declaration of Arbroath on the American Declaration of Independence.

For those involved in Tartan Day organisation therefore it has sometimes proved difficult to persuade homeland Scots to become involved. Some American Scots who were interviewed expressed their disappointment at this but believed that, as a result of the early success of Tartan Day, there would eventually be a more equal input from both sides of the Atlantic:

> It's a two-edged sword, if you will. Nobody owns Tartan Day. We wanted it to be a grassroots manifestation and that's really what it's become around the country. Tartan Day events are taking place, which are organised by local people in celebration of the event. Where it got a little complicated is that, when I was looking at the event, I saw the opportunity for Scotland to have a platform, to kind of present itself as it is today. So we encouraged, with some difficulty I have to say initially, the Scots to get involved.
>
> But in 2000, when we were running the Tartan Day event in Washington dc, we revived our Wallace Award, and our Wallace Award was presented to Senator Trent Lott, then Senate majority leader for the Republican Party. Why him? Because he was the sponsor of the legislation that created the day in the first place. We recognised him, and because of his position in the Senate we were given the Capitol Hill steps where the president gets inaugurated, we had a whole panoply of senators and congressmen on the dais. It was a truly magnificent affair. In the audience were George Reid, Patricia Ferguson and Henry McLeish, I think Struan Stevenson and maybe one or two others.[1] But those key players looked and thought 'Well,

1 In 2000, Henry McLeish, George Reid and Patricia Ferguson were all Members of the Scottish Parliament. Henry McLeish was First Minister of Scotland 2000–2001 and George Reid was later the Scottish Parliament's presiding officer 2003–2007. Struan Stevenson has been a Member of the European Parliament for Scotland since 1999.

> wait a minute. There's something here to build on.' So they went back
> to Scotland and thought well, maybe we should engage with Tartan
> Day. So Scotland's engagement then escalated. My issue that I have is
> that it is not as joined-up as I believe it should be. There isn't enough
> communication between the two sides. (N10)

During the twelve years since the passing of the Senate resolution establishing Tartan Day, the scale of the celebrations has increased, with events
taking place across the country. The main events, however, continue to be
in New York and, to a lesser extent, Washington DC.

Tartan Day today

The New York celebrations have grown significantly over the years and
soon became Tartan Week — although the Scottish government prefers
to refer to it as Scotland Week. In 2007, because 6 April fell on the Easter
weekend and it was not possible for the parade to take place at its usual
time, it was scheduled a week later. Tartan Week events therefore stretched
over two weeks, becoming Tartan Fortnight, although this was not a
phrase used by the organisers.

There are now a significant number of events that take place. In
the arts, there are a large number of musical events, featuring Scottish
bands, sometimes performing in pubs, sometimes in open-air concerts.
Theatrical performances have also entered the programme and, in 2007,
an Edinburgh Festival Fringe play, *Did You Used To Be R. D. Laing?* was
performed at the American Theatre of Actors. In 2008, the Scottish
Youth Theatre performed at the Algonquin Theatre for a week. Events
involving Scottish writers such as Andrew O'Hagan, Ian Rankin and
Alexander McCall Smith have also featured on the programmes in the
last few years.

Lecture programmes have also been developed, featuring speakers
on various aspects of Scottish history and culture, and sometimes incor-
porating music and film. In 2007, the lectures were held at the New York
Historical Society; in 2008 at the New York Public Library. History is also
celebrated in the annual Tartan Day heritage event on Ellis Island, organised by the Clan Currie Society.

Other events of a more 'one-off' nature have included an exhibition
of the work of Scottish silversmiths, entitled 'Silver of the Stars' and held

in the Forbes Galleries in 2007, a reception to recognise and support the work of the National Trust for Scotland, held in the Metropolitan Club in 2008, and in 2010 a photographic exhibition of the work of Harry Benson.

Sport is also part of the programme. On the first Sunday of Tartan Week, the annual 10k Scotland Run takes place in Central Park, an event started in 2004. In 2006, the New York City Tartan Army launched an annual football (soccer) match between its own members and visitors to the city; this usually takes place at the Pier 40 Soccer Complex. Thus, events are being launched regularly with some rapidly becoming annual 'traditions'.

Social events vary enormously. The New York Caledonian Club organises a pre-parade ceilidh while the New York City Tartan Army organises a post-parade one. The latter develops into an evening event, held in a pub and lasting well into the night. More formal (and expensive) is the St Andrew's Society Cocktail Reception and Tartan Ball, while the society is also responsible for organising the Kirkin' o' the Tartan, held in the Central Presbyterian Church on Park Avenue.

Between 2005 and 2007, there was also a 'Scottish Village' in the Vanderbilt Hall of Grand Central Station, featuring a number of retailers, heritage and tourist agencies. The Village appeared small and rather insignificant in the vastness of Grand Central and raised the question as to whether a larger trade event, showcasing Scottish products, might not have made more of an impact. But:

> The Scottish Village is run and organised by VisitScotland and for them it's primarily a tourism promotion. To be honest, I haven't heard others say it's small and lacks ambition. The bigger companies already have a profile and a network and an ability to get their goods to market here. The Pringles and the Baxters of this world, and I suppose Walkers as well. You're right, it's a limited space, but it has developed over time. The Village looks quite different this year from how it looked two or three years ago. One of the big things they've been able to do this year is allow people actually to sell goods in the Village, which didn't happen until this year. I think that's a step forward. (N8)

The growth in the number of events throughout Tartan Week was mentioned by a number of individuals in interviews:

> And what's happened is, over the years, it's become much more than

just the Tartan Day. There's much more going on, from the Scottish Village in Grand Central Station to cultural activities — dancers, singers and so on. Most years, they've had 'Dressed to Kilt' with Geoffrey Scott-Carroll, which has got a little bit out of my price range now. There's been a number of events organised by Alan Bain of the American-Scottish Foundation. (N11)

'Dressed to Kilt' has been one of the most high profile events in Tartan Week and almost the only one that regularly merits column inches in the New York newspapers or in *Time Out New York*. It is a major fashion show, usually featuring tartan fabrics, and attended by celebrities such as Sir Sean Connery and his wife. In some respects, it is more a part of the world of fashion than of the Scottish diaspora and it was perhaps no surprise in 2008 when it was rescheduled to take place in the autumn, rather than in April, to fit in with the fashion world calendar. However, in 2009, it was moved back to Tartan Week.

The largest event in Tartan Week is, of course, the main parade, on Sixth Avenue. In many respects, this is the culmination of the week and in some years it has had a major impact — for example, when Sean Connery led the parade. But some people have questioned the format, remarking that it perhaps compares unfavourably with the size of the Irish Americans' St Patrick's Day celebrations:

Let me just talk about the historical side [of Tartan Week]. It was the parade up Sixth Avenue, when Sean Connery went up with 10,000 pipers — that was great publicity. But the truth is there's typically 2,000. Unfortunately it looks awfully small on Sixth Avenue. Considering that St Patrick's parade is three weeks earlier, which attracts, what, a million? And basically the police and the fire people take the day off so they can go to the parade. So I don't know what the numbers are — certainly tens of thousands. So purely from a positioning and marketing point of view, the parade itself, using the same format, up a city street in New York is kind of a losing proposition. And if you ask people around, many connect Ireland and Scotland and think the Irish are having another march. So I don't think it's possible to win that one. Maybe they shouldn't change the format — keep the pipers — but maybe have it in say Battery Park. It will be 2,000 pipers, it'll be great. But unless you've got a wide angle lens, you're going to see it's empty. So from the point of view of Scotland, and representing Scotland, I'm not critical of the parade, I just don't see how that format can work. (N3)

Personal observation would support this. In 2007, for example, the parade consisted of seventeen separate pipe bands, seven clan societies, nine Scottish American organisations, a Scottish university and a collection of Scottish dogs. The pipe bands were impressive and filled the street with both their presence and their music. But when representatives of the clan societies and other organisations were walking past, then there was much less to engage the spectators. What then might the impact of Tartan Day actually be?

The impact of Tartan Day

Opinion appeared to be divided as to the impact of Tartan Week and, specifically, the Tartan Day parade. Undoubtedly the presence of Scottish politicians in places such as New York and Washington will enhance the connections between the two countries, and the involvement of organisations such as the American-Scottish Foundation is likely to lead to enhanced business links. But a number of interviewees made a comparison with the St Patrick's Day event as referred to above, believing that Tartan Day suffered as a result. Nevertheless, Tartan Day was undoubtedly growing in significance:

> I think it is becoming a big day. Certainly, in and around this city, New York, it's gained a reputation. People expect it. People look forward to it. They understand what it's about. So I think it's certainly something that the Scottish-American community in New York look forward to. But I know that there are Tartan Week celebrations happening all across the US and I'm in touch, more or less regularly, with a whole host of organisations across the US and small and large things are happening. I don't think we've ever seen it — or even the Scots-American community whose invention it was — ever really saw it as in some sense trying to rival or outdo or to get near what St Patrick's Day has become. It's a celebration of their heritage and it's an opportunity for us to tell modern Scotland's story in the US and I suppose that's what we're about. (N8)

> **R:** I would say it's becoming significant in the calendar of the Scots Americans. It's not universally known or appreciated but I think you'll see on Saturday the sort of crowds that are coming to watch are getting

larger and larger.

I: And is it having a spin-off in terms of how it's expanding?

R: In terms of bringing people in, I get the sense it's growing. I get the sense that people are getting involved, but I think only if they already have the Scottish association. I think St Patrick's [Day] is probably unique in that everyone takes part. I mean, from now through the autumn, there's a parade in New York almost every weekend. The Greeks, the Germans, the Puerto Ricans. And I think in most cases, it's people with that background that participate. (N11)

This interviewee implied that participation in Tartan Week events would perhaps be limited to those who were already involved in Scottish organisations of one kind or another. Events would not therefore appeal to a wider audience. Certainly, this would appear to be borne out by the general lack of publicity about the various events, with only 'Dressed to Kilt' receiving any significant press coverage. In 2007, for example, the *New York Times* appeared to be the only city newspaper that carried a photograph of the parade. Thus only those who were members of associations or on relevant mailing lists would know what was taking place:

I: I get the impression that the Tartan Day parade isn't well publicised.

R: That's right. So if you're part of a club or a society or whatever, then you get to hear about it. But otherwise, not in the press, you never get to hear about these things. When you were there, did it look as if people had actually come or had people just come across it?

I: A bit of both, I think. There were some people there in kilts, who had made a point of coming to watch. But you're right. There were some people who were doing their shopping and had stopped and watched just because it was a parade.

R: Well, the only times I've watched it is when I've accidentally come across it. In fact on Saturday I was actually down Sixth Avenue doing some errands and the street was closed off before the parade had started. But I could hear in the distance someone practising on their bagpipes. So I realised it was the Tartan Day parade. (N13)

....

R1: You don't hear much about Tartan Day. You don't get much media coverage. It's really talking it up, the clansmen mentioning it to other people. We just run one bus in, with maybe forty people. It's small. It's not vast, but it's always in our calendar, knowing that we're going to march and the clan that will march with us, although most of the clansmen are bandsmen too.

I: So will most people know what the parade actually is?

R2: Some of those involved in Scottish organisations will go there. I have a group of friends who come down by train from Connecticut, from Hartford I think. Some past years, we've had pipe bands come from Tokyo, Australia, Germany, France, all over the place. That kind of thing has died out because it's expensive. And Tartan Day is still a fairly new holiday in the United States, it's only nine years old. It's not like it's the St Patrick's Day parade. But there are parades in New York City every weekend — Puerto Rican Day, Greek Day, Russian Day, Cuban Day. Then you have the Veterans Day parade and it goes on and on. So most of the people who watch the parades in New York City are not people from New York City, they're tourists. (N14)

While accepting that those who are members of Scottish organisations will be much more likely to be aware of Tartan Week events than the general public, there also appeared to be a division between expatriate Scots, who had actually been born in Scotland but were living in America, and diaspora American Scots, who had ancestral links with Scotland. The former tended to view Tartan Week as having perhaps less relevance for themselves, and thought of the whole event as being essentially a Scottish-American one. The position was articulated in an interview with an office-bearer of the New York City Tartan Army:

R: When [Tartan Day] started, for a lot of people in the Tartan Army, there was a feeling that this wasn't much to do with the Scotland we know. For one thing, it's kind of artificial, like it's a copy of St Patrick's Day or something. So a lot of people thought that this was about shortbread — a, you know, 'tinned' image of Scotland and people didn't want that much to do with it. A couple of years went by and it was pretty small, then we thought well you can ignore it, which is kind of cynical and the easy thing to do, or you can make the most of it and try and have fun with it. So we started having parties and things and we're on our fifth year of parties and our fourth year of taking part in the parade. The first year I think we had six people. The second, it was twelve. And then the next year it was maybe thirty or forty. And then last year, there were too many folk for me to count, who took part as part of the Tartan Army. The parade has a couple of thousand people in it so we're one of the larger groups, although we're a little bit disorganised which may be a bone of contention with some of them.

I: Do you think then that's it's become an important day on the calendar?

R: It's difficult to get a feel for what it means to be Scottish American in New York, I think. Our group is predominantly expats, Scottish born. There are a few exceptions. And I think some of the more traditional groups have many Scottish born in them, but also second, third, fourth generation. And I think it means something different to them. If you're part of a Scottish organisation, it's become a date around which you can organise things. Obviously, April 6, while it's a historical day, it wasn't something that was actively part of your calendar. I think Burns Night and Hogmanay were really the only dates. I mean even St Andrew's Day, Battle of Bannockburn, weren't things that were really celebrated. So I don't know how important it is to people. (N5)

In other parts of America, Tartan Day events are generally quite small, although they are often seen as still having some impact. In the main, they consist of dinners, dances or ceilidhs, piping displays or contests, whisky tasting and various family 'fun days' and galas. In Washington DC, there is a reception on Capitol Hill, which is a high-profile event but outwith Washington and New York few cities hold large parades. Sometimes, there is a belief that local people will not really be aware of the event, although local politicians have occasionally been persuaded to take part.

For example, within Colorado, there was a general recognition that the annual Tartan Day parade had made only a limited impact, but it was perceived as growing:

There is a Tartan Day celebration. It's held at Civic Center Park in downtown Denver. Near City Hall and the State Capitol here and between them there is a park. That's where it's been the last few years. Has that influenced people? I don't know, maybe a few. I think people wander by due to curiosity. You see the same people you see at the Tartan Day festival at all the other Scottish things, but I am sure there are occasional people it's had some impact on. (C2)

It's very small. This was something that was passed by the US Congress and then the Colorado legislature introduced something very similar. They have this annual ceremony on 6 April. They always invite Senator Allard[2] out who claims to be of Scottish origin. They invite a few other people. To be perfectly honest, they never turn up. (C6)

Well certainly [it's] not as big as we'd like. There again I think it's resources mainly. In New York, Sean Connery and some of the societies there put together 10,000 pipers on Tartan Day. So we'd love to grow that and have the same kind of celebration that the Irish do. We have something like the third largest St Patrick's Day celebration in the country here in Denver. We can certainly top that! (C8)

R: I think across the country, it is having a huge impact. It's the first time that the Senate took time to recognise the Scottish contribution to America. To have the Senate resolution and to have a day set aside when you recognise Scots. In a lot of towns maybe it's only a dinner, but there is something going on in almost every community now on Tartan Day. New York has had big parades and they get the national publicity but I think Tartan Day is going to have a huge impact. Will it ever be as big as St Patrick's Day? Probably not. The Irish overwhelm us in terms of their numbers.
I: It will grow though, you think?
R: I think it will, absolutely. (C16)

For some, the relatively small size of the Denver event was seen as something positive, in that it could be more of a family occasion than the large east coast parades:

> The other thing is family. I don't know if it was 9/11 and the Towers and all that which made you realise family was important. At the festival it seems that it's all about family. (C15)

One particular spin-off of the publicity surrounding Tartan Day has been the growing interest in tartan itself. As the event has grown in Colorado, for example, the state has taken the opportunity to establish its own tartan:

> **R:** I think the first [Tartan Day parade] was three or four years ago. The

---

2 Wayne Allard was a member of the House of Representatives 1991–1996, when he was elected to the Senate as one of Colorado's two senators.

last one we had, we had a great number of clans; we had a fairly large event, much more so than the first couple we had, where it was a quick get-together in a place downtown here in Denver. So it has grown. We now have a Colorado tartan — to many of us that was a very significant happening. The governor has a tie of the Colorado tartan. One of the pipe bands here in Colorado now uses the Colorado tartan for their kilts. I may end up getting a kilt in Colorado tartan because it identifies me as Coloradoan as well as Scottish.

I: What does Colorado's tartan involve?

R: Well, it has purple for purple mountain's majesty, it has blue for the sky, it has white for the snow, it has green for the forests. It is a very attractive tartan. It was designed by a reverend in Colorado Springs and he did a very nice job. (C4)

Finally, we have already seen how, for some Scottish-American organisations, there is often disappointment at the low level of participation in Tartan Week from Scotland itself. Such individuals believed that Tartan Week represented an important opportunity to develop business relations between Scotland and the United States and they expressed surprise that the Scottish government itself had not made more use of the event to promote links between the two countries:

I think it would be important for the Scottish Executive[3] to help Americans celebrate Tartan Day. I know there was some criticism about how much money they spent on their trips to this country last year, but they need to send their national leaders to America — and not just to New York or Washington. They need to scatter them across the country. The governor of Colorado is on his way to Europe. He's going to stop in Glasgow and Edinburgh. Colorado is the sixth largest state in terms of export/import with Scotland. They have yet to have a government official come to Denver and visit with the Scots. They need to help us do that. I know the press is going to raise all sorts of hell about how much money they are spending but I think in the long run it's going to pay dividends for them. (C6)

3 The term 'Scottish Executive' was initially used to describe the devolved government of Scotland following the establishment of the Scottish Parliament in 1999. In May 2007, following the victory of the Scottish National Party in the Parliamentary elections, the title was changed to the simpler 'Scottish government'.

Conclusion: The future of Tartan Day

So far, Tartan Day has apparently been successful across the United States, although the events vary enormously in number and scale, from state to state. While the celebrations have been fairly minimal in some places, those in New York are significant and there is now a range of different events taking place during Tartan Week, as it has now become. The parade in particular has been seen as hugely important in marking the identity of Scottish Americans, with pipe bands led by Scottish celebrities such as Sean Connery.

That said, the parade has apparently become a victim of the current recession. In April 2010, by order of the Police Department, it was allowed to walk along only ten blocks of Sixth Avenue, instead of the previous thirteen, a result of New York City's budget deficit. As noted above, there are some people interviewed who have, in any case, questioned the format of the parade and, in particular, its timing, coming as it does so soon after St Patrick's Day. Perhaps the enforced changes to the parade might lead to a rethinking of the format of future Tartan Day celebrations.

Despite these difficulties, there is no doubt that America has embraced the symbolism of Tartan Day because, for Scottish Americans, tartan is a badge of membership within the Scottish community and of clan affiliation. It is therefore part of the celebration of identity (Ray, 2001a). The nature of the celebration itself may be different from equivalent events in Scotland, but Tartan Day is specifically aimed at the Scottish diaspora and so the tradition that is being created is a recognisably American one.

How then might Tartan Day develop? There is no doubt that, within Scotland itself, the whole concept of Tartan Day is viewed with some suspicion. Partly this may be due to a dislike of seeing Scotland defined by the image of tartan, partly because, for Scots at home, Tartan Day in America is not necessarily viewed as actually being *Scottish*. The tensions are usefully summarised as follows:

> I am sure that many found this more than a bit uncomfortable. It seemed, at least from this distance, to arouse that old *bête noir* of Tom Nairn's, the tartan monster and its excesses. Be that as it may (and how can we tell?), it raised nicely the question of who is a Scot. That dubious statistic of 15 million Scots abroad reared its head. However that calculation is done, it does raise the issue of what defines Scottishness. I guess that much of our native discomfort with Tartan Day is that

many of us living in Scotland do not care very much for an ancestral, an ethnic, definition of Scottishness. 'My mother's a McTavish' does not do a lot to measure the commitment and contribution to Scotland in our scale of values these days. (McCrone, 2001a, p. 20)

From the American side of the Atlantic, the tensions appear to be less a matter of concern. Interviewees appeared to see no difficulty in both celebrating Scottish-American heritage and providing a platform for modern Scotland to promote itself:

I don't think it's a choice and I don't think we have to make a choice. My strong view is that we can do both in Tartan Week and we should do both, because one of the ways in which we are able to tell modern Scotland's story is because people have an understanding about Scotland and there's a positive reaction about Scotland that's about the history and the more traditional things. We need to use that, we need to celebrate it for what it is because it's valuable in itself. But also use it as a hook for getting messages out about what modern Scotland's about. I don't think there's a tension. You may speak to some people who think that there's a problem there. I think we ought to be able to celebrate our heritage, our culture, the impact that Scots have had on shaping this nation, as well as modern Scotland's story. I think there's room for both of those things and, in some senses, they meld into each other as well. (N8)

Despite some misgivings about the name of the event, it does appear that Scottish politicians and business leaders have increasingly come to recognise its importance and have begun both to attend and to use the opportunities available:

I am still very uncomfortable with the name 'Tartan Day'. I think we could have done a lot better than that. But it is what it is and we may as well get on with it. I think if you are of Scottish heritage or an expatriate, I think you do want to celebrate the haggis and tartan part. I think there is a tension because clearly a lot of people in Scotland would say, 'Well, you know, we're twenty-first century Scotland, we don't want all this stuff to stereotype us.' But I think it should be seen as a means to an end. It's a starting point, a talking point. But we need to get that balance between showing that we're not just in the last century, but we're in the current century. (N11)

Scottish politicians and business leaders both recognise the necessity of participating in Tartan Week and a current Scottish government minister stated in an interview that he believed that Scotland needed to make more of the links with its diaspora. This suggests that the government is becoming more relaxed about the 'tartan connection' and seeking to resolve the tensions between the differing aims of the Scots in America and at home:

> I think we beat ourselves up unduly in this country about Tartan Day. It's about a continuation of the cringe. If it is tartanry, so what? It's like people coming into this hotel, having Scottish nights. Shock, horror! Imagine that! Since when has it been an offence to dress up in tartan and play the bagpipes? If that's what some of our expat community like, then good on them. Rather than whinge and whine about Scots who've left, we should actually be grateful that they actually retain an interest. You know, numerous other peoples who have left their countries have abandoned any affinity to the country that they've left. And yet these are people who left, whether it was two years ago or two centuries ago, that retain an affinity and an affection. That's something that's quite incredible and we should welcome that. I think Tartan Day is useful as a symbol of Scottish identity in North America. I think we have to retain that, we have to build upon it. (S2)

In the event, the Scottish government announced in April 2008 that, as far as their contribution was concerned, they would be using the term 'Scotland Week' rather than Tartan Week, so that the country's name became more prominent during the celebrations. The name of Tartan Day for 6 April when the main parade takes place, however, remains.

What is interesting, however, is that although homeland Scots clearly have great reservations about the term 'Tartan Day', the country is itself is beginning to use the term as a peg on which to hang various events. Thus, within Scotland itself, a number of local authorities such as Aberdeenshire, Angus, Dundee, East Renfrewshire and Perth and Kinross have launched Tartan Day events. These include family fun days, piping displays, ceilidhs and, with a nod to the diaspora, the Dundee Family History Centre uses the opportunity to hold an open day for those interested in genealogy. Coupled with the designation of 2009 as the 'Year of Homecoming' for the diaspora — described in more detail in Chapter 7 — it would seem that the use of heritage and tartanry as a way of marketing the country is actually growing in significance. There may be a market justification for this approach but it may also perhaps be seen as rather backward-looking.

Certainly it seems clear that Tartan Day will continue to be a significant date in the calendar of American Scots and apparently now within Scotland itself. The Scottish government is increasingly seeking to engage with the Scottish diaspora, most notably through the 2009 Year of Homecoming (and future Homecomings), and will almost certainly play a greater part in American Tartan Day celebrations in the future.

Chapter 5

Maintaining a Scottish identity

We have already begun to explore the importance of a Scottish identity for those born or living in America but with a Scottish ancestry or heritage. I have also discussed the range of Scottish organisations that exist in America and their importance in enabling American Scots to meet socially and celebrate that heritage. It is intended in this chapter to focus on the nature of the Scottish identity which is being celebrated, and how individuals maintain this over the years.

In many countries, of course, issues of identity are closely tied to citizenship and, within Europe, this has been defined in a number of different ways. In Germany, for example, citizenship law dates back to 1913 and is based on the principle of *ius sanguinis* ('blood law'). In other words, German identity and citizenship are inherited by descent through the father. Postwar citizenship laws have been influenced by German political experience and are designed to protect Germans who may have been forced to move out of the country after 1945. More recent legislation on employment and welfare benefits all control access to those who are German citizens. Thus the *Gastarbeiter* (guest workers) in Germany are excluded from many benefits, despite being resident in the country on a more or less permanent basis (Ginsburg 1994), and this idea of a 'blood right' makes it very difficult for any foreigner to obtain German naturalisation (Smith and Blanc, 1996).

In many other countries, citizenship laws are based on the principle of *ius soli* ('land law'), where citizenship depends upon place of birth, regardless of one's individual ancestry. In France, the Jacobin tradition of universalism has led to the notion that 'Frenchness' is open to all who immerse themselves in the French language and culture (Miles, 1993). The United Kingdom too adopts this approach, while in the United States there has been a positive encouragement to subscribe to American values, as a means of welding a disparate group of people together into one nation, sharing American citizenship (Kymlicka, 1995). Thus:

> the implication of *ius soli* is that birth in a country and familiarisation with its customs and ideals make a good citizen of anyone fortunate enough to have the opportunity. In this sense, the USA prided itself in taking in all comers and making 'good Americans' of them, corresponding to the French confidence in being able to create good Frenchmen and women, wherever French language and culture were permitted to exercise their natural elegance. (Fenton, 1999, p. 206)

Yet although the American position has been to encourage the assimilation or integration of migrants into a common American identity and citizenship — the concept of the melting pot, which I have already discussed — many groups have sought an additional identity based on their ancestral ties. The descendants of Scottish emigrants, now resident in the United States, continue to assert their Scottishness in part through the existence of such organisations as Scottish societies, clan groups and Highland Games (Jarvie, 1991). They are thus claiming Scottish identity through their ancestry or blood line and therefore subscribing to the principle of *ius sanguinis*.

The markers of national identity are therefore rather unclear. Kiely *et al.* (2001) have attempted to define what 'Scottishness' actually is and, while there appears to be widespread agreement that being born in Scotland confers Scottish nationality on the individual concerned, there is dispute about other identity markers. These might include ancestry, place of residence, upbringing and education, and commitment to place. American Scots would probably assert that ancestry confers 'Scottishness' on them whereas this might not be accepted so unquestioningly in Scotland itself. This chapter explores these issues of 'Scottishness' and Scottish identity and how American Scots seek to maintain this.

Choosing to be Scottish

It was evident in the discussions on 'symbolic' ethnicity in Chapter 1 how many Americans have become quite selective about their ethnicity, choosing from a range of different ancestries the one to which they wish to belong. Waters (1990) suggested that Scottish ancestry had once a fairly low status and its popularity had declined prior to the 1970s, but it would appear from the revival of interest in Scottish organisations and the expansion of activities, such as Highland Games, that 'being Scottish' is now increasingly popular. Some interviewees recognised that they had a multiplicity of ancestries but explained how they had come to focus specifically on their Scottish connections:

> I had a vague awareness of Scottish ancestry until I discovered the Scottish culture and music — that really grabbed me. At that point, the fact that I had Scottish ancestry really became important to me. I'm a mutt. I have a fair amount of German, Scottish and a little bit of Dutch and Swiss ancestry. There's also one French woman there and some English. I think all the Irish is going to turn out to be actually Scots. So I am a mixture. I speak German well. It is clearly the Scottish ancestry with which I identify. (C12)

A second interviewee had felt an immediate affinity for the Gaelic language, which had helped to cement her sense of 'Scottishness':

> **R:** It's tough, I don't know. I don't feel as if I can really be Scots American. I haven't lived in Scotland, I've thought about it. As opposed to any other identity and I certainly have some ancestors from other places, Scottish is the only other one that I feel is really a part of me.
> **I:** Why?
> **R:** I honestly don't know. It's just like hearing the language. Why would I have any connection with the language?
> **I:** It just struck you and you identified with it?
> **R:** Yes, and I speak other languages and I like other languages, but I never had that response to a language before. I don't know, I can't explain it. (C3)

A third acknowledged her mixed ancestry, while still claiming the importance of the Scottish connection:

> I have kind of a mixed bag in here. I'm the kind of person that appreciates and loves the whole international community. I lived in Brazil for seven years. I speak Portuguese. I speak Spanish. I don't have to speak another language to go to Scotland. I think it's important to know your heritage and where you come from and where your roots are. I felt really comfortable and at home in Scotland, but I can also feel at home in Brazil. I'm just an international body. (C7)

For other interviewees, 'being Scottish' was not something that they had thought about and they did not really feel that it had been a conscious choice. Rather it had been an automatic or unquestioned identification with Scotland. Others spoke of their enjoyment in participating in Scottish events and the friendships they had made. They had similarly not really thought to question their identity:

> Today it's kind of an automatic thing, like I feel like I'm in the club. It's just something that is. (C21)

....

> What's interesting is about the first paper my daughter wrote in college. She wrote about all these years mom made me go to Scotland and now it's in my blood and I don't know why. It was a great paper. I don't remember the genealogy or Scotland being anything we ever talked about in the family. It was just kind of there. (C18)

Individuals often spoke at some length about their ancestry and their interpretation of it. One interviewee claimed to be completely Scottish, although only two of his grandparents had actually been born in Scotland. It is unlikely that, in Scotland itself, his claim of 'Scottishness' would have been accepted completely unquestioningly:

> **R:** I'm 100% Scottish. Both my grandfathers were born in Scotland. Both my grandmothers were born of Scottish emigrants. [Scotland] is important because my family came from there. It's just a fact that I'm 100% Scottish.
>
> **I:** Would you not feel American? Or is it a bit of both?
>
> **R:** A bit of both. I'm just proud to be Scottish. They're a great race. They populated the world. So many writers and brilliant people. (N2)

Other people, however, were more realistic and recognised that such identity claims were open to challenge, particularly as time and the generations put more and more distance between individuals and their 'homeland':

> I play traditional Irish music and I look out over the audience when I play on St Patrick's Day, and everyone's dressed in green. They say things like 'I really belong on the other side', meaning in Ireland, and I think that, after a generation, they can't really pretend that they truly belong there. You see people dressed in tartan, kilts, sporrans and sgian dubhs, and they speak with New York accents. But I think you can only truly get away with wearing a kilt in Scotland. (N1)

For many individuals, their choice of identity was linked — at least in part — to the Scottish organisations with which they had become involved. One woman stated that she had both English and Scottish ancestry but her long-standing involvement with the Colorado St Andrew Society had 'given her an identity'. Another suggested the American Scots were inventing a tradition for themselves (see Trevor-Roper, 1983) and that this was having an impact:

> One friend of mine said the Scots are inventing themselves a history here. Somebody else said, 'Why not, everybody else does', which is to some degree true. Something you learn down your family like you learn music. I woke up to Scottish tunes when I was a baby and learned to sing those songs at a very early age and know most of the verses to some of these songs. You're getting it in that way but in another way you think, 'Well I am this' and you wonder 'What does that mean?' So, you start looking and researching. There are a lot of people who are beginning to rethink what it would be like to be a Scot and to bring those traditions in. (C11)

Adherence to traditions within the context of Scottish organisations represented an important marker of identity for American Scots and reinforced their view of being Scottish. Indeed, there was sometimes a sense that they believed they were maintaining traditions that were under threat in Scotland itself. Music and Gaelic culture were mentioned as specific areas where the American interest was thought to be particularly important:

> There's been a real movement of our generation in moving ahead. With a strong re-identification of these things. If we don't, it will be lost and that would be sad because the culture, the music, especially the music — we all respond to Gaelic rhythms — it just needs to be nourished. (C11)

Another strong marker of identity, as has been seen, is the American Scots' strong sense of their ancestral ties and this, for many, has helped to offset the fact that most had not been born or brought up in Scotland — markers of identity that would rank more highly among Scots within Scotland itself (Kiely *et al.*, 2001).

For those interviewees who had in fact been born in Scotland, an additional, and significant, marker of identity was accent. Not only does this indicate nationality or identity but it can also influence other people's perceptions of the speaker, for example in terms of geographical place, questions of belonging and of class and status. Charlesworth (2000) showed how speech and dialect embed individuals into particular social worlds. Those Scots in the sample who had retained their accent were keenly aware of it, while others mentioned how their families looked for changes in accent as being examples of creeping 'Americanisation':

> Years and years ago, I was in Tokyo and there was a Scottish business delegation and I got chatting to one of the guys, a chief executive of a company or whatever. He said to me, 'You haven't lost your accent, son'. I said no. His response was, 'It's your passport around the world. Never lose it.' And that's been a lesson. I've never deliberately gone out to retain my accent but it's certainly what differentiates me. I will always say that I'm Scottish before I'm British if given the chance. I find that if I'm on the telephone here and I'm speaking to companies and want to get in to see them and the girls outside have trouble, as soon as I get on the phone, as soon as they hear my accent, lo and behold the door is opened. The point is you've differentiated yourself. I absolutely think of myself as 100% Scottish. Scottish history, Scottish culture. Americans actually take an interest but only because you're different. To be different in America means quite a lot. (C6)

> Well, the last time I went home, everybody says to me, 'Gee you're so Americanised', and I didn't feel I was. Well, I'll tell you this much. If you come over here as a female and you don't work, I think you turn out different. But if you're in the workforce, you have to try and get rid of that accent. I haven't really got rid of it and when I go home I go right back into it again. Thing is, here people ask you things just to hear the accent and I get a lot of that. So that's how I had to lose it a bit. (C10)

> In business, being a Scot is a big advantage. That's why I haven't lost my accent I don't think. I think the Scots that were before us were very trustworthy, very honourable men. So anytime you strike a deal, I think if you're Scottish they know you're going to live up to that deal. There's an honour there that's unwritten. It's very helpful. (N14)

This particular individual also believed that a Scottish accent was more acceptable outside Scotland, as it could less easily be placed in class terms.

Thus, in Scotland itself, a Glasgow accent might be viewed by others as being working class, but elsewhere such markers of class disappeared:

> Everything hinges on getting a better living. That's why I came across here. Not to make millions of dollars. But in Scotland there was a class society, so if you talk with a Glasgow accent I always felt I was down one rung on the ladder. Going down to England and talking with a Scottish accent put me up a rung on the ladder. Coming over here put me up two or three rungs on the ladder, just with the accent. (N14)

It can therefore be seen from the responses of the various interviewees that their Scottish identity was very important to them, although most had actually been born and brought up in America. How then did they negotiate this hyphenated identity, being both Scottish and American at the same time?

Being Scottish or being American?

All interviewees were asked if they considered themselves to be Scots or Americans or a combination of both. For those who articulated a clear hyphenated identity, the interviews sought to explore the extent to which the Scottish element was important. The interviews did not, however, ask the question in the level of detail that has been used in Scotland to define individuals' sense of 'Scottishness' or 'Britishness' (Moreno, 1988; Brown et al., 1966). Individuals who participated in these Edinburgh-based studies were asked to distinguish the *extent* to which they felt Scottish or British, and the results have shown a strengthening of 'Scottishness' and a sense of Scottish identity, at the expense of a 'British' one. The studies have been used by some politicians to suggest that the concept of 'Britishness' and, by implication, the British state itself are increasingly outdated.

Within the United States, the position was rather different in that the majority of interviewees were American citizens and so in terms of citizenship they were not Scottish — or indeed British. They appeared, however, to be able to distinguish between being *American*, an identity in which they took a great deal of pride, and being *Scottish* in the sense of having a Scottish ancestry. Thus the two identities could co-exist side by side, neither threatening the other in any way. This echoes the findings of Waters (1990), that many young people are exploring their ethnic roots while simultaneously being patriotic Americans. Being American is the

primary identity which most individuals rarely question, while a hyphenated identity is something more personal:

> I think it's fair to say that I'm an American. Outside of a particularly
> friendly community, I don't know that I would say that I'm Scottish
> American. It's just that I'm an American who identifies strongly with
> my Scottish ancestry and my modern Scottish connections. (C12)

> I'm an American. But I talk about being Scottish all the time. (C18)

> We're absolutely Scottish American and we'll say, 'I am as proud of
> being American as I am proud of being of Scottish ancestry.' It's not
> one over the other — they are both present. (C11)

> **R:** I tell everyone I'm American made with Scottish parts.
> **I:** But the Scottish bit's important to you?
> **R:** Yeah. Anybody that I spend a lot of time with knows I'm Scottish.
> (N14)

In some cases, interviewees were able to discuss some of the subtle-
ties of identity. One suggested that an individual's strength of identity was
related to generational distance from Scotland. He believed that those individuals whose Scottish ancestry was several generations distant could not
identify as readily with Scotland as those with a more recent connection:

> I think that, when you're studying Scots in America, you really have to
> divide them into two categories. One is Scottish Americans — that's
> what I am, with three grandparents born in Scotland, raised in the
> Church of Scotland, raised with all the admonitions to work hard and
> save your money and all that kind of thing. Then there are people who
> are Americans of Scottish descent. By that I mean people who maybe
> are a sixteenth or a thirty-second or a sixty-fourth or a hundred-and-
> twenty-eighth Scottish. They found a Scottish ancestor and they're
> happy with the kilts and all that tartanry and call themselves Scottish
> Americans. But I call them Americans of Scottish descent. Their ideas
> and motivations are quite different. (N6)

There was also a recognition that some Scottish Americans might have their
claim to Scottishness challenged, particularly by 'homeland' Scots. But they
were often unable to see what other identity they could possibly claim:

> I am first an American, OK? Second of all, I am a Scottish American.
> The fact is I'm Scottish — but probably not. But that's my orientation,

because what other orientation would I have? It's not that we're trying to be Scottish. That's not the issue. I'm an American. (C8)

....

Well, I know a lot of people born and raised in Scotland, such as yourself, might perhaps question whether I should say what I'm going to say right now. I consider myself to be a patriotic Scot. That's the difference between a Scottish American and a person of Scottish ancestry. My grandparents spoke the way you do. They raised us to be Scots, all the manners and all the traditions that go with it. I could sing and play on the piano fifteen or twenty Scottish songs by the time I was twelve. I consider myself a Scot. I'm an American also. I'm proud of both. But other people will say, 'You're not a Scot. You don't have any vote here.' There are even people who say I shouldn't wear the kilt. There are a lot of people in Scotland who think like that — 'it's *our* national dress and *you're* not a citizen.' (N6)

Of course, such hyphenated identities are commonplace within America. It was recognised by many interviewees that the sense of belonging to America while, at the same time, having pride in one's ancestry would apply equally to other ethnic groupings within the country.

Thus people seemed to have a strong — and comfortable — sense of identity, which manifested itself in a dual attachment to both the United States and to Scotland. This strong awareness of Scottish ancestry had led a number of individuals into exploring genealogical sources in an attempt to find out more about their ancestors. This in turn helped to strengthen an individual's sense and awareness of his or her heritage:

I'm definitely an American. I started dancing before I even knew I had Scottish heritage. Just as a lark, I started looking back and on the LDS[1] website and looked into finding Scottish ancestry. So I'm definitely an American more than Scottish. That's the way I view myself. I do run around in a pleated skirt every once in a while though. (C2)

We have already seen that an increasing awareness of one's identity is often related to greater wealth and leisure time, both of these making it possible for individuals to take the time to explore genealogical sources. These are Novak (1971)'s 'Saturday ethnics'. Interviewees in this present

1 The Church of Jesus Christ of Latter-day Saints (the Mormons) has a large Family History Library and an extensive website, which can assist genealogical research.

study sometimes showed an awareness that this was the case for them or their friends:

> **R:** I believe it's affluence. Affluence is all it is. People have enough money to spend to buy books about Scotland, to read about the Munro clan and they take it up as an interest.
>
> **I:** So it would be a very middle-class interest then?
>
> **R:** I think so, yes. I think you have hit the nail on the head there. It's a middle-class activity. I lived amongst computer people for twenty-odd years. If you are in the computer R & D side, nobody ever talks about being Scots-Irish or Italian American or anything like that. They are Americans and they are in the computer business. But socially I meet an awful lot of people who tell me they are prepared to spend so much more money on researching their heritage than I ever would. (C20)
>
> ....
>
> **R:** Some of it has to do with the affluence.
>
> **I:** You mean once people have more money they have more means to explore?
>
> **R:** Yes and also the society as a whole became more affluent so they had more time to do things.
>
> **I:** Do you think the genealogy and the exploring are a whole middle-class thing?
>
> **R:** Probably. People who are scratching out a living don't really have the time or maybe the extra money. (C21)

Indeed, the time-consuming nature of genealogical research had prevented some working people from doing it and they relied on retired members of their family to help or relatives with some spare time:

> **I:** You were saying that your aunt's very involved in exploring groups and doing this genealogical research. You haven't done that yourself?
>
> **R:** No. She does it for me. It's time consuming and I still work a full-time job. I trust what she does because I know her and she is very, very detailed and very specific on everything, that's just the way she is. That's her hobby, it's very time consuming, it's hard to do, very hard to do. (C1)

A number of interviewees described their excitement at discovering relatives through their researches and of making contact with them. This again helped to reinforce the sense of Scottish identity and pride in Scottish heritage:

I met a distant cousin through the first Gaelic immersion in Boulder. We had a group from New Mexico that came up for the immersion and we were sitting in a tavern after the event on Sunday evening. I was talking to G_____, my teacher and I happened to mention Polk County, Missouri. That's where my family originated in Missouri. One of the students sitting near by said, 'What about Polk County, Missouri?' I said, 'I have family from Polk County.' He said, 'Oh, I do too. What's your name?' 'It's Mitchell.' Well, his great-grandfather and my great-grandfather were brothers. Here I am at a Gaelic class in Boulder, Colorado with someone from New Mexico and we have a common ancestry. That's how it ends up sometimes. (C4)

Scottish-American activities

We have already seen in Chapter 3 how important Scottish organisations are in enabling American Scots to maintain their identity and celebrate their heritage. In fact, it is well nigh impossible to establish just exactly how many Scottish organisations exist within the United States today. There are large numbers of St Andrew societies, Burns clubs, Gaelic language groups and Scottish dancing organisations, as well as independent bodies organising specific events such as Highland Games or Tartan Day celebrations. Some organisations are affiliated to American federations of Scottish societies; others are branches of Scottish-based organisations such as the RSCDS or An Comunn Gàidhealach. Hewitson (1993) estimated in 1993 that there were more than 200 clan societies and family associations, more than a hundred Scottish societies and around 125 pipe bands, including the splendidly titled Nae Breeks Pipe Band from Millville, Illinois.

The figure is substantially larger today and I have already noted the work of Hague (2001) in exploring the growth in the numbers of Highland Games in America, from around seventy-five in the mid 1980s to more than 200 today. As interest grows in genealogy and heritage and, as more individuals embrace their 'symbolic ethnicity', then the numbers of other Scottish organisations are also likely to increase. This range of Scottish activities is in turn serviced by a number of American-based federations of organisations, as well as various magazines and other publications. There is a 'Scottish Coalition' comprising national organisations serving the Scottish-American community.

The range of activities pursued by societies may be illustrated by perusal of the websites of almost any of the various St Andrew societies around the country. They hold regular meetings, Burns Night Dinners, Highland Games and often Tartan Balls and country dancing classes. Many societies also sponsor a pipe band, participate in National Tartan Day, run informal social events such as whisky tasting, golf outings and sometimes 'fun' events such as 'haggis shoots'. They usually also organise an annual 'Kirkin' o' the Tartan'. Some of these events would be familiar to people in Scotland; some such as the 'haggis shoot' are run for amusement.

The Kirkin' o' the Tartan has already been referred to on several occasions and it is perhaps worth describing it here in more detail, not least because it is an interesting example of the invention of a tradition, one which would be completely unfamiliar to homeland Scots.

The event was established in 1941 by the then president of the St Andrew's Society of Washington DC, the Reverend Dr Peter Marshall. He was pastor of the New York Avenue Presbyterian Church, and later chaplain of the Senate. The service began as a gesture of support for British troops during the Second World War and Dr Marshall was a regular speaker in support of British War Relief. From 1952, the event became established at Washington National Cathedral.

Essentially, the Kirkin' is a prayer service that generally begins with a local pipe band leading a procession of officers and members of the St Andrew's Society, together with any honoured guests. During the service, members parade to the altar, to present the tartans or clan banners for blessing. There are various hymns and prayers to St Andrew, before the Pipes and Drums then lead the parade out of the church and often the Kirkin' is followed by a social event or by a concert or dancing display. One might expect a Kirkin' to take place in a Presbyterian church, following the Scottish tradition, but this is not necessarily the case. Indeed, it appears to have moved out of the Presbyterian church tradition and into the Episcopalian one. MacDonald (1992) suggested that the blessing of a piece of cloth would appear very Roman Catholic to most Highland Presbyterians and they would probably frown upon this type of activity. Ray (2005c) has also commented upon the quite militaristic format of many Kirkin's.

The Kirkin' o' the Tartan became a regular feature of many Scottish organisations across America and often took place on the Sunday following local Highland Games, or around St Andrew's Day. More recently, it has been scheduled to take place around 6 April, to coincide with National Tartan Day celebrations. It shows how Scottish societies in America do not necessarily reflect the structures and activities of organisations within the Scottish homeland but have adapted and introduced their own ceremonials. It is common for St Andrew's Day itself to be celebrated in America, for example, whereas it is often ignored in Scotland and is not officially a public holiday — despite recent attempts to make it so.

Many interviewees in the sample spoke of Kirkin's which they had attended and of their pleasure at being present. There was also some recognition that it was a Scottish-American, rather than a Scottish, tradition:

> **R:** The Kirkin' o' the Tartan at St John's is a huge event. There are smaller churches that have a Kirkin' like that. People show up and walk their plaids down and get them blessed.
>
> **I:** Are they inventing a tradition? That's a very American tradition. That wouldn't exist in Scotland at all.
>
> **R:** No. But there it is. It is not an American generic tradition. It's a Scottish-American tradition. (C11)
>
> ....
>
> **R:** When I went, it was about five years ago and the cathedral was so crowded. That was actually an Episcopalian church, so I don't know how the Presbyterians are doing with all of this.
>
> **I:** This is one of the things I have never understood. Most of the Kirkin' o' the Tartan ceremonies take place in Episcopalian churches.
>
> **R:** I know. It doesn't make any sense to me. I thought maybe they just did it at St John's because it is a Gothic structure and the sound is phenomenal. I think that is real strange, I don't have the answer, sorry. (C18)

Many other events have invented traditions, by introducing their own specific rituals. At the Grandfather Mountain Highland Games, for example, there is a torchlight procession on the evening before the Games start. One member from each clan takes position at one of four points on the field, their positions apparently symbolising the return of clans to Grandfather from the four points of the compass. One by one, the clans announce their presence and build a single, fiery pyre in the centre of the field. This has all the hallmarks of an ancient tradition but actually it dates back only to the 1980s.

Websites for the numerous Highland Games lay great stress on the opportunities presented to visitors to research their ancestry at the various clan tents in attendance. The presence of these clan tents is a specific feature of American Highland Games and they are relatively unknown at Games held in Scotland. When vendors participate at a Scottish gathering in Scotland, they are generally selling food or local produce, rather than Scottish books, CDs and clan paraphernalia, as sold at Games in the United States (Ray, 2003). This rather backward-looking approach has been defined as 'filio-pietism' or an exaggerated respect and admiration for one's ancestors (Hook, 1999). Accounts of the Scottish influence in America have not always succeeded in avoiding it.

That said, it is important to recognise that Highland Games in North America fulfil an important community function. It is easy for visitors from Scotland to adopt a rather condescending attitude towards American Scots and their continuing affection for the Highlands. But:

> It is a simple matter, for example, to make fun of the enormous pomp and ceremony surrounding events such as the Glengarry Highland Games [in Ontario] ... But to adopt such an attitude is simply to demonstrate one's own failure to comprehend the distinction between symbol and substance. What is being celebrated at the Glengarry Highland Games and similar festivals is the profound sense of community generated over the last two hundred years in the homesteads and the villages established with such difficulty in this little bit of North America (Hunter, 1994, pp. 86–7).

The Glengarry experience may be rooted in a Highland past but the present sense of identity which is being celebrated is rooted in experiences that owe little or nothing to Scotland, and that are essentially Canadian. Thus the Glengarry Games, like many Scottish organisations in North America and like Tartan Day itself, exist to serve the Scottish diaspora, and their traditions are as much North American as purely Scottish.

Some myths and images

This disjunction between the activities and traditions of American Scots and homeland Scots has been a recurring theme throughout this book. Clearly, part of the discomfort which is evidently experienced by many homeland Scots, in relation to Tartan Day and the activities of Scottish organisations in America, appears to stem from a fundamental difference of opinion regarding 'Scottishness'. For many homeland Scots, it is difficult to appreciate that individuals born and brought up in America, and whose ancestors may have left Scotland centuries previously, should nevertheless still believe themselves to be Scots. Such individuals seem to be identifying with a country and a culture of which they may have little or no direct experience, and one they may never have actually visited.

This apparent conflict about the whole notion of Scottishness is usefully summarised by the journalist Alan Taylor, reflecting on being a Scottish 'exile':

> But then exiles are curious, tortured creatures. Edinburgh, wrote Muriel Spark, the doyenne of exiles, 'bred within me the conditions of exiledom'. She left, she said, because it was 'a place where I could not hope to be understood'. A few lines later, she adds: 'Nevertheless, it is the place where I was first understood'. For her, exile ceased to be a fate and became a calling.
>
> Had I stayed in London, I suspect it would have been my fate, like all those itinerant Scots around the globe who hanker constantly after things they'd been desperate to abandon, from Oor Wullie[2] to haggis suppers. We are, it seems, constantly in conflict with the notion of Scottishness, afraid to embrace it too wholeheartedly lest we be accused of chauvinism or sentimentality or hubris. No wonder Scots are not natural enthusiasts. How such a cautious nation has achieved so much never fails to amaze me. (Devine and Logue, 2002, pp. 259–60)

'Scottishness' is indeed defined in very different ways. As noted earlier in the chapter, Kiely *et al.* (2001), for example, have attempted to examine how people set about the task of constructing and maintaining national identities. They explored different markers of identity and nationality, including place of birth, ancestry, place of residence, length of residence, upbringing and education, name, accent, physical appearance, dress and commitment to place. Those markers that were seen by participants in their study as being the strongest in defining a person's claim to Scottish identity were place of birth, ancestral ties, upbringing and education, and possibly residence.

2　Oor Wullie is a cartoon character, whose adventures appear every week in the Scottish *Sunday Post*.

Yet 'Scottish identity is neither static nor simply defined. Rather, it is flexible and open to redefinition and reinterpretation by different people and organisations depending on the context of its evocation' (Hague, 2006). The position in America, for example, is particularly complicated, with some people becoming Scots by choice, as they rarely have the usual markers of national identity, with the possible exception of ancestry. Thus:

> There are several ways to identify Scottishness overseas. One is through individual self-ascription; anyone can be Scottish if they feel Scottish, a piece of wisdom you will hear often enough at social gatherings like Burns Suppers in Winnipeg, often attended by more 'chuks' than 'macs'. Another is by concentrating on the symbols and public expressions of Scottishness: the kilts, the pipes, the tartans, the Gaelic language and the creation of a membership in various Scottish organisations. The symbols are, of course, meaningless 'tartanry', and the public expressions, including instruction in Gaelic, Gaelic newspapers and Scottish societies, usually signal the decline of a culture rather than its vitality, since they are often made to prevent perceived cultural loss. (Bumsted, 1999, p. 97)

A more important question therefore may be why Scots abroad choose to associate with other Scots — in other words, why is being Scottish so important? This question is one that was asked in relation to Ireland by the late journalist Pete McCarthy (2000) in exploring his Irish roots. How, he wondered, can one feel a sense of belonging towards a country, in which one had never actually lived? He suggested a parallel with the Celtic monks who would wander around Europe before finding a place for a community, which they called their 'place of resurrection'. They believed that they were beneath the spot in the firmament that would one day lead them to Heaven (McCarthy, 2000).

MacDonald (1992) referred to a self-rating questionnaire, entitled 'How Scottish are you?', which appeared in the *Scottish-American* newspaper. There was no mention of identifiers such as place of birth, nationality or name. Instead the questionnaire focused on the frequency with which individuals visited Scotland, and the number of kilts they owned.

Indeed, many Scottish organisations within the United States do not necessarily require their members even to be of Scottish ancestry, or married to someone with a Scottish background. The websites of many St

Andrew's societies make clear that membership is very open and so societies are not exclusively Scottish. As Ray (2001a) emphasised, the Scottish-American community is, indeed, the Scottish-*American* community. No matter how proud of their Scottish heritage individuals may be, and no matter the interest in things Scottish, people are essentially underscoring their pride in being American. By honouring their Scottish identity, they are also honouring the roots of their American heritage.

Perhaps this helps to understand why home-based Scots and Americans view Scotland in such different ways. This was illustrated most famously by the film director Arthur Freed who visited Scotland in 1953 to seek a location for shooting his forthcoming film, *Brigadoon*. He returned to Hollywood, having found nowhere in Scotland that actually looked — in his view — like Scotland. The film itself has subsequently come to stand 'for all that is awful in tartan and sentimentality — a degrading perversion of Scottish culture'. There is a certain satisfaction in Freed having been unable to find anything 'sufficiently phoney to meet his purposes' (Bruce, 1996, p. 37).

On a similar point:

> Under the wide limbs of oak trees, four girls are dancing. They cock one hand on a plaid-skirted hip, fling the other in the air … Just a hammer's throw away, tomato-faced, big-necked young men, chests bare over MacKenzie or MacLeod kilts, vie with each other to chunk what looks like a telephone pole across the lawn. On the porch of the old house nearby, four bearded pipers play 'Scotland the brave'.
>
> This isn't Scotland of course: Scotland isn't so self-consciously *Scottish* … This is, in fact, Jefferson County, Florida. The food is more barbeque than haggis and half the guys in kilts also wear Florida State T-shirts. But they've come to celebrate a place — or at least the idea of a place — most of them have never even seen. (Roberts, 1999, p. 24)

Strathern and Stewart (2001) suggested that the activities of such American Scots, in promoting tartan and the kilt as symbols of Scotland abroad have actually done much to strengthen them at home. The negative connotations associated with tartan and the kilt have tended to disappear and 'association with military prowess and gentlemanly rank has prevailed'. Certainly the kilt has grown enormously in popularity within Scotland itself in recent years, becoming *de rigueur* for many weddings and formal occasions.

Perhaps the basic issue is whether or not it matters that homeland Scots and American Scots have different perspectives on identity and nationality. Highland Games and other Scottish activities are essentially fun and the desire by many people to indulge in periodic wallowings in Scottish nostalgia should perhaps not be taken too seriously. The point was made forcefully in an interview with a Scottish government minister:

> The media criticism is frankly a cheap shot. It's a continuation of the Scottish cringe. Why do we denigrate our own culture? Why is it a figure of fun and it's something to be castigated that people march and follow a pipe band in kilts? If you were to do that about Greeks or Pakistanis in their national dress, you would correctly be told you were being racist. So why is it that a section of our society in Scotland — and some in the media — are so denigratory of who we are? We should be proud of who we are. It's part of a growing Scottish self-confidence. (S2)

Perhaps the only time potential embarrassments arise may be when American Scots visit Scotland itself and, perhaps like Arthur Freed, find that the reality does not entirely match the imagination. The experience of American Scots attending a clan gathering in the 1970s is interesting in this regard:

> The incongruity between the culture of the home country and that of hyphenated Americans is also pointed up by the experience of a group of affluent Americans of Scottish descent who returned to Scotland in 1977 for the International Gathering of the Clans. Replete with kilts and bagpipes, they spent two weeks searching the countryside for their roots. According to the *New York Times*, the Americans were met with ridicule, not only for making a spectacle of themselves, but also for fraternising with the wealthy clan chiefs whose ancestors had driven their ancestors out of Scotland. (Steinberg, 1981, p. 62)

Fry (2003) agreed that Americans returning to Scotland are often apt to misjudge the occasions when kilts may be worn. As he pointed out, normal workaday Scotland often has little time for historical consciousness, 'least of all for the fake historical consciousness of foreigners'.

During the 1960s, the Scottish comedian Jimmy Logan used to perform a song entitled 'American Scot', about an expatriate returning to his homeland. The humour in the song came from references to the American being proud of belonging to 'the Finkelhoffer clan' and his return to the 'hills of

Scotland' turned out to be a return to Maryhill, a down-at-heel working-class district in Glasgow. But the song is also affectionate and captures the dual identity of the individual involved:

> So he sailed for America
>
> And he helped to build America
>
> And, although he was the leader of his clan,
>
> He was proud to be a son of Uncle Sam.[3]

The song demonstrates very neatly the mixture of pride that American Scots have in their Scottish heritage together with a pride in being American.

Visiting Scotland and searching for one's roots

As was shown in Chapter 2, most of those people interviewed as part of this research were able to talk about the move to America which had been made either by themselves or their ancestors. Indeed, there appeared to be a high level of awareness of family history and many people had undertaken genealogical research. This had led to a desire to visit Scotland and to see where their ancestors had moved from.

Research suggested that many members of the diaspora have a rather romanticised notion of Scotland, one that has little basis in reality (see, for example, MacGregor, 1980; MacDonald, 1992). MacGregor actually recounted the story of a conversation with a justice in Iowa who had Scottish ancestry and a strong interest in Scotland. But he had never actually visited in case he was disappointed and the reality failed to measure up to his (perhaps rather idealised) view of it. In the interviews carried out for this book, however, it became clear that many American Scots had a quite detailed knowledge of Scotland in general, and family history in particular, and had developed significant links with Scotland. This had given them a perhaps more realistic view of the country.

Thus, of the twenty-one interviews conducted in Colorado, in fifteen cases the interviewee(s) had visited Scotland at least once during the previous four years; only four people had never visited Scotland. In the New York sample, all interviewees had travelled to Scotland within the previous four years, as the majority were Scottish born and had Scottish relatives. The availability of cheaper transatlantic flights in recent years appeared to

3 I am very grateful to the late Mrs Angela Logan for permission to quote from this song.

be making travel relatively straightforward and enabling members of the diaspora to visit — in some cases on a fairly regular basis. There are daily direct flights from New York (Newark) to both Glasgow and Edinburgh and direct flights from many other American cities to the UK. Many individuals in the Colorado sample had taken advantage of a direct flight from Denver to London, introduced a couple of years previously. Such developments had made travel very much more straightforward than before.

In a number of cases, families simply visited Scotland for a holiday because they liked the country, and in some cases there was the added attractions of hill walking or golf:

> Jan's been four times and I've been twice. Our first trip was to orient me with respect to a great deal of Scotland. We did a grand tour, so to speak. In two weeks we put 2,000 miles on the car. We saw a little bit of everywhere. Our next trip we tried to stay mostly along the west coast without having to drive nearly so much and we spent three nights on Mull which is my wife's favourite island and I just fell in love with also. We have future plans to go to very specific places where we haven't been. We want to go to the Orkneys and the Western Isles and the Hebrides. (C4)

> Probably a lot of my curiosity and drive to visit Scotland are very much related to golf. I really was anxious to play some of the courses and try them. I love golf. I like the mental challenge. I am not a very good golfer. I think golf, as much as my family background, is what got me there the first time. (C18)

One family had visited for a holiday but had ended up buying property, which they then used as a base for future visits, although such purchases appeared very rare:

> **R:** We did a house exchange in Troon. So the people in Troon lived in our house while we lived there. Then we met really good friends in Troon through that house exchange. It's almost like a whole separate set of friends that we have, that we have maintained … Their children and our children are very good friends. We ended up buying a house together as an investment. [We] formed a Scottish corporation and bought a little house down at Dunure. We're renting that house out. Sometimes I use that house but sometimes I stay with friends.

I: You actually have a base now that you can use for holidays?

R: Yes. (C18)

In two instances, the holiday in Scotland had actually been a honeymoon, as couples made their first Scottish visit a particularly memorable and romantic occasion:

> My first trip was in 1996. My wife and I went there on our honeymoon. We had a Scottish wedding here. We were going to get married in Scotland. Her ancestors are also Scottish, back about as far as mine are. But we found out that we had both been single for so long, we were in a middle-age status, each had a failed marriage, that if we would have gone to Scotland where our families couldn't have attended we both would have been strung up and hung by our families, so we had a Scottish wedding in Denver and went to Scotland for our honeymoon. We returned two years later and we always have plans to go back (C4).

> **R1:** We've only been once.
>
> **R2:** That was our honeymoon.
>
> **R1:** In September of …
>
> **R2:** Right after 9/11.
>
> **R1:** Yes. We left six days after 9/11.
>
> **R2:** But we had the trip planned and it was our dream trip of a lifetime because we both wanted to go and neither of us had been there before. So we went anyway and it was wonderful. (C13)

For many people, of course, a visit to Scotland is used as an opportunity to explore family ancestries. A number of those interviewed subscribed to the *Family Tree* newspaper,[4] and this had helped them to begin searching historical and genealogical sources. In many cases, initial searches could be conducted online, but as people became more immersed in family history it was thought to be important to visit sources in Scotland. Some people had therefore taken advantage of Scottish visits to go to Register House in Edinburgh, where records of births, marriages and deaths are held.

Others spoke of exploring the histories of their clans, either by visiting the local area or attending clan gatherings. This 'roots tourism' has been described by Basu (2004; 2005) in his studies of, first, the 1999 Orkney

---

4   Published in Georgia by the Ellen Payne Odom Genealogy Library.

Homecoming event, in which 150 Canadians of Orcadian descent participated and, second, the visits made by members of the Scottish diaspora with links to Clan Macpherson to Newtonmore in the Scottish Highlands for clan gatherings and events.

One New York interviewee spoke at length of her search for her relatives during a visit to Scotland and how she had brought members of her family together after many years of separation. It is a long story but it provides an interesting insight into the importance of rediscovering family links for members of the Scottish diaspora and so is reproduced here:

> **R:** My grandmother arrived in Toronto, and she never really left that area. She lived in downtown Toronto all her life. And she was from a small town called Renton[5] but unfortunately she never kept in touch with her family, for her own reasons, and she never really had the opportunity to go back to Scotland. I adored my grandmother, she was my best friend and I grew up in Toronto listening to her talk about her homeland. So I always had this incredible ache to go there.
>
> So how I went to Scotland myself was back in '93, I was an actor in Canada and I decided to take a summer course at the National Theatre School of Great Britain. I thought, well I'm going to be over there for three weeks on the course, so I thought I could stay longer and trek up to Scotland. I had my grandmother's birth certificate and a couple of photographs and some general information about Renton, where I needed to go.
>
> After the school was over, I got on a train and went up to Glasgow. I was incredibly moved the whole way and I felt my grandmother's presence with me — she was still alive then. So I landed in Glasgow and transferred trains and took the train to Renton, thinking I could stay in Renton, that there was a hotel.
>
> **I:** And there was no hotel.
>
> **R:** I found that out quite quickly! I was walking towards the main street and a fellow was coming from the pub and I said, 'Excuse me, could you point me to the centre of town?' And it was 'Ach, lassie, you're standing in it; this is it!' So I realised I would have to go back to Glasgow to stay in a hotel.

5 Renton is a small, former industrial, town in Dunbartonshire, west of Glasgow and close to Loch Lomond.

But I found out that the other half of my family were the S_____s who run the boats on Loch Lomond. My great-grandmother's maiden name was Mary Jane S_____.

The next day I went back up to Renton and I was walking around the streets, and they could tell that I was definitely not one of the locals. Someone said to me, 'Are you lost? Can I help you?' And I said, 'Well, I'm looking for Burns Street'. And he showed me where to go. I found there were no houses on the street. My grandmother said that, when she'd lived on the street, she could look out her window and see Dumbarton Rock. There's a nice park there now.

Then this person said, 'Why do you want to know where Burns Street is?' and I said, 'Well, my grandmother was born there.' So they asked her name and I said, 'Mary B_____. Her brother's name was Benjamin B_____'. He said, 'Benny B_____! I know his son Billy!' He had had about nine sons and Billy happened still to be living in the area. So they said, 'Well you come in with me and we'll call and we'll see if Billy's home.' We called and Billy's son picked up and said he would be home at a certain time and said I should go by the house at 4 and meet the family. So I did and walked in and I said, 'I think we're related. My grandmother is your aunt. Did you have an aunt that went to Canada?' And he said, 'Aye' and I said, 'Obviously she wasn't spoken of a lot', and he said, 'Well, not really.' And I said, 'Well, I'm her granddaughter and I'm bridging the gap, because she never had the chance to come back.' His wife brought out a picture, the exact same picture I have of my grandmother in service in Crieff. A neighbour had given it to her saying one day somebody's going to come looking, you know, and in case they do this is proof. And I said, 'That's my grandmother — that's the same picture I have back at home, of her in service, sitting outside the school she worked in.' And she said, 'Well, you look like a B_____!'

So I got my grandmother on the phone and she was very frugal, she didn't want to waste money on anything. But I said, 'Granny, I'm phoning long distance, you have to accept the charges. I have a relative here. I have your nephew on the line. I'm speaking to Benny's son, Billy. Billy's here.' So they finally got to speak.

I finally got my mother over there in '99 and she met them. (N12)

Not everyone had such detailed family knowledge, allowing them to make direct contact with relatives. But others visited areas and places associated with their families.

Many individuals had traced their ancestry back over several genera-tions, and, even though emigration from Scotland might have taken place centuries earlier, the Scottish connection remained extremely important to them. For most, it was essential that they knew something about their roots and 'where they had originally come from'. They stressed the rela-tive youth of America as a country and the fact that, with the exception of Native Americans, everyone was an immigrant with an ancestry rooted elsewhere. This reflects the work by Waters (1990) on the 'particular American need to be "from somewhere"' (Waters, 1990, p. 150):

> It's kind of nice to have something to hold on to. Here in America, nobody is actually American, with the exception of the Native American Indians. Nobody is actually an American; everybody is something else. It's kind of pleasant to have some kind of identity from historical roots. (C2)

....

> **R1:** To me [Scotland's] kind of like the motherland. This is a second-ary motherland really. I really feel that connection with my family over there. I would love to learn more about my background and how we came over here. When I went to Scotland and we went to Dunstaffnage Castle, which was built by the MacDougalls, I felt completely at home. I felt like it was familiar. It felt wonderful to be there, to walk on the soil that my ancestors had walked on. It was really exciting. It really felt great.
> **R2:** It's weird, I'm almost more proud of being a Scot than I am of being an American.
> **R1:** I think I am too.
> **R2:** We heard that term when we were over there of a 'blown-away Scotsman'. If you're Scottish, you're Scottish. It doesn't matter where you are born, you are just living someplace else for now. (C13)

The reference to a 'blown-away Scotsman' is interesting. This particular perspective was echoed by another interviewee who likened being Scottish to being Jewish; both identities for him transcended national boundaries, a position recognised as 'transnationalism' (Smith and Guarnizo, 1998). The interviewee recognised that he could never be Scottish in the strict sense of being born, brought up or living there, and could never have that set of experiences, but he argued that this did not detract in any way from his sense of 'Scottishness'.

One interviewee was the Colorado convenor of the Clan Mackintosh of North America and had found his Scottish visits a useful way of contacting other clan members:

> **R:** The first time I went, I scoped out my own path and found bed and breakfasts on the internet and I fell fortunate. I got to stay with a Mary McIntosh on the Isle of Skye. I didn't know these people; I do now. I correspond with them. Then I got to stay with Elizabeth and John McIntosh in the Inverness area. They're farmers. Then I got to stay with Ken McIntosh and his wife Irene. The weekend I stayed with them, there was a Scottish festival right next door, in Nairn. I got to watch the piping competition and what goes on there.
>
> **I:** Specifically were you looking for McIntoshes?
>
> **R:** I wasn't, but they started popping up and what can you do? You can't ignore them. (C8)

Although genealogy was an important interest for many people, they were aware that some Scots have tended to view with mild amusement the interest that many members of the Scottish diaspora have in their heritage and their family roots. For Scots still resident in Scotland, genealogy is perhaps not seen as being of such significance. Certainly, one couple spoke of spending time in a guest house in Mallaig, where the hotelier was openly hostile towards what he saw as a continuous stream of Americans asking questions about their origins. They believed that their presence on holiday, rather than on a search for family origins, helped to redeem them in his eyes:

> **R1:** It was really quite marvellous because he has a bed and breakfast. When he has extras, he will open his house but he doesn't like to open his house that much, especially to Americans, because Americans are there usually to explore their roots and little else.
>
> **I:** Is that a bad thing do you think?
>
> **R1:** Well, from his point of view, because it's what we would call a Texan exploring your roots. 'I'm superior, I come from the biggest state. You should feel glad that I am here spending my money in your bed and breakfast.' He had little time for that. So his first question for

us while we were unloading our luggage, was: 'Do you have ancestors in Scotland? Why are you here? Are you looking for your ancestors?' We explained that we knew those things pretty much and we were just here to enjoy a couple of castles and soak up a little atmosphere in pubs and not make ourselves conspicuous. We passed the test.

R2: There were several other tests. We got into this long conversation with him about something that we have kind of an idea about, which is that when our families came over they were living a certain lifestyle that had certain habits or patterns in them. They froze, they didn't continue changing. They became Americanised perhaps, or they died out or you kept them but you kept them intact. People who lived in Scotland went on and became far more anglicised in some ways. That's one theory. We had a very long conversation about that with him.

R1: But the fact is that we did have those conversations. (C11)

A large number of interviewees had become involved in Scottish cultural activities. There are a number of Gaelic learners groups across North America and An Comunn Gàidhealach, which promotes the Gaelic language, has an American branch. Some Gaelic learners visited Scotland to take advantage of summer schools and immersion courses at Sabhal Mòr Ostaig, the Gaelic college on Skye. Others had learned Scottish country or Highland dancing and others were involved in musical groups, with several bagpipers among them. These activities provided another reason for visits to Scotland:

> We last went three years ago. It was a two-and-a-half-week family vacation motivated by a week of instruction for me at Sabhal Mòr Ostaig in Skye. We took our youngest son who had never been to the UK or out of the US ... My expectation would be to go to Scotland maybe every three years or so. I also spent a week at the Gaelic college in St Ann's, Nova Scotia last summer. I want to go back there as well. (C12)

....

> **R:** The first time I went for three weeks and got my feet wet after finally going to Scotland after many years. I visited Sabhal Mòr Ostaig. But I didn't do any formal study until 1992. I was there for two weeks and then in 2000 I studied with them one week.

I: Is it like an immersion class that you go for?

R: It's quite good. It's not quite an immersion but you could make it one if you hang out with the teachers during the class breaks and the dinners. In Nova Scotia at the Gaelic classes there, they have what is called an immersion week proper, where there are activities all day into the evening. When you are in public you are expected to try and speak Gaelic. That's more of an immersion. (C21)

A year and a half ago, we took some dancers over, because we set up a dance exchange with the Inverness Scottish Dancers. So we had them come over two years ago in August and they stayed with us for two weeks, and then the next year in May I took eight dancers with me and we went over and stayed in Inverness with them for two weeks. So that's going to be an ongoing thing now. (C1)

We caught one day in Glasgow where our son was playing at the World Pipe Band Championships. So we got to see him play. His band last year won fifth in the world. This year they won third. So they're excited. (C7)

Those interviewees who had actually been born in Scotland had, as might be expected, a rather different perspective in that Scotland remained their birthplace rather than a place to explore ancestry. Nevertheless, it remained extremely important as their homeland and some people still talked of visiting family as 'going home':

To me it means home, it really does. I still say 'I'm going home.' I go home every year. My husband used to say this is my home and I would say this is just where I live. My home is Scotland. I have such a pride and love of Scotland. To me it just means my roots, to put it in an American thing, because they are all looking for their roots. It is where I came from. It is where, even today, where I have the most fun. (C17)

Scotland is home and will always be home. It's where my heritage is from. Go to the graveyards and see family members going back hundreds of years. That's an intrinsic part of me, even if I never go back to live there again. It'll always be an intrinsic part of me. You pick up a history book and it's part of my family, even though their names aren't there. My family went through all of the various things that happened. (C19)

Some of those born in Scotland attempted to draw distinctions between themselves, with a detailed knowledge of their origins and where they had come from, and American Scots, whom they felt were still searching for their roots. Scotland-born individuals, while acknowledging that their knowledge of family history might be incomplete, did not feel that it really mattered:

I: Let me ask you, I mean speaking as a Scot, why do you think being Scottish is so important then to Americans? What's the difference in their approach to yours?

R: It's incredibly different. I knew all four of my grandparents. I was very close to my grandmother on my mother's side. My parents' grandparents I had no idea about and I really couldn't tell you who they were. I've got their birth certificates and I know their names but I've often thought, should I go and research this? It's easy enough. I could do it. But why? It doesn't have that kind of importance. I know where I belong. I feel that a lot of the American Scots are grasping for belonging somewhere other than the United States. (C20)

....

I: With your view as an outsider coming from Scotland, and meeting Scottish Americans, why do you think there is this constant need that Americans seem to have to explore their roots — in a sense to differentiate themselves from each other? It's as if somehow being American isn't enough?

R: That's a really interesting question. That's something I've constantly asked myself. I can only assume because they're a young nation. We forget that modern-day America has only been in existence for about 250 years. It's constantly changing. If you would listen to Americans how they speak now and Americans as they spoke, say, in the 1950s or on radio broadcasts through the 1930s, they almost had a British accent. If you listened to an old recording you ask, 'Is that American?' You struggle to hear the difference. Plus Americans are constantly on the move. It's something that amazes me. People will leave New York and go to Denver in search of a job, moving 1,200 miles. It's like moving from London to Cairo. There's a cultural thing there of course, but we wouldn't do that in the UK. Americans are constantly on the move and I think it's because of that that they need to have some sort of fallback of where they come from. (C6)

The children of these Scots-born interviewees had almost all been born in America and their approach to Scottish visits varied quite significantly. Some were interested in visiting their parents' home and meeting relatives but, for some, there was little interest:

> **I:** Does your son visit as well?
>
> **R:** No, he's an American. He can mimic me with a Scots accent and he's got a sense of humour but this is home to him. (C9)

Finally, some interviewees visited Scotland on a more formal basis to do business. For them, the establishment of the Scottish Parliament had been significant and two people in particular spoke of meetings with Scottish government ministers. There were also significant links with other bodies in Scotland:

> I don't know how many times I have been to Scotland but it has been a number of times. I have a lot of connections. Part of my duties as president is to make connections and form bonds back and forth. So I served on the patron's committee of Glasgow University when they had their 550th anniversary. I am on the American board of the National Trust for Scotland, which should take me back to Scotland, but it hasn't very often. We've had great relationships with the city of Glasgow. The last three lord provosts have all been to visit and developed relationships and friendships. (C16)
>
> ....
>
> At the moment I probably go back home once a year. I was home in March of this year. That was merely a flying visit because I was on official business in Northern Ireland and took advantage of being there to go home for a couple of days. I'm going home again in November because the British government has invited Governor Bill Owens [of Colorado] to visit the UK for a week as the guest of the government. We will have three days in London and I'm taking him up to Glasgow and Edinburgh for two days. (C6)

In recent years, the Scottish government has sought to improve links between Scotland and the diaspora, while the development of Tartan Day in the United States has provided an opportunity for Scots to travel to America to participate in the celebrations. I will return to this issue of the continuing links between Scotland and its American diaspora in Chapters 6 and 7.

Reading about Scotland

For those who are unable to travel to Scotland, there is, of course, a wealth of written material available about Scotland. Books about Scottish history seem to sell well in the United States and a number of interviewees referred to specific volumes. In addition, there are a number of magazines produced both in the United States and in Scotland, aimed at the Scottish-American community and one of the interviewees in New York was actually a regular writer for one of these.

The American-based magazines include the *Scottish Banner,* published in Dunedin, Florida and which claims to be 'the only monthly Scottish newspaper in the world aimed at Scots at home and abroad. For more than twenty-six years, the *Scottish Banner* has linked Scots with their ain folk. Through these pages, Scots have made friends across the world.' Another publication, *Scottish Life,* produced in Hull, Massachusetts, is a rather more glossy affair with articles about history, travel, Scottish culture and sport. The autumn 2003 issue, for example (which was published while the Colorado interviews were taking place), contained articles on Wigtown (Scotland's book town), Urquhart Castle, Manderston (a country house in Berwickshire), on woodcarving in Arran and on the Museum of Scottish Country Life. The New York interviews in spring 2007 coincided with an issue of *Scottish Life* featuring the House of Dun (in Angus), the Palace of Holyroodhouse, and the archaeological treasures of Orkney. The magazine also contains features on people who have realised their dream of moving to Scotland, on music and books, and there is a calendar of events in both North America and Scotland and extensive advertising by American clan organisations.

Produced in the same offices as *Scottish Life* is *The Highlander,* apparently the oldest of the Scottish-American magazines. Published bi-monthly, it has articles on historical events, Scottish life and traditions, clans, music, genealogy and on 'famous Scots'. These have included Robert Burns (perhaps inevitably), St Margaret and, curiously, General George Wade. Wade was an Irishman serving in the British army and was sent north by the Hanoverian government in the 1720s to construct military roads aimed at policing the Highlands; one might not have expected to have found him regarded as a 'famous Scot'.

There are also a number of magazines with a rather more specialist focus. *Scottish Tales* is an online journal that features stories and cartoons with a Scottish focus, aimed at younger readers. *Celtic Heritage*, which circulates in the United States although published in Nova Scotia, has a focus on music, folklore and the Gaelic language. There are also regionally based magazines such as the *Sunbelt Scots Magazine*, which serves Scottish-American communities in the southern United States.

Within Scotland itself there are a number of magazines published, such as the *Scots Magazine, Scotland Magazine* and *Scottish Memories,* which have wide circulations among the diaspora in North America and elsewhere. Some Scottish newspapers such as the *Sunday Post* also circulate widely among the diaspora communities.

Interviewees were asked if they subscribed to any such magazines or to Scottish newspapers, and most in fact did so. Generally the most popular ones seemed to be those produced within America, namely *Scottish Life, Highlander* and the *Scottish Banner,* with around four or five interviewees subscribing to each. Apart from these, the publication that was most frequently mentioned was *Family Tree,* which is aimed at those with an interest in genealogy. Of the magazines produced in Scotland, *Scotland Magazine* was mentioned the most frequently; others were *Scottish Field, Scots Magazine* and *History Scotland.* There were also some people who subscribed to other magazines with a UK focus and *British Heritage* and *This England* were mentioned:

> I used to get the *Sunday Post.* I used to subscribe to a lot more. I sub-scribe to *This England,* maybe because of the photography in that. I subscribe to the *Scotland Magazine.* I used to get the *Sunday Post* sent to me all of the time until this cousin died and no one else took it on. I get the *British Heritage* but that includes Scotland. (C17)

....

> **R:** I did up until the time I left Minneapolis. Are you going to ask me which one it was?
>
> **I:** Yes.
>
> **R:** The *Scottish Field.* My sister always claims that she would like to live in Scotland but she's out of touch completely. She has only been back about four times in fifty years. (C20)

In this case, the respondent's sister, who had been responsible for the subscription, clearly held to the view that she might one day return to

Scotland, but it was suggested that this 'myth of return' (Anwar, 1979) was unrealistic.

Gaelic learners subscribed to more specialist magazines. One person mentioned the newsletters and publications of Cli, based in Inverness, and An Comunn Gàidhealach America. Another subscribed to *Am Braighe*, which is a Gaelic newspaper published in Canada.

> What I subscribe to are things that are Gaelic oriented. I just don't have time for *Scottish Life* and these other things. I really don't have time for the Gaelic ones but I get them anyway. So I am a member of Cli out of Inverness. They put out a quarterly. I get a quarterly from Nova Scotia. I get two magazines from there. ACGA has its own quarterly. Slighe nan Gaidheal[6] I am a member of, although a nominal one. They have an occasional newsletter. That's basically it. I don't have the time to read about other things. (C21)

The newsletters of local Scottish organisations themselves, such as the various St Andrew societies, Gaelic language and dance organisations, were mentioned by a large number of interviewees, although such publications rarely appear to contain information beyond local society news. In one or two cases, individuals were members of organisations based in Scotland and received newsletters and magazines. One person referred to Historic Scotland and three to the Royal Scottish Country Dance Society.

Few people subscribed to Scottish newspapers, although two people had periodically received copies of the Aberdeen *Press and Journal* and two the *Sunday Post*.

Finally, there are also catalogues, such as the *Scottish Lion*, published by a firm of importers in New Hampshire, which sell Scottish goods to Scottish Americans and these were also mentioned.

The meaning of Scotland

Given the obvious importance of the Scottish connection and the great efforts made by American Scots to maintain it, is it at all possible to sum up what Scotland actually means to them?

Certainly, the romance of Scotland and its heritage exist as potent aspects of a Scottish identity for many people. A study carried out by

6 Slighe nan Gaidheal is an organisation established to support and promote the Gaelic language, based in Seattle.

TNS System Three (2007) for the Scottish government sought to identify the images that people held of Scotland, as a means of inputting to the government's strategy for promoting the country overseas. In American focus groups, Scots were seen as hearty, traditional, family-orientated, fighting and principled people, images that apparently derived partly from the Hollywood movie *Braveheart,* and partly from the character of Groundskeeper Willie in *The Simpsons.* Those who had actually visited Scotland referred to scenery, golf courses and castles. There appeared, however, to be little awareness, however, of Scotland as a place for trans-acting business.

These findings were echoed in a number of interviews in the survey:

> I know modern-day Scotland doesn't want to accept this, but you have to accept the fact that Americans have a mystical relationship with Scotland. Modern-day Scotland wants to be known as comput-ers and whisky and manufacturing and education and medicine but Americans have this mystical relationship that defies definition. It's bagpipes and clan wars and castles. It's there and, whatever it is, it's real. It makes the American Scot look back to that romantic past, to go back and trace their ancestors, to go back to the castle at Edinburgh. We all know that Scotland is a very modern country and leads Europe in the production of computers and all of that. It's a very difficult question to answer. (C16)

....

> I'm one of those Americans, and they're very common, who in touring the Highlands and listening to Celtic music and so on, had an emo-tional connection that's really inexplicable. It's a very romantic period and experience in my memory. I've never been any place where I had the same kind of feelings about connectedness. I would say in dis-covering the music, I've been a musician all of my life, but never had a genre that grabbed me, that this is what I should be doing. That's my feeling about Celtic music. I feel very much at home with what I know of Scottish historical culture and music. If I believed in genetic memory I would cite this as evidence for existence because of the kind of feeling. My wife had the same feeling. She has no Scottish ancestry but she identified with it. (C12)

> Scotland is fantasy. I suppose we dream of going to Scotland like many
> Scots have dreamed of the American Dream. The history of Scotland is
> so old, so interesting. We have done a number of articles. I am wearing
> a torc, which for me is a symbol of Scotland. My Celtic ear-rings are a
> symbol. Probably Scotland's a symbolism. I think of heather, I think of
> moors, I think of sheep dogs. It's the fantasy part and I think that's what
> we are living over here. Most of us who are doing this are living a fantasy.
> But there's a reality behind it all. I don't know how else to say it. I really
> would love to visit Scotland. It's mountainous, it's beautiful. (C14)

There were a surprising number of people who referred not just to
Scotland but to a 'Celtic' heritage, particularly in relation to music, and
some made connections between Scotland and Ireland in this respect.
Such individuals were perhaps 'cardiac Celts' in Bowman's (1995) phrase.
That is, they felt Celtic in their hearts — although it is doubtful if they sub-
scribed to all the various aspects of Celtic history, such as paganism.

More recent migrants to America, who had been born and brought
up in Scotland, had as expected a different — and less romanticised — understanding of Scotland:

> I think it means different things, depending on what group you're
> talking to. Scots-born people, who have lived in Scotland, maybe
> grown up there or worked there before moving to the US, have an
> understanding of modern Scotland, what modern Scotland's all about,
> that, for obvious reasons, the more distant Scots-American commu-
> nity don't have. So they are distinct groups. And for the more tradi-
> tional organisations, what they're doing is celebrating their heritage
> in the US and that's fantastic and that's where Tartan Day came from.
> They're quite distinct groups, both are very valuable to us in the work
> that we do in the Executive and in the embassy promoting Scotland.
> But they have different concepts of their own identity I think. I'm sure
> it's the same with other ethnic groups as well.

> One thing that always strikes me about America is how, across
> the ethnic groups, how proud people are to be Americans. For
> Scots Americans, maybe they would always describe themselves as
> Americans first. But they're people in this modern age, who are more
> interested in their roots, where they came from. They're more able
> to trace that on the internet and with all these other tools. There's a

general raising of awareness of people's ethnicity and where they came from. I deal with people every day who are hugely proud of where they come from. But they're Americans first and foremost, they're Scots Americans second (N8).

The meaning of Scotland had perhaps changed somewhat as individuals travelled to Scotland on holiday or to visit relatives and the impact of both the internet and greater frequency of visits to Scotland were both specifically mentioned in interviews.

Scotland's achievements and the Scottish character

Although there were variations between interviewees as to what precisely Scotland meant to them, there was nevertheless a considerable pride in Scotland's achievements and a related pride in having Scottish ancestry. A surprising number of people mentioned Arthur Herman's (2001) book, which had apparently had a considerable impact in the United States:

> **R:** Some of the best television programmes here are BBC programmes and they cover Scotland. There is a lot published about Scotland and the Scots. The Clearances and all that kind of thing. There have been books published over here that become bestsellers because they have 'Scot' on the front cover. I'm sure Bob and Margaret talked about one …
>
> **I:** The Scottish enlightenment one, the Herman book? Yes, several people have mentioned that to me. I'm surprised how many people have mentioned it.
>
> **R:** Everybody has read it because it's an insight into the history of Scotland that I didn't have. (C20)

....

> **R:** I have been involved with it so many years and have read books about Scotland, and what they have done for civilisation.
>
> **I:** Herman's book?
>
> **R:** As well as Duncan Bruce's *The Mark of the Scots*. It just gives you a sense of pride to know that those people have done so much. In many cases they started out with nothing but had the perseverance to keep on until they really made something of themselves and left a mark for others. I am not really good about putting those kinds of things into

words. I have a little English blood and probably some French too, but it seems to me I will only claim Scottish. (C16)

Some of the books that interviewees mentioned might be described as hagiographic rather than presenting a balanced and research-based approach to Scottish history. Many appear to have been deliberately designed to instil pride in the Scottish expatriate. Bruce's (1996) book, for example, has the rather over-blown title, *The Mark of the Scots: Their Astonishing Contribution to History, Science, Democracy, Literature and the Arts.* The other book mentioned, by Herman (2001), has — interestingly — been titled quite differently in Britain and in America. In Britain, it is *The Scottish Enlightenment: The Scots' Invention of the Modern World,* but in America it has a rather different emphasis as *How the Scots Invented the Modern World: The True Story of How Western Europe's Poorest Nation Created Our World and Everything In It.* One might take issue with Scotland being so described at the time of the Enlightenment but the description appears to have struck a chord with expatriates who sometimes referred to Scotland as a 'poor country' in interviews:

> From my personal research, it just kind of makes you proud to know where you're from and who your ancestors are. To me, it's nice to know that you're a Scot, because when I read, even though Scotland is one of the poorest countries in Europe, no offence, a lot of the ideas for the modern world came from Scotland. The banking industry, psychology, anthropology and all that was researched in Scotland. I just read lately that in the eighteenth century, 1750 or 1760, I can't remember, 65% of the Scots were literate already and could read. I think it's because John Knox wanted to be able to read the Bible. Is that true? (C1)

Some people drew comparisons between aspects of the Scottish and American characters and expressed their irritation at the perceived insularity of America and a general ignorance about other parts of the world, including Scotland:

> **R:** It's a lot of things. It's to enjoy fun, to enjoy life. It's to enjoy people. I think Scottish people are some of the most hospitable people in the world. I think they just love people. I don't think you would ever take a walk in Scotland and walk by somebody without talking to them. You don't have to make people say hello to you. Here, I've been here for thirty years and I can tell you today I belong to a hiking group and

I also do a lot of walking. I have to say good morning. I force people to say good morning to me. In Scotland it is not that way.

I: Being Scottish is still important to you?

R: Very important. And look at all of the things we did way back. So many Americans are blind to how not just Scotland but the rest of the world invented things. It was not invented in America.

I: You are saying they are quite insular in knowing the background?

R: Yes. I used to be very angry about this but I've become more tolerant of it. But now, 9/11 made them realise there was the rest of the world. But most Americans, when I first came here and for many, many years after I came here, knew very little about other countries. So I started excusing them after a while, because why would you, when you are 3,000 miles from coast to coast? You're so big in your own self. If you live in Colorado, to know something about Utah and about Kansas and Mexico and Nebraska is probably about as much as us knowing something about Scotland and England. But then we seem to know more. I think our education was way better. (C17)

Indeed, the quality of Scottish education was mentioned by a large number of people, partly relating to personal experience but also to the experiences of their ancestors. There was a very strong belief that women in particular, in Scotland, had benefited from education to an extent that was unusual for the time; this had then proved beneficial after emigration to the United States (Moore, 2006):

R: I think I developed an appreciation for the Scottish society, and its values, as a member of the Presbyterian Church that I grew up in. My great-grandfather was one of the founders of the church in that town. It was more of an appreciation and an expectation of women to be educated and to do well. I saw being raised like this as being very different from how my friends were raised in a small town.

I: The education was always important?

R: Yes, especially for women. The women could be deacons in the church and the women were expected to be well read and to take part in arguments. Whereas the other two dominant churches in that community, Lutheran and Catholic, did not feed my girlfriends the same line. I started questioning that and I read a lot about John Knox and the Reformation as a kid. Then I read more about the Scottish society,

which way back was matriarchal. It was interesting. It was something I
did on my own within the context of a Scottish heritage. (C18)

There were also some references made to the role played by Scots in
creating the American constitution and the American legal system. Thus
many of those who helped to frame the Declaration of Independence were
Scots or descended from Scots (Fry, 2003) and this has been discussed in
the previous chapter, on Tartan Day.

Although, as noted above, some people made reference to Scotland
being a poor country, others emphasised areas of strength. Family ties
themselves were seen as strong and some people emphasised the need
for strength of character to enable Scotland to remain as a separate and
distinctive country:

> I felt a really strong sense of self-esteem, knowing that I came from a
> strong family in Scotland. I think a lot of us here don't have a lot of
> family history because our families have only been here 100 or 200
> years. I think I miss that history of the way back, of feeling that I was
> part of something that had been around for a long time. I needed that.
> It really helped me to feel like I was a part of something lasting (C13).
> I think it's a wonderful little country that has wanted to be free for
> many years and have its own personal identity away from England.
> With the advent of *Braveheart* and some of the other American movies
> it has come out with, I think over here we're even more cognisant of
> the struggle that Scotland has had over the years. But it's very special. It
> has such its own character and its own identity. (C5)

The Scottish family

The strong sense of Scottish identity which was expressed by many interviewees, often strengthened further by exploring genealogy and ancestral
roots in Scotland, was often displayed publicly. We have seen the renewed
interest in Scottish organisations in America, in Highland Games and in
learning Gaelic. For some families, being Scottish influenced family occasions such as weddings and often had profound influences on the children
of American Scots. Thus younger generations were also active in maintaining a Scottish identity and a connection.

During interviews, a number of people used the opportunity to talk
about family weddings, often accompanied by photographs. In fact,

although such ceremonies were intended to be 'Scottish', they would probably not be recognised as such by homeland Scots. In some cases, the ceremonies had been adapted to fit a rather mythical sense of what a Scottish or a 'Celtic' wedding might have been. In other cases, the photographs revealed a remarkable variety of 'Scottish' dress, with kilts worn with a great range of accompanying garments. The scale of the ceremonies tended to be very large but there appeared to be no dancing afterwards, as would be the norm in Scotland:

> These are pictures here of a wedding that was this summer of our youngest son. What's laid out here on the ground is a big circle and then a smaller circle and then this kind of arbour and then a star pointed in here and then these are the two clan plaids. When his wife came up, they were hand-fasted because it was a Native American Celtic ceremony basically. So, you can see all the guys are in kilts. Degan gave them sgian dubhs for their groom's gift. So they not only see themselves as Scottish American, but they have also taken as much of an interest in furthering traditions and redefining them, so that they have meaning for them. Hector is Degan's good friend and a Native American teacher, so he and his wife did the service. They put together as many of the Native American elements and the Celtic elements as they could and they went together very well. (C11)

....

I: You talked earlier about your Scottish wedding.

R1: We both felt so strongly about it.

R2: I wouldn't marry a woman that wouldn't let me wear my kilt at the wedding!

R1: Show him the picture, honey. All the kids were in their kilts. I felt the same way. I wanted him to wear it.

R2: I absolutely would not have married a girl that would not let me wear my kilt.

R1: Yeah. We had such a great time. Probably 80% of the men that were there that day were in their kilts too.

I: This is in Denver?

R1: It was actually in the mountains, in Evergreen. We had about 280 people there. Maybe half of those were men and the majority of them were kilted, almost all of them.

R2: We told everybody that we wanted to have a Scottish Renaissance-type wedding. We asked them to be kilted if they liked. We wanted it to be fun and laid back.

R1: All the kids were kilted. The same kilt actually. That's McDougall. These are my sons and my nephews.

R3: That's my brother.

R2: Vic and his friends wore Johnstone. His two cousins had Johnstone. His two friends — we rented kilts for them that were similar to Johnstone.

R1: That's my dad and he's McDougall. My brother has his on. It was fun to see the blue kilts and then the red ones.

R2: Even the dog had hers.

R1: Yes, the dog had a red plaid bow on. (C13)

....

R: Our oldest son gets married next month and he gave strong consideration to doing the wedding in a kilt. Through me, he has developed a mental connection to his Scottish ancestry. His name is Ian.

I: Did he decide against the kilt?

R: He did. I think that was his fiancée's influence. It's entirely up to him. I would have come in mine, of course, if he would have come in his. (C12)

....

I: How would your children regard themselves? Do they also get involved in these activities or have they become just American?

R: Some of them more so than others. One of my granddaughters loves to go on the re-enactments with us, and she's now twenty-two years old. She's been doing that her whole life and she's known as a Scot also. My second oldest grandson lives out in Arizona but, whenever he comes to visit us on the east coast, he wants to know 'What are we doing this weekend, Grandpa?' so he can dress in a kilt. (N14)

Thus, many of the children of American Scots appear to have followed their parents in developing an interest in their Scottish ancestry. Sometimes, this was linked to holidays or visits to Scotland:

I: I was interested in what you said earlier about your daughter having a Scottish wedding in Buffalo. Would your children also regard themselves as being Scottish, or Scottish American?

R: Scottish American. Because when they were little, I used to take them with me to the Games and when I'd go visit I'd always drag them with me to Scotland. The one that got married in Buffalo — when she graduated from high school, for a graduation gift I sent her by herself at eighteen to Scotland for two weeks. I gave her plenty of money, a credit card, her ticket bought and the only thing was she couldn't go to Edinburgh or Glasgow, she had to stay up in the north because she was just eighteen. She had to go to visit the little towns where I wouldn't have to worry about her. Nothing against Glasgow or Edinburgh, they were just big cities and she was just a kid. I had a lot of friends over there already and she stayed with a friend of ours.

I: Did that help her to give her a sense of Scottish identity so that when she got married she wanted to do the whole thing?

R: Oh yes, yes she thought it was great! Yes, yes, I guess it is. They've been there, they just take it for granted, they just think they're Scottish, they just know it. (C1)

Hunter (2005, p. 19) related the similar experience of a young American Scot visiting Skye as part of a journey around the UK. He became so caught up in the experience that he remained on the island for a couple of weeks. He claimed to feel totally at home, identifying completely with his Scottish heritage. Indeed, this seems to be increasingly the case with many younger people, who have rediscovered their Scottish ancestry and identified extremely strongly with it:

I: What about your kids, would they consider themselves to be Scottish or Scottish Americans?

R: I think our son would probably say Scottish first. I think so. (C7)

....

R1: He wears his kilt to school.

I: Do you?

R3: Sometimes.

R1: Not something he does every week.

R2: They have Tartan Day in America on April 6. So that's a day you can get away with it.

R1: A couple of days during the year he will wake up with a wild hair and throw it on.

R2: Or he'll put it on and go out and play and be *Braveheart*. He does that often. A lot of times when we have a family get-together, a lot of kids will wear their kilts. (C13)

....

I have a son in Virginia Beach, Virginia. We went down there to the Loch Norman Games. Immediately our son and one grandson were in our extra set of kilts and went to the Games. They became a part of it. I went up to Spokane, Washington. My daughter lives up in the tri-cities area. I took along extra kilts and I had two grandsons up there immediately in kilts and we went to the Games. (C14)

The names that families gave their children were often Scottish:

[The] discussion for our first grandchild is 'what is his name going to be?' His name is William Angus. So there is something about naming your children in this old tradition as well. (C11)

His name's Rory and his younger son is Rowan. They wanted to use Scottish names. I have a brother and sister and since I got excited about it now they have and my parents are. It's kind of spreading through the family. (C13)

But there were also some children for whom the Scottish connection held little interest. Interestingly, this applied most commonly to the children of native-born Scots, who appeared to be keen to integrate within American society rather than retaining their parents' identity:

My son will still tell people that he came from Scotland. But he's American and he's not into soccer or anything. He's into car racing and football. (C9)

That's funny — we had the same discussion while I was on vacation. I wonder, are they going to go back and try and find out their roots? Of course they don't need to because I have all that information. I really think they feel American. I don't think they feel for one moment, except my youngest boy, Brian, would probably say I was born in Georgia but my mom is from Scotland. We have family reunions every five years in different places back home and here in different states. We've worried about the fact that the next generation doesn't all come to the family reunions. Some of it is expense and there are all kinds of reasons. We are concerned that when we are gone that there won't be no more family get-togethers. (C17)

My only son, he's more interested in punk rock than anything else. He knows I run around in a kilt every once in a while but that's about the only association he has with Scotland. (C2)

Thus there appeared to be generational differences in relation to feelings of Scottish identity, which appear to be hard to explain and hard also to predict just how interest and identity would develop across the generations.

The apparent renewal of interest in Scottish organisations and Scottish identity in North America would seem to indicate that, for the most part, that identity is strengthening within the expatriate community. The involvement of many of the children of American Scots would also suggest that this trend will continue, although not all children, of course, remain interested. The expansion of existing Highland Games and the establishment of new ones, the continued interest in genealogy and the establishment of Tartan Day would all suggest that the Scottish expatriate community is relatively strong. This view was explored with the various interviewees.

Is a Scottish-American identity strengthening or weakening?

There appeared to be an initial division of opinion as to whether the Scottish-American identity was strengthening or not. But eventually this resolved itself into a widely held view that, while the *Scottish-American* identity was strengthening, as evidenced by the expanding interest in Scottish organisations, Highland Games and the like, a truly *Scottish* identity was being weakened as a result of reduced immigration to America from Scotland itself. A large number of interviewees ascribed this growing sense of Scottish-American identity to the influence of films such as *Braveheart*. Thus:

> **I:** Would you say the identity of Scots in America has become stronger?
> **R:** In my experience, yes. I see a lot of people doing some pretty unusual things at these Games. Part of it I think is due to — I hate to take offence — due to the movie *Braveheart*. A lot of people became interested in Scotland and being Scottish as a result of that movie, as inaccurate as it is, as I am sure you are aware. (C2)
> ....

> I was working for the festival before *Braveheart* came out, and since then it seems like there has been a lot more interest. Whether it's from that or just general interest, I don't know. Those movies seem to really have peaked an interest. If people really do want to know if they have Scottish roots, they're going to find out more about it. (C5)

Films such as *Braveheart* and *Rob Roy* (both released in 1995) were credited not only with strengthening American Scots' view of their own identity but also with 'promoting' the Scots identity within America as a whole:

> I believe it was a very important thing for *Rob Roy* and *Braveheart* to come out at the same time. In some respects they competed against each other at the box office, I believe. It created, I believe, an interest in things, especially among the kids. I think there were a lot of kids that saw this, that may have started asking questions, like maybe they were named McPherson and the family didn't do much and all of a sudden we have a McPherson and hey we need to look at this. I think it probably did have an impact on increasing interest. (C4)

Some of those actually born in Scotland, however, were somewhat bemused by the tremendous impact that the film had made:

> I've only been here three and a half years, so I'm not able to speak on any long-term basis. But certainly I think things like *Braveheart* made a huge difference. You have to go to some of the sporting events here to understand, but some of the clips from *Braveheart*, and particularly the charges and the battle cries, are played at sporting events almost to encourage your supporters to ride. That's really quite an interesting phenomenon. (C6)
>
> ....
>
> Well it certainly didn't impact on me, because the accents were horrendous. Well, Mel Gibson looked pretty cute in a kilt but, um, certainly a lot of people since have come out and said, 'Where are you from? Oh, *Braveheart*.' They want to connect the two. (C19)

A related influence appears to have been the successful export to the United States of BBC programmes such as *Monarch of the Glen*, shown between 2000 and 2005 and based on the novels by Compton Mackenzie. They have appealed to the American view of Scotland, and have been widely shown on the Public Broadcasting Service (PBS) channel. For one interviewee, it represented a 'more accurate' picture of Scottish life than historical films, although residents of Scotland itself might feel somewhat differently about it:

> **R:** More recently, *Monarch of the Glen*.
> **I:** Do you get that over here?

R: Oh sure, I subscribe to BBC America just to get it. I stumbled on that. I was watching PBS one day here and I really wasn't watching. I was messing around on the computer and I hear this Scottish country dance tune that I recognised. So I turned around and looked at the TV and there were all these guys doing some jig or reel. Then I started watching it and got interested in it. That's probably more accurate than movies are about life in Scotland and as a result we took a trip up to Aviemore. Couldn't get in there but I got a picture of my wife against the backdrop of Loch Laggan.[7] So that's another thing that has influenced some Americans. (C2)

Other interviewees referred to the Highland Games themselves as having an important role in strengthening Scottish identities in America, because of their high visibility as a tourist attraction. And tartan was also mentioned as having an immediately identifiable link with Scotland and being Scottish, although one person felt that Americans became confused between 'tartan' and 'plaid':

In part it's commercial … Tartans have become very commercial. There's great business in all of these Scottish things. Here in the States it's the same thing. You go to the Games and the vendors are there, it's immense what they have to sell. What's immense is that the people buy it. The world has gotten much smaller because of the internet and the communication is much faster. I don't think sixty years ago there were clans around in the States. I don't think there was the education of people about their names that goes on today. So I think there has been a substantial increase in Scottish interest. (C4)

....

I think here, people don't really use the word 'tartan'. It's plaid or 'plad' I guess they say here.[8] If you go into a store, even a Scottish store, here that sells tartan stuff, if you ask for tartan they usually look at you a bit confused and say plaid. It's always plaid. It's plaid skirts and plaid kilts and plaid scarves. (C19)

7 The programme was filmed on the Ardverikie estate, on the shores of Loch Laggan, between Fort William and Aviemore. The popularity of the programme led to its being used for local tourist marketing purposes.

8 In Scotland, the word 'plaid' would normally be pronounced to rhyme with 'paid', but in America, it would always be pronounced to rhyme with 'pad'.

Wearing the kilt was seen as an obvious identifier of 'Scottishness' but this was viewed in a rather ambivalent way. Some people expressed their pride in wearing the kilt and felt it was extremely important to them:

> I used to like to, before I was married, to wear my kilt to pubs. I never once received a derogatory comment from anybody. Everybody who came up would be, 'Oh wow, cool' and they'd start asking about it. Never did I get anything about somebody say I was wearing a skirt. (C13)

But others suggested that this was merely reinforcing the rather romantic view which many other Americans had of Scotland:

> **R:** Most Americans have probably never been to Scotland and don't know anybody from Scotland. People from Scotland are pretty much just like people from America. You don't run around in kilts all the time. You don't drink whisky day and night and have swords and knives and things. You're just pretty much normal people.
>
> **I:** You're saying a lot of people haven't been to Scotland, so do people have quite a romantic notion of what it's really like?
>
> **R:** I think so probably, because in America Scotland is perceived as castles and golf and seascapes. I think that's what people perceive as Scotland. (C2)

There are a number of issues that arise from this discussion about the possible strengthening of Scottish-American identity. Quite apart from the influence of Hollywood films, there is the continuing importance of Scottish events such as Highland Games and the significance of the kilt and tartan as identifiers of 'Scottishness'.

Conclusions

What has emerged in this chapter is the importance of identity to American Scots and the lengths to which individuals will go to maintain it. Identity in this expatriate context is essentially rooted in ancestry, rather than in a Scottish birthplace and it is clear that, for some, distance lends enchantment. American Scots sometimes adopted a sentimental view of their homeland and many of the activities designed to maintain the Scottish connection — such as Kirkin' o' the Tartan — would not be recognised in Scotland itself.

That is not to invalidate the claim of individuals actually to be Scottish. Research in Scotland into the markers of identity (McCrone, 2001b, p. 73) showed that ancestry is readily accepted by many Scots as an indicator of Scottishness. Most would see it as being of less significance than birthplace or upbringing but it remains an important marker.

Many of those who claim a Scottish connection often wish to take things forward by actually visiting Scotland and, frequently, undertaking genealogical research. So for those who travel to the 'homeland', what do they find? In many cases, Scotland itself has changed significantly over the years and so the relationship between American Scots and modern Scotland may be a complex one. It is to this relationship that I now turn.

Chapter 6

The relationship with modern Scotland

A changing Scotland

I have discussed in previous chapters the importance to members of the diaspora of maintaining a connection with the homeland and the continuing significance of their Scottish identity. The connection and the identity are maintained in different ways by different people but key roles are played by Scottish organisations, by Highland Games and other events, and by the growing importance of Tartan Day. Not everybody plays an active part in these organisations, although in cities such as New York American Scots and expatriate Scots are perhaps more regularly in contact with Scotland for business purposes. So some people have a very realistic and up-to-date view of the Scottish homeland and do not necessarily see it through a nostalgic lens.

But when we speak of a relationship between modern Scotland and the Scottish diaspora, precisely what kind of a relationship is this likely to be? Scotland itself has changed so substantially in recent years that emigrants may find it hard to keep up to date. Is their relationship truly with *modern* Scotland or is it with an idealised homeland? It is perhaps important therefore, at this point, to say something about the ways in which Scotland as a country has changed, particularly in political terms.

The early 1950s are often regarded as a high point of Britishness in the UK, in the aftermath of the Second World War and before the disintegration of the British Empire (Devine, 1999). But the UK emerged from the war nearly bankrupt and had to be rescued by American loans. Scotland, in particular, was in bad shape and in desperate need of industrial reconstruction and diversification. The Attlee government's approach was the establishment of the postwar welfare state and the nationalisation of key industries, such as coal and steel. While this allowed for reorganisation of these industries, the nationalised industries had their headquarters in England — usually in London — and so key decision-making was removed from Scotland. During the 1950s, UK regional policy succeeded in encouraging new investment, such as motor manufacturing plants at Linwood and Bathgate, and a new steel mill at Ravenscraig, near Motherwell, but these developments only served to highlight how much of a branch economy Scotland had become.

This was particularly true of the electronics industry, which expanded significantly in Scotland during the 1960s and 1970s. Although initially viewed as a major success story, with the term 'Silicon Glen' being coined to refer to the Scottish version of California's 'Silicon Valley', the developments were essentially branch plants of American companies. These included IBM, NCR, Burroughs and Honeywell, later joined by a number of Japanese companies (Payne, 1996). By the end of the twentieth century, some of these plants had closed, as companies retrenched.

At the same time as Scotland was experiencing mixed economic fortunes at home, the decline of the British Empire was reducing opportunities abroad. During the 1950s and 1960s, the UK appeared unsure as to its future direction and it was not until 1972 that it joined the European Union (then known as the European Economic Community). This allowed Dean Acheson, American secretary of state in the early 1950s, to make his famous remark that Great Britain had lost an empire but not yet found a role. This lack of direction led many in Scotland to question whether the union with England continued to be a meaningful one and, after the discovery of North Sea oil with its power to transform Scottish economic fortunes and which would make an independent Scotland economically viable, the union came under particular strain. By 1977, Tom Nairn could write of the likely 'breakup' of Britain (Nairn, 1977).

The late 1960s therefore saw the growth of political nationalism in Scotland. The Scottish National Party (SNP) had been founded in 1934, following the merger of some smaller predecessors, but had had only limited political success (Lynch, 1999). But its breakthrough came with a by-election victory in Hamilton in 1967 (Ewing and Russell, 2004), after which the party has had continuous representation at Westminster.

The reference to the loss of empire is an important one. Many people in Scotland watched as a series of British colonies became independent, and this process inevitably raised the question as to whether Scotland itself ought to be independent — or, at the very least, have a measure of home rule. Thus:

> In a television programme in March 1998, Ludovic Kennedy said that he was present to report for the BBC at scores of hand-over ceremonies in former British colonies where the Union flag was lowered and the flag of the newly independent country was raised. 'I started to think', he said, 'if these little places, and some of them very small and very poor, can have self-government, why can't Scotland?' (Scott, 1999, p. 58)

The success of the SNP — and its equivalent, Plaid Cymru in Wales — led the government at Westminster to look at the ways in which Scotland was governed and to move to establish a legislature in Edinburgh, to deal with Scottish domestic matters. A referendum in 1979 failed to gain enough support to ensure the establishment of a Scottish Assembly, because of electoral hurdles contained within the legislation (Devine, 1999) but, by 1997, the unpopularity of the Conservative government and growing support for devolution ensured that a second referendum resulted in massive support for a Scottish Parliament. This was formally established at Holyrood in Edinburgh in 1999, although not without some predictions that it would in the long run help to destabilise the union (Jeffery, 2008). This view appeared to have some truth, after the SNP's success in the Holyrood elections of 2007, after which they formed a government for the first time.

The establishment of the Scottish Parliament and the growing support for the SNP appear to be reflected in a stronger sense of national identity within Scotland. As the sense of 'Britishness' has declined, there has been an equivalent growth in feelings of 'Scottishness'. A series of election and attitude surveys over time have shown convincingly that the numbers of individuals within Scotland identifying themselves as Scottish rather than British have grown steadily (Stone and Muir, 2007) and these changes have been reflected in a range of political and social attitudes and responses (Paterson, 2002). Commentators reflect on a growing confidence within Scottish society.

It can be seen therefore that Scotland has gone through massive societal, economic and political changes in the sixty or so years since the end of the Second World War. The country is now very different to that from which many people emigrated and it is possible that some American Scots may find it harder to identify with it. How then have these changes affected the ongoing relationship which American Scots have with their homeland?

The post-devolution relationship with Scotland

In the face of the changes that have taken place within Scotland, it is perhaps worth asking whether the North American experience of Scottishness has any relevance for Scotland itself. Cowan (1999) pointed out that emigrants are notoriously conservative. French people, for example, often have great difficulty in recognising the French values preserved in modern Quebec and, similarly, Calabrian emigrants retain a view of their homeland which few there would share. Some would therefore regard the Scottish Americans as irrelevant:

> There's certainly a temptation to dismiss the Scottish-American scene as a superficial hotch-potch of bagpipes, caber-tossing and swirling kilts, peopled by groups of slightly eccentric enthusiasts trapped in a 'loch and glen' mentality, a past which effectively vanished after Culloden. (Hewitson, 1993, p. 282)

On the other hand, while Scottish Americans may be emotionally tied to a Scotland of the past, and possibly less familiar with contemporary issues, there is perhaps a challenge to Scots living in Scotland to help make Scottish Americans more aware of other aspects of what they perceive as their homeland:

> Would a broader picture damage their attachment to Scotland? I'd like to think not. Perhaps we've reached a crossroads where these misconceptions can be corrected and the Scots diaspora reminded that Scotland is a nation still, a complex people with complex aspirations, not a theme park. (Hewitson, 1993, p. 283)

A similar challenge is delivered by Alan Bain, president of the American-Scottish Foundation, who remarks about the ways in which his admittedly romanticised view of Scotland frequently bumps up against reality in his work for the foundation (Devine and Logue, 2002). He also noted how Tartan Day, which is clearly important to American Scots, is not seen as particularly relevant within Scotland itself. Yet, as Bain pointed out and as discussed in Chapter 4, Tartan Day could be used as a vehicle for Scottish business to promote itself within North America. He argued that more could be done to use the Scottish diaspora as a resource, with Scotland's business, tourism, cultural and academic institutions working more collectively and strategically, to the benefit of all.

It may also be the case that the view of Scotland held by American Scots will in time become more realistic. As recently as the 1960s, air travel was difficult and expensive and there was little opportunity for Scottish emigrants to return home. Indeed, the first time that many American Scots had had the opportunity to visit their homeland had been as servicemen fighting in Europe during the Second World War. Some events that were introduced from the 1950s onwards for the benefit of Scottish expatriates, such as the MacLeod clan parliaments at Dunvegan Castle in Skye, could not have taken place if it were not possible to fly easily to Scotland from other countries (Hunter, 2005).

For those unable to return 'home', memories of homeland inevitably became overly nostalgic, reinforced by literature popular in the emigrant market, such as magazines like the *Scots Magazine* and *Scottish Field*, and reinforced also by tours by Scottish entertainers such as Andy Stewart and Jimmy Shand (Cameron, 1998). The late comedian Jimmy Logan reflected in his autobiography on his various tours of North America, playing to 'remarkable' audiences; on one tour, the opening night show in Montreal had lasted four hours (Logan, 1998). Today, air travel is relatively cheap and commonplace and it is easy for American Scots to travel 'home'. The internet provides an immediate set of links to Scottish websites, which can inform those elsewhere of what the issues in Scotland really are. Such technological advances have made it easier for expatriates to retain more realistic transnational values and involvements (Eckstein, 2002). Thus, the images that are held of Scotland may change significantly over time.

Many of the interviewees stated that they travelled regularly to Scotland and attempted to keep in touch with developments through the internet. It was important therefore to explore the extent to which the significant political and societal changes within Scotland had made an impact on American Scots.

Interviewees were asked if they were aware of the process of devolution within the UK. There certainly appeared to be a strong awareness of the new Parliament and some people had either been in Scotland at the time it opened, or had been to the Scottish Parliament's visitor centre at Holyrood:

R: I know the Scottish Parliament was reconvened because that happened about four years ago and we were there. The Queen was there. I
think it was about four years ago.

I: It was exactly four years ago.

R: We were there, so I was aware that the British had finally allowed the
Scots to have their Parliament reconvened.[1] I do know that there's a new
House of Parliament being built down by Holyrood because we walked
right by it. (C2)

....

I stayed up till three o'clock in the morning to watch the Queen open
Parliament, on television. I wouldn't want to profess to know a lot
about it ... I should be ashamed that I really don't know what has happened since then. (C17)

One person thought that the establishment of the Parliament would have a
significant effect on strengthening Scottish identity and had been aware of
an increased use of the Scottish Saltire on public buildings:

One of the things that we picked up on ourselves was that I didn't
notice the Saltires flying as much in 1996 as in 1998. That was also
during the World Cup. Unfortunately, Scotland didn't do well in the
World Cup that year. But we did notice a significant increase in Scottish
flags between our two trips and we talked about it while we were there.
I believe it was mostly out of the devolution procedures (C4).

There was thus some awareness within America of a growing sense of Scottish
identity at home. To my own surprise, I had some experience of this while
shopping in New York in spring 2007 in a small clothing store in the west
midtown area. When I went to pay for my purchases, the shopkeeper examined my Bank of Scotland credit card. 'So', he said, 'you're from Scotland?' I
agreed that I was. 'And are you Scottish or British?' he asked. 'That's a very
good question!' I replied, somewhat taken aback at being asked. My ques-
tioner appeared to have no connection to Scotland whatsoever, yet clearly
appreciated some of the issues of identity affecting Scots within the UK.

Other people, however, have relatively little awareness and some of my
interviewees suggested that America was too insular a society for Scottish
devolution to have made much of an impact:

1 The terminology here is interesting. The term 'British' appears to be equated with
'English', as if the Scots were not also 'British'.

I remember when the Stone of Scone went back to Scotland,[2] and devolution, when they first broke ground in the new Parliament. I mean that was in the news here, whether that was in the main news or the BBC I can't remember. But it was on the news. You know America's a very insular society. It could be an earthquake in South America and twenty million people died and it would come after the sports. I mean, literally, Americans know very little about what's going on in the world in general. (C19)

There's very little interest. Americans are very insular. They are very inward-looking. They hardly take an interest. They will take an interest in what's going on in Colorado because that's relevant to them. They will take less of an interest in what's going on at the federal level unless it's something really big. It would take something as major as the recall in California[3] for them to take any interest in what's going on in California. They're not interested in anything that's going on in Illinois or Texas or Arizona, it's of absolutely no interest to them and less so overseas. Constantly, tests are being taken by youngsters who have no idea where Canada is in relation to the United States — or Australia. If you try and put a map of Europe and ask which country is where, they fail miserably. There is really very little interest unless it's specialised, someone with a specific interest. (C6)

There appeared to be a very wide support for the establishment of the Scottish Parliament, although the reasons for this support were many and varied. For some, Scottish devolution could be compared with the American War of Independence as a blow against British imperialism:

Personally I don't like British imperialism. When I go to the British Museum, all I see is things that England plundered from other parts of the country and, while I view myself as an American, my British [ancestors] were in Wales and Scotland which were both conquered and subjugated by England. That's my feeling. That may be an archaic notion on

2 The Stone of Scone is a block of sandstone that was traditionally used in the coronations of Scottish monarchs. It was taken to England by Edward I in 1296 and, although it was briefly repatriated to Scotland in 1950 by student nationalists, it was only officially returned in 1996. It is now kept in Edinburgh Castle.

3 The recall election in California took place in autumn 2003, at the time of this interview. The then Democrat governor, Gray Davis, was 'recalled' by a petition of electors and forced to stand for re-election. He lost to the Republican candidate, Arnold Schwarzenegger.

my part from 500 years ago, but that's kind of the way the English ran their world years ago. Fortunately here in the United States they lost. We revolted and we won. You Scottish lost. (C2)

For others, devolution had acquired a certain romanticism:

> It's hard to describe that feeling. It's kind of like in *Braveheart*. We have a country of our own. I hate when they mention Scotland as Britain. That's just wrong. We're not British. We're Scottish. (C13)

There were a number of interviewees who made historical allusions, linking the establishment of the Parliament to the return of the Stone of Scone, the Declaration of Arbroath and other events. There were also references to more recent history, with one person recalling the long struggle to achieve devolution during the 1980s and 1990s, with supporters camped outside the Royal High School building on Calton Hill in Edinburgh, which had been identified as the venue for a Scottish legislature:

> I feel I'm very well informed about it. There was a picture of Sean Connery getting recruited by the SNP people to rally round the troops. There's a little movie out there called *Interrogation of a Highland Lass*[4] and it's about the repatriation of the Stone of Scone back in 1950, 1951. I admire the fact that people are still willing to fight for that. The Declaration of Arbroath — am I pronouncing that correctly? — how that has gradually led to an identity. (C8)

> You know, you keep abreast of what's going on with the Stone of Scone being returned and all of it. That was quite an unusual thing that happened. I think these things are meaning a great deal to the Scottish who are finding their roots through things of that sort. (C14)

> I can say that in 1993 I remember the guys all camped out at the old Scottish Parliament on Princes Street in Edinburgh. Then along came the Corries and '*Flower of Scotland*'.[5] (C18)

---

4   This is a film that was shown on the BBC in December 2000, to celebrate the fiftieth anniversary of the taking of the Stone from Westminster Abbey. It was made in Gaelic (titled *An Ceasnachadh*), with English subtitles, and dramatises the interrogation of one of the participants, Kay Matheson, by a less than sympathetic detective inspector, who is unable to comprehend either the language or the strength of national feeling involved. It would appear that copies sell well in America.

5   *Flower of Scotland* is Scotland's unofficial national anthem. The song was written by the late Roy Williamson of folk band the Corries.

Levels of awareness of the details of devolution were similarly very varied. Some people knew about the distinctions between the powers of the Scottish and Westminster administrations and drew parallels with the United States and the distinction between state and federal powers:

> Oh, yes. You've got to have it locally. With the ties to Downing Street and all of that, you still have an international, British, Parliament with world affairs. In Scotland, in Edinburgh, it will have to do more to be more prominent, education wise and road building and all of that. (C9)

> It is kind of like in the United States, where we have state versus federal government. To me I think that Wales and Scotland and Ireland should all have their own Parliaments. Then you have the major Parliament, which happens to be in London, but could be somewhere else and it is like the federal government. So, yes I support it, for each country to have their own. (C17)

Others appeared to be confused between Scottish devolution and independence:

> Yes, but do you think Scotland can manage on its own? (C10)

> I think any country should have their own independence, even though they are a part of Britain. (C14)

Some people were supportive of the Scottish Parliament but had some initial concerns about its performance. They suggested that it would take time to establish itself. It appeared as if some of the negative publicity, which has appeared in the media within Scotland about the Parliament and, in particular, the cost of the Holyrood building, had reached the United States:

> I've read a little bit. It's going to take a while to get things organised. The Parliament itself is a little overpriced, so to speak. Some of the purchases and changes to the building that were going on cost a fortune. It's going to take a while because it's a change from always going to London for funds or whatever, to having to do it yourself. This is a new thing. I am not saying Scots are not up to it. It's going to take some time to do it that way rather than the old way. (C7)

> I don't know too much about it because you don't hear much about it over here. But from what I do hear, there's been an awful lot of squabbling, even over the building. (C9)

For some people who were involved in business, the Scottish Parliament had become extremely important in terms of access to opportunities, and some individuals had met with Scottish ministers and Parliamentary officials:

> At one time I had several connections with the Scottish Parliament. Wendy Alexander was a friend who is now out of power. I also met Donald Dewar and had two or three opportunities to visit him. (C16)

> While we're there, we're hoping for meetings with the First Minister and the presiding officer perhaps, and some Members of the Scottish Parliament [MSPs]. (C6)

I have already discussed the numbers of interviewees who were involved in learning the Gaelic language and how this seemed to affect the way they approached the issue of devolution. Some had relied on Gaelic newsletters and the like to keep them informed, while others saw the establishment of the Scottish Parliament as an opportunity to revive a language to which they themselves were committed. They had some concerns, however, about how quickly this would actually happen, believing that support for Gaelic had been a relatively low priority for the Parliament thus far:

> I have kind of followed it in the news, including the news in the Gaelic learners' community. I certainly have had a positive attitude about it. Even though I am an American and I consider myself American, not Scottish American, I feel it's extremely important for Scotland to pursue those things that help it maintain its national identity. It's important to me as an American, including support for the Gaelic language and other things. The establishment of a Parliament is a very positive step in my point of view. (C12)

> **R:** Most of what I know is through Radio nan Gàidheal. They have news and stuff, either through listening to them or through a page of news briefs.
>
> **I:** So you listen to it online?
>
> **R:** Yes. That's where I get news, or what Clì puts out in their publications. I don't keep abreast of it real close. I just don't have the time. I know of a few things going on. When I was a teenager, I would be ardent for independence and that. Today I see things through the Gaelic lens. In the past before devolution, one could argue that London had done more for Gaelic than Edinburgh ever had.

I: In what sense?

R: In the sense of applying money. As I understand it, after 1707, Scotland still had control over their education system and the Act of 1872 was a big turning point for putting Gaelic down in the Highlands and the Islands. That's the kind of thing that I judge that on.

I: You're aware of the new Bill by the Scottish Parliament?

R: Yes. I want the Parliament and the Bill to succeed as well but I still approach it with a grain of salt. (C21)

This interviewee was referring to the 1872 Scottish Education Act. While introducing compulsory schooling for all children, it had a negative impact in parts of the Highlands, in that the use of Gaelic was (often unofficially) discouraged in schools. Many teachers were English-speaking and children were often punished for speaking Gaelic. In relation to the Scottish Parliament, there were some initial attempts by SNP MSPs Mike Russell and Alex Neil to introduce legislation, but eventually the Scottish government itself did so, passing the Gaelic Language (Scotland) Act in 2005. The legislation strengthened the body, Bòrd na Gàidhlig, which promotes the use and understanding of Gaelic; and placed a duty on public bodies to consider the preparation and implementation of Gaelic language plans. There was also further support for Gaelic medium education. Subsequent to the legislation, a digital Gaelic television channel, BBC Alba, was established in 2008. Such moves were seen as welcome:

> I wish there would be a stronger Gaelic commitment by some of the current Scottish government, but they're doing a lot more than we would have ever gotten done. Not me, being a native, but the Scottish Gaelic community, did not get any support to speak of from the Crown, whereas now I believe they are getting some significant support. It still needs to be more. But I'm encouraged by what I read of the Scottish students now starting to take Gaelic. They're starting to teach Gaelic more in Glasgow and other places. (C4)

Attitudes to independence

As is evident above, a number of interviewees appeared to confuse Scottish devolution and independence, and so the opportunity was taken to explore attitudes towards full independence for Scotland. As with devolution, attitudes were divided.

Some supporters of devolution saw independence as a logical next step and were enthusiastic about the prospect, although there was some uncertainty about what might be involved in such a move:

> Scotland's pseudo-independent. That's not a political statement, it's simply a reality and from an economic and cultural development point of view, its image abroad is pretty important … If you look at countries that have split, like the Czech Republic, then there are certain criteria. Where do the people look to their leadership? I would say the people look to Edinburgh. They don't look to London as their spiritual leader. Where the people look is ultimately where they want to be governed. (N3)

> **I:** So would it be desirable for Scotland to become independent?
> **R:** Well I think so. Just to be clear, in our organisation, we discuss this often and there's not a universal view on that. I find myself, living away from home, with an increased sense of patriotism and connection with my home country. But I also think that if you're living there, you're too close to see this identity issue. There's all kinds of arguments on the economy and stuff. But whenever we get together to discuss how Scotland fits in with America, it always gets round to thinking that things would seem different if Scotland were independent. If the union was something that everyone in Scotland was 100% behind, and saw themselves as part of Britain, then we'd probably have a fairly clear identity that way as well. But there is a split. (N5)

A significant number of interviewees made comparisons with Ireland. On the one hand, Ireland was seen as being a comparable and successful country, despite having only limited natural resources. There was a belief that Scotland could perhaps learn from the Irish experience. On the other hand, there was a recognition that Americans should beware of getting too closely involved, as had been the case in Ireland, with organisations such as the Irish Republican Army (IRA) receiving substantial support from American sources (Wilson, 1995):

> [There's] a lot of debate between friends over there. The older folks said it's ridiculous; we don't have a tax base. There's no way we can be independent from England. We don't have any of the resources. The young kids saying they wanted it. Being in Ireland on June 1, 1999 was a very

interesting day. We were doing a house exchange there in Northern Ireland. Two things happened that day. The truce with the IRA fell through and they put in the first presiding officer [in Edinburgh]. Then we went over to Glasgow about ten days later for a wedding. It was kind of a big deal. I remember saying, 'Wait a minute. I don't know why you can't be totally independent, even though you say you have no resources, because Ireland basically has no resources.' It is one of the strongest economies going right now because they have done it on just pure education and a whole lot of campaigning. (C18)

....

I have never looked at the numbers to be honest but what I will say is I look at Ireland with a smaller population and probably less resources than Scotland and I see them being very successful. I did a lot of work with Finland, another small country like Scotland, remarkably successful based on high-tech, 100% internet connections and so on. So my uneducated feeling is there's no reason why Scotland shouldn't be a successful independent member of the European Union. I see the European Union as absolutely necessary. We're not going to be out there as a Norway, for example. Emotionally, I'd like to see Scotland independent. I think what it would do is create an accountability. You know, for years and years, we blamed the English for everything. I think to get to independence is a very tough pill to swallow, so you'd have to go through say a five-year transition. I think it would be tough ... Logically, if Ireland can do it, if Finland can do it, if Denmark can do it, why shouldn't Scotland be able to do it? You know, we've got the educated workforce, we've got the infrastructure. (N11)

....

I see parallels between Scotland and Ireland. Until the 1980s, Ireland defined itself by not being British in many cases. But membership of the European Union, Mary Robinson, Jack Charlton and the football team, all coalesced and they became confident about their Irishness and being European, and they didn't become fixated on the 1916 Rebellion. They saw themselves as being proud to be Irish. I think Scotland has to move in that direction — to stop saying we were sold out in 1707, and say, 'Frankly, we're sorting out our health, education, justice systems'. So our quality of life is better and how we'll judge

Scotland versus the World is how we do for ourselves, not what was done to us. I think these things are changing. (S2)

Some interviewees were somewhat sceptical about independence, doubting that Scotland had a strong enough economy to survive independently of the UK:

I don't know. I think if Scotland could have had the money from the North Sea oil field, and they could have kept that in Edinburgh instead of sending it on to London, they would have had a financial base. I don't know economically if they can exist without the United Kingdom. (C16)

The only thing I would worry about is if they can make it, financially. From my perspective, maybe I'm incorrect about this, but a lot of their resources have just been coveted by London for the longest time, and if they were independent they could take a look at what their situation was. (C8)

Others likened independence to an American state breaking away from the union, something that seemed unthinkable:

To break away, it would be like Colorado breaking away from the union of the United States ... This is also how my older friends feel ... All of them said almost the same thing. 'Gosh, we're such a small country, why do we need to break away?' It's just like our Civil War. Why would you take these states and separate them, when together we're so much better off? (C1)

I don't think I would support [independence]. The best analogy I would give is I would not support a state breaking away from the United States government. I think there are certain things that can be done on a state level, but there are many things that you need to have consistency throughout. I think that if everybody broke off, that you would have all these piecemeal things that when you go from one place to the other you don't know what the rules are. (C17)

The comparison with Ireland, which emerged in discussions, is an interesting one. There are a number of Irish organisations that have had a relatively high profile in America over the years, of which perhaps the most significant was the Irish Northern Aid Committee (Noraid), which was established by Michael Flannery and Martin Galvin following the start of the Troubles in Northern Ireland, in 1970. Noraid was involved in raising financial support for the nationalist movement within Northern Ireland and was accused by the British, Irish and American governments of being a front for the IRA. This was always denied, however, and Noraid claimed the money was intended for 'humanitarian relief' in the province. The fact remains that if Irish Americans wished to donate money to Ireland, there was little alternative to Noraid for many years (Wilson, 1995; Dezell, 2002).

The Scottish nationalist movement, on the other hand, appears to have had a very low profile within the United States and there was simply no Scottish equivalent to Noraid. The SNP itself has not had a North American network, although there are a number of individual members. Unsurprisingly, a large number of interviewees had either not heard of the party or knew little about it or its policies:

> I've heard of them. I don't know much about them. I know a few years ago I was in Canada and there was a group selling a little button for a donation. It was a little yellow button with a little symbol on it. It was symbolising the drive for Scottish independence. That was the only place I've ever seen this. It was in Vancouver. (C7)

There was, however, widespread recognition of one of the SNP's most high-profile members, Sean Connery:

> Over in America, we Americans have an idol and his name is Sean Connery. He has done an incredible amount for Scotland in terms of bringing it into the public view. In all seriousness I think he has done a hell of a job, especially in America. Everybody knows him. (C20)

Keeping informed

The level of awareness which American Scots had of the significant social, political and constitutional changes that have taken place within Scotland raises the issue of how individuals managed to keep themselves informed about developments in the homeland. For most people, the internet had made a huge difference, enabling them to access almost immediately a range of information about events in Scotland. The BBC web pages were mentioned by a number of people and it became clear that the BBC was held in high regard within the United States. A significant number of people also subscribed to BBC television programmes or else they simply watched the BBC world news on the PBS channel:

I do watch BBC. We have that, it's on twice a day on the PBS station. It's so much better news because you get a totally different viewpoint of more areas of the world that you don't see on local or national stations. (C14)

I do it with BBC Scotland. I go online. My wife has the BBC ticker running on the bottom of her computer at her office. I'll go in and I'll listen to some of the Gaelic programming on the internet. I'll also get on BBC Scotland and see what's going on. (C4)

Several people mentioned accessing newspaper websites and they proved to be another significant way in which people kept in touch with Scotland:

I have listed, amongst my favourites, *The Scotsman* and the *Daily Record* and as much as anything else I would be checking up on sporting results, but when you go into *The Scotsman* website, anyway, the first page that comes up is what is going on in Scotland. So if there's anything that grabs me I just click on that. (C6)

I go online quite regularly to *The Scotsman* and *The Glasgow Herald* and so forth. And also the *P and J* [*Press and Journal*] in Aberdeen to see what the teuchters[6] are still up to. (C19)

The change in ease of communication resulting from the internet was highlighted by a Scottish government minister, comparing the difficulties in communicating with his brother in London in the 1970s with communicating with the United States nowadays:

I find it easier, at the start of the twenty-first century, to keep in touch with friends I've made in New York now, than I did to keep in touch with my brother when he went down to London in the early '70s. You know, you couldn't get the papers unless you queued up at Victoria station to get a *Record* or a *Scotsman*, you couldn't read the papers online, phoning home was very expensive and you did it maybe once a fortnight on a Sunday, flying home was impossible unless there was a family bereavement and you did it as a matter of urgency. The road journeys were long. I keep in touch with friends in New York, they

6 The term 'teuchter' is sometimes used by Lowland Scots to refer to Scots from the North or the Highlands. Opinion appears to be divided as to whether it is amusing banter or merely offensive. In this case, the interviewee was referring to Aberdonians in this way.

come over, it's easy for us to get back and forward. The world has changed, attitudes have changed. (S2)

Other people simply mentioned reading books about Scotland and reading magazines, either in print or, occasionally, on the internet.

Looking to the future

The continuing links with Scotland and with Scottish organisations raise the issue of whether some of those interviewed might, at some point, consider returning to Scotland. As noted earlier in Chapter 5, one interviewee and her family had become very friendly with a Scottish family in Troon, following a house exchange. This had eventually led to the two families jointly purchasing a house in Dunure, on the south Ayrshire coast. But the actual purchase of property appeared to be very rare and most interviewees appeared much less certain about 'moving back'. There was a recognition that it represented a huge step, and one that might not prove to be a sensible one:

> I would like to [live in Scotland]. But I have so many children here and grandchildren that it would be kind of hard. The perfect scenario would be to live in both places, just to stay there more than two weeks, maybe six months. Buy a house. Three or four years ago, some of my friends and I got together and we were going to put in money together and buy a £50,000 to £70,000 house and take turns using it. (C1)

In the event, the money that had been earmarked for this potential purchase had been used for a family wedding.

Some interviewees had visited Scotland and had seen what they regarded as the house of their dreams. The difficulty was in being able to afford the dream:

> **R1:** I would not hesitate for a minute, if I could, to move to the Isle of Skye.
>
> **R2:** We even know of a house that we would love to buy, but we don't have the money.
>
> **R1:** It's out of sight.
>
> **R2:** There's an old manor house on the Isle of Raasay — Raasay House. But it's going down badly. It's still at the state where it could be restored but it needs a big injection of funds to do that. I keep telling joking like, if we ever win the lottery, we might.

I: But you wouldn't hesitate if the circumstances were right?

R2: I would seriously consider it. Part of the reason is now both of our sets of parents are gone, so we don't have to worry about being here to take care of them. We've done that, so we're pretty free now. The kids are grown and educated and on their own, so we're free now. (C7)

Indeed, a number of interviewees spoke about whether the notion of moving to Scotland was a genuinely realistic one. A few believed it might be possible to live in Scotland for periods during the summer, but did not anticipate moving permanently. For one couple, there was a concern that expatriate Americans might not be welcome if they were seen to be using their wealth to buy properties in areas of housing shortage like the Highlands. They suggested that they needed to be seen to be sensitive to local concerns:

R: Yes. We thought about it. We thought about looking for a house that we would buy for our family, for future time. Once I had been to Scotland, there was a sense that it would be a little bit of an occupation. I have a lot of money in comparison to some of the people we stayed with when we were in Scotland. I am more ambivalent about it then I was before, because nobody said, 'Won't you come here and be with us, we would welcome you back.' There was none of that. It was a sense of, 'This is who we are and this is what we are about and thanks for your money.'

I: Are you saying that if you were to go and buy property there that you would be somehow outbidding somebody local?

R: You would be taking somebody's house, one, and secondly you would be those people from America that took that house.

I: Do you think you might not be made welcome?

R: Yes. I agree. There is a sense of that. (C11)

Other interviewees felt that moving to Scotland would be like moving into the unknown and that it might lead to great unhappiness, if migrants found it difficult to settle. One likened it to people in Colorado who decided to live in the Rocky Mountains because of the attractiveness of the scenery but eventually found the existence there — particularly in winter — too hard to endure:

It's just like you think about moving up to the mountains. You think about moving up to Nederland or Estes Park. A lot of people go up there and spend all this money with these really expensive houses.

They stay one year. And then they come back down the hill. The weather is horrible up there. The wind blows and howls and screeches up there. It snows up there. You could get killed up there or get eaten by something, and it's a year. They sell the house, they move back down. I know that might happen to me too. You have to be a realist, you can't be a romantic. You have to face the facts. (C1)

Even those who had been born and brought up in Scotland acknowledged that, while they had a periodic hankering to return, it was essentially a nostalgic feeling and was not necessarily realistic. They recognised that family and friends back in Scotland had often moved on and so they would be returning to very changed circumstances. In some cases interviewees knew of Scots who had returned to Scotland but had apparently found it very difficult to settle, and one interviewee knew of similar experiences involving friends who had returned to Ireland:

R: I don't know. I must say we have seen a lot of couples here go back [to Scotland] and with one exception they all came back.

I: They couldn't settle back?

R: No. Even one of my nurse friends. She went back but she was back again. She just couldn't …

I: Hard making the adjustment?

R: Hard — and she went back to family. You miss your family, you do, but …. (C10)

....

R: I think the Irish have been very successful in attracting investment and many Irish retire there and find it appealing. Some come back [to the USA] again because they find they're not really part of that culture any more.

I: You mean people go back to Ireland and …?

R: They go back to Ireland but, after a while, they say, 'What am I doing here? I'm from New York.'

I: So it's not been perhaps a comfortable experience for people?

R: Well for some people. I know people who have done that in England also.

I: Because the country's changed from what they remember it as?

R: Well I think a lot of people don't remember. Their *grandparents* emigrated. They've never been there in their life, some of them. (N2)

Others were far from nostalgic, making frequent return visits to Scotland, but were unimpressed with some of the things that they saw. They believed that Scotland's social problems would deter them from moving back:

> When my husband last visited a year or two ago, he went out for a drink with some friends. On his way home late at night, going through the centre of Glasgow in Union Street, he said it was like a scene from Dodge City. Young people coming out of the bars at closing time, drunk, fighting, throwing up in doorways — young boys and girls rolling around on the ground fighting. When one of my family visits her NHS doctor she is surrounded by young drug addicts waiting for their methadone prescription. I know this probably sounds a bit harsh and obnoxious of me to say these things. I love my country and there are a lot of great things about it, which I feel proud of. But it has a lot of social problems which need to be addressed before it becomes an attractive place to live. (N13)

Having recognised that, in most cases, relocation to Scotland on anything other than a temporary basis was probably impractical, interviewees spoke of their likely continued involvement with Scottish organisations within America. In most cases, this was likely to mean a continuation of their existing activities, such as dancing, or helping to organise the Highland Games, or learning Gaelic. Some felt that demands on their time already prevented them from extending their involvement:

> I'll probably keep dancing. I probably won't get involved with the St Andrew Society because I don't know what they do. I go to their events. I'm a member. Would I get active in that? No, I think dancing is enough for me, with all the other things that I do. (C2)
> ....
> I certainly would like to help at the Highland Games and stuff … From what I've seen so far, most of the things [the St Andrew Society] has organised so far are the St Andrew's dinners and Burns dinners and it doesn't seem to be the sort of get-togethers like 'sit and chat' or guest speakers talking about say castles or whatever that people could come and listen to. (C19)

There is an implicit criticism here of the local St Andrew Society and there was a distinct sense that the society was not an especially thriving organisation, with a relatively small number of activists. This appears to reflect a wider issue about the membership of many Scottish-American organisations across the country. Although there is a wide range of societies, clan organisations, Gaelic learners' groups and so on, many seem able to operate only because of a small group of dedicated and active office-bearers. Despite there having been a substantial expansion in the number and range of Scottish organisations across the USA — for example, the increase in the number of Highland Games in the calendar — many of these appear to be the result of individual enthusiasm and initiative and may not reflect the existence of a large number of activists. Many of those interviewed for this study, particularly in Colorado, were in middle age and this appeared to be an accurate reflection of organisation membership, as observed. There were relatively few younger people willing to take on the running of these organisations in the future:

> The Gaelic language, I enjoy it thoroughly. I'm going to continue. I'm the only person out of the class of thirteen that started five years ago that's left. That's pretty typical. (C4)

> We have to pass it on to the younger ones. We can't hold on forever. I've tried … But there is a time when somebody else has to take it, and I am not at the helm of anything. (C16)

At an individual level, however, there was an enthusiasm to continue:

> **I:** Assuming you're going to stay where you are in Colorado, will you continue to have the involvement with the Gaelic group?
>
> **R:** Yes. I don't know how much I will teach in the future but I see this involvement in some form or another as something I do. People could ask you why you do it and you could give them all kind of reasons for it but it's being kind of involved in something I do, like I put on my socks. It's part of my landscape now. (C21)

> When my husband passed away we couldn't decided what to do. So, each year I give a sword to the premier Highland dancer in his memory. It's called the Douglas Pollock Woodward Longs Peak Memorial Sword. Usually Kent or I present it to the dancer. This is the seventh year I've done that. The youngsters have said they will do the same when I depart. They'd carry it on, because once you start something like that it becomes tradition and it means so much … It keeps my husband's name out there. He was very popular among the clans. We

have a lot of friends. He helped the Hendersons get started, He helped the Camerons when they were getting started. A lot of people came to him because they knew he had a strong interest in it and could help them and I followed along, dedicated. (C14)

Conclusions

During the period following the Second World War, Scotland has changed in many ways, socially, economically and politically. The most significant change has perhaps been the devolution of political powers from the UK government at Westminster and the establishment of the Scottish Parliament in 1999. But although such changes are significant domestically, they might well not impinge on the Scottish diaspora overseas.

Given the sometimes nostalgic view of Scotland held by the diaspora, there is perhaps an expectation that there would therefore be a low knowledge of change in the homeland. But, in fact, many of those interviewed appeared increasingly knowledgeable about events taking place in Scotland. Knowledge is not perfect of course and there is sometimes confusion, for example in regard to the extent of political change and to devolution and political independence. But the spread of the internet and the expansion of cheap transatlantic air travel mean that it is now much easier for expatriate Scots to travel 'home', to be better informed and to maintain contact with Scotland.

Although contact remains important, few individuals saw themselves actually moving back to Scotland, with the possible exception of one family who had bought a house in Ayrshire. Moving back after several generations — or even after several decades — was recognised as being difficult and so the continuing connection between Scotland and its diaspora is likely to remain at arm's length.

Within Scotland itself, however, there is a growing recognition of the importance of the diaspora and a growing commitment to maintain and develop those connections from the Scottish 'end'. Chapter 7 therefore explores the ways in which the diaspora can be 'cherished' by homeland Scots.

Chapter 7

Cherishing the diaspora

We have observed the ambivalence that a number of homeland Scots occasionally demonstrate towards members of the Scottish diaspora. American Scots returning to Scotland to explore their family roots and their heritage are often regarded with mild amusement as such concerns are perhaps not so important for Scots who live in Scotland and whose 'Scottishness' is taken for granted. There is too a commonly held belief that diaspora Scots have an overly nostalgic view of Scotland — one which is often at odds with the realities of twenty-first-century Scotland.

However, while this is sometimes the case, it is not necessarily that simple. First, members of the Scottish diaspora have not necessarily looked to the homeland at all times — rather they have often gone their own way, establishing their own traditions and events. So the Kirkin' o' the Tartan has no equivalent within Scotland itself, while Tartan Day is very much a diasporic celebration rather than a homeland Scottish one. Even Highland Games, which have been successfully exported to countries such as America have a very different format there than in Scotland. So it may be said that the Scottish diaspora is not solely interested in traditions and heritage within the homeland but has gone a considerable way to developing its own.

This is recognised by a number of authors. Hunter (2005), for example, referred to two members of the Scottish diaspora — John Tutterow (an American whom he interviewed) and the writer Alistair MacLeod (a Canadian). He suggested that neither Tutterow nor MacLeod was trying to be or become Scottish. Rather 'they simply want to get a handle on the Scottish component of backgrounds which are essentially Canadian in Alistair MacLeod's case, American and Southern in John Tutterow's' (Hunter, 2005, p. 25). Dezell (2002) noted a similar process in relation to the Irish in Ireland and the Irish in America, to whom she referred as 'two grand people separated by notions of a singular culture'.

Secondly, whereas Scots who emigrated before the 1970s were constrained in terms of their ability to keep in contact with and to visit their homeland, this is now far from being the case. We have seen how the advent of cheaper transatlantic air travel and the internet have made it so much easier for homeland and diasporic Scots to keep in contact with each other. This means that members of the Scottish diaspora are now able to have a much more realistic understanding of twenty-first-century Scotland — and not one that is overlain with a mist of nostalgia. As society becomes ever more global and as business (including tourism) transcends frontiers and boundaries, then the transatlantic links between Scotland and America have become ever stronger.

Within Scotland itself, the key event of recent years has been political devolution from London and the re-establishment of the Scottish Parliament. This has already been summarised in Chapter 6. In relation to the diaspora, the Parliament has been of huge significance as it has enabled Scotland, its politicians and policymakers to engage directly with its diaspora for the first time. This chapter therefore focuses on this engagement and how Scotland, like Ireland before it, is beginning to 'cherish' its diaspora.

At a basic level, devolution has meant that Scottish politicians are able to travel to America and directly support Tartan Day, something that UK politicians were unlikely ever to do. In addition, events such as Tartan Day have provided a platform for Scottish ministers to promote the country and to engage in dialogue with politicians, policymakers and business people in America. This was demonstrated very effectively in April 2001 when the then Scottish First Minister Henry McLeish met with President George W. Bush — scheduled to be a ten-minute meeting but which lasted for twenty-five. Reflecting later on the visit, the Edinburgh newspaper, *The Scotsman,* suggested that 'the visit indicated that a devolved Scotland had the beginnings of international recognition ... and that there were enormous possibilities to develop for the future (McMahon, 2002).

This enhanced relationship between the Scottish Parliament and the Scottish diaspora was commented on in a number of interviews:

> It's an activity that Scotland really didn't do until devolution. This whole engagement with our diaspora abroad is a product of devolution and the creation of a Parliament in Edinburgh. It gave Scotland the ability — and the confidence I think — to go out and engage and seek

to tell our modern story. So I think, in some senses, we're behind some other nations but I think there's a real serious determination across the board — and this is not party political — that Scotland should be an outward-looking nation and one of the key things we should be doing is engaging with and involving and understanding our diaspora, and trying to work with them so they understand what modern Scotland's all about. I think we're making big inroads, there are huge steps forward that we've had since devolution. Who knows what will happen on the 3rd May?[1] But the administration that comes in, nobody's going to go back from that international engagement. It's only going to increase and I think that's a good thing (N8).

I think Tartan Day is a manifestation of what is going on organically elsewhere. Part of it is to do with the renaissance in Scotland, with the restoration of our Parliament. I remember being in Chicago talking to a young Scots girl, basically being gobsmacked having seen the Parliament on TV ... And that is having an effect on people, the fact that we as a government are going to be much more outward-looking, sometimes in conjunction with our British colleagues, sometimes not. We're going to reach out to our peoples (S2).

It is probably fair to say that, in developing policies in relation to the diaspora, Scottish politicians have been influenced by the experience of Ireland. As another small west European country with a large diaspora — and as a country with many links to and similarities to Scotland — Ireland has been seen as perhaps holding some lessons for Scottish policymakers. It is useful therefore to consider the Irish experience.

The example of Ireland

Irish Americans, like many Scottish Americans, have had a complicated relationship with their 'homeland'. Dezell (2002, p. 189), for example, described the 'amazement and irritation the Irish-born feel for Americans' fervid attachment to things Irish — or things they think are Irish'. Sometimes such attachments are romantic and sentimental; sometimes

---

1   This interview took place shortly before the Scottish Parliamentary elections on 3 May 2007. The Scottish National Party became the largest party and formed a minority administration. They continued to work with the diaspora and support Tartan Day along broadly similar lines to the previous Labour/Liberal Democrat administration.

they appear in different ways. For example, the Irish dancing phenomenon of Riverdance owes its existence to the drive of Michael Flatley, born and brought up in Chicago and 'a consummate example of Irish Americanism in overdrive. He brought to an Irish folk art the utterly American conviction that bigger, faster and flashier is better.'

But part of the key to Ireland's engagement with its diaspora was the determination of Mary Robinson, after her election as Irish president, to ensure that Ireland was an outward-looking country with strong international links. As part of this strategy, she argued that the country should 'cherish' its diaspora, referring in her inauguration address to the seventy million people worldwide who claimed Irish descent. In 1995, she made an important speech to the Houses of the Oireachtas in which she spoke of Irishness as not simply being territorial and urged Irish people to 'turn with open minds and hearts to the array of people outside Ireland for whom this island is a place of origin' (Robinson, 1995).

While Robinson's message appears to have had an important impact at home, there has been a continuing disjunction with the Irish Americans. Thus, while Robinson was vowing to lead a country that was open, tolerant and inclusive, organisers of the Boston St Patrick's Day parade had (in 1995) won a Supreme Court ruling allowing them to ban lesbian, gay and bisexual marchers.

Despite these continuing tensions between homeland Irish and their American counterparts, the Scottish media have reflected on the relative success of Ireland in engaging with its diaspora. On 3 April 2002, *The Scotsman* newspaper reported:

> The Irish, as in so much else these days, provide the template. They latched on early to the fact that good relations with America were crucial to economic development and international recognition. On Saint Patrick's Day, half the Dublin Cabinet was in America. So were Gerry Adams and Martin McGuinness. Even David Trimble has become a White House fixture. But the Scots, a sister nation sharing a common culture and a similar sense of victimhood, have somehow never made the effort.

The Scotsman suggested that Ireland had been more successful over the years because Dublin had been a seat of government for decades. The Edinburgh Parliament, by contrast, was in its infancy, but provided the opportunity for Scotland to engage directly and more effectively with its diaspora in the future.

Another issue highlighted by *The Scotsman* was the importance of the Irish vote in America and I have already discussed the way in which Irish politics (particularly in relation to Northern Ireland) impinges upon the United States. American fundraising has been an important source of money for a number of Irish political causes. But there does not appear to be any 'tartan vote' and no significant Scottish lobbying of American politicians.

In interviews, a number of individuals referred to the Irish experience as providing an important model for Scotland to follow:

> Well, I think in many ways Ireland is the role model for Scotland. The Irish have done a fantastic job over the years in promoting Ireland, everyone in the US knows the Irish, knows what they're about, knows their songs and their heritage. Less people understand Scotland. They may confuse Scotland with Ireland or they may not totally understand what Scotland's all about. Now clearly part of that is that Ireland is a separate country and so I think it's a little easier. (N11)

There was also a reference to a greater Irish governmental presence, which has allowed engagement with the diaspora. Scotland, as part of the UK, has had to work through British governmental channels up to now and, although there is now a Scottish government presence in Washington, it is a small office with a single civil servant.

The difference between an independent Ireland and a politically devolved Scotland may be seen in relation to the issuing of Green Cards to allow individuals to work in the US. The Green Card Lottery provides more work visas to countries with lower rates of immigration to the US and no visas to countries that have sent more than 50,000 immigrants to the US in the previous five years. On this basis, Ireland is an eligible country but the UK is not; thus, by being part of the UK, Scotland is therefore excluded from the Green Card Lottery system:

> There are complicated factors like visas and things. The Irish are able to go through the Green Card Lottery but Scotland is part of the UK so doesn't qualify for that. (N5)
>
> ....
>
> There's this whole Green Card Lottery thing, which seems to work well for the Irish but I don't think works well for the British. (N11)

Since the establishment of the Scottish Parliament, there is no doubt that Scotland has tried hard to 'catch up' with Ireland and there are now a number of significant developments that illustrate its progress.

Developments in Scotland

Some of the developments during the last ten years have related to tourism and the encouragement of expatriate Scots to visit their homeland; others have had a more long-term aim, such as the encouragement of reverse migration.

It is in relation to reverse migration that one of the first initiatives was developed, directly responding to projections which suggested that Scotland's population was both ageing and in decline — although the decline appears to have been reversed in the last two or three years. Certainly, the economic implications of population decline have been well understood at government level, and the Scottish government therefore sought to address the issue — in part by encouraging in-migration. The Fresh Talent Initiative, aimed at encouraging people to consider coming to live and work in Scotland, was formally introduced in a statement in the Scottish Parliament by the then First Minister, Jack McConnell, on 25 February 2003. It followed the publication of a policy document entitled *New Scots: Attracting Fresh Talent to Meet the Challenge of Growth* (Scottish Executive, 2004), setting out how the Scottish government intended to operate a scheme of managed migration. Some of the measures included in the scheme have involved allowing non-EU graduates from Scottish universities to remain in the country for two years after graduation without requiring a work permit, the establishment of a relocation advisory service for people considering settling in Scotland, and assistance to Scottish universities to offer bursaries to overseas students.

But a particular strand in the attraction of in-migrants has been a focus on the Scottish diaspora. The *New Scots* report stated:

> There are many thousands of Scots living and working elsewhere and we will actively encourage these expatriate Scots to return home. The extent of the Scots diaspora means that there are millions of people across the globe who have a strong emotional and cultural link with Scotland. Friends of Scotland and GlobalScot[2] will be reorganised to

2 Friends of Scotland and GlobalScot have been set up by government to promote

create a more focused relationship with this group, to encourage some
of them to live and work in Scotland (Scottish Executive, 2004, p. 7).

The Scottish government's approach demonstrated that there is an increasing awareness of the diaspora as a resource and as a possible source of business investment and this was recognised by interviewees. One individual
who was active in both business and the arts believed that the initiative
could and should be extended:

> **R:** I think [Fresh Talent's] a good initiative. I think it's much too
> restricted. It's targeted at people who've had a formal education,
> meaning universities — and let's try to keep them there. In terms of
> economic development, I'm very much on the whole concept of the
> creative economy, that the only negotiable asset is people's creativity.
> If you look at places that are really vibrant and thriving, then they're
> inevitably driven by individuals — an accountant, a lawyer, a profes-
> sor — and if you look at where that growth happens then it's where
> those creative individuals are attracted to. And they're attracted to
> environments where there's culture, where there's diversity, tolerance,
> there's infrastructure. And that's why we're sitting in New York and not
> Topeka, Kansas. And once you see that dynamic, then my opinion
> is that Scotland is particularly adept — it could apply that to Fresh
> Talent. The issue shouldn't just be about attracting the talented guys at
> universities and getting them to stay there. It's a good initiative, but not
> bold enough, For the highly qualified entrepreneurial people that they
> want to bring back, there's the option to put tax relief in, seeing that
> Scotland has its own laws.
>
> **I:** But not control over taxation?
>
> **R:** No but there is the ability to differentiate over other UK taxes.
> There are opportunities under Scots law for greater protection for
> intellectual property as opposed to elsewhere. (N3)

A Scottish government minister believed that the Fresh Talent Initiative
could be successful to the extent that, if the Scottish economy thrived as
Ireland's had, this would very definitely encourage reverse migration:

> I remember being in Chicago and the point was made to me by
> Chicago Scots and a lot of them are first-generation Scots working

---

Scotland internationally. See http://www.FriendsofScotland.gov.uk (accessed April
2011)

in finance — HBOS,[3] that kind of thing. But nobody had ever had anybody coming to them and saying, 'Want to come back?' Now part of that's down to the state of the Scottish economy. In Ireland, it was the turning round of the economy that saw the bars empty in Boston and New York. Now there are people in places like New York — well, America is for them. But there are plenty of others, if you said, 'Look, we're actually looking for a senior analyst in the Royal Bank of Scotland and we can pay you big bucks', a lot of people would say, 'Time to go home and have a family or whatever, it's a good place to live.' The problem is there aren't the opportunities and we're not looking for them. (S2)

It is unclear if, in reality, many individuals would actually relocate, because of the considerable personal upheaval that a move 'home' would involve — quite apart from the uncertainties created by the recession. Certainly, few of the people interviewed could imagine themselves relocating to Scotland, in part because of the difficulties in leaving behind family, friends and existing employment. This echoes the findings of Boyle and Motherwell (2005) in their study of Scots in Dublin. They found that most Scots working there, while recognising the possible advantages of moving back, felt that they were unable to do so as employment opportunities in Scotland were thought to be poorer than in Ireland. Only a limited number had thought seriously about it, believing that the 'quality of life' was better in Scotland.

This issue of Scottish economic opportunity was raised again in evidence to the Scottish Parliament's European and External Relations Committee Inquiry. In the absence of clearly identified employment opportunities, the Fresh Talent Initiative was thought to be asking potential economic migrants to 'bet on a long-term future in Scotland'. Many migrants would be unwilling to bet in this way and the uncertainty as to job prospects in Scotland would be likely to act as a deterrent.[4]

Nevertheless, between 2005, when the Fresh Talent Initiative was launched, and June 2008, there had been almost 8,500 successful applications

3   The Halifax Bank of Scotland, headquartered in Edinburgh until its merger with Lloyds Banking Group in January 2009.
4   http://www.scottish.parliament.uk/business/committees/europe/reports-05/eur05-01-01.htm; accessed April 2011

to the Initiative. Most of these appear to have been international students wishing to stay in Scotland, however, and there has been limited reverse migration. The Fresh Talent Initiative came to an end in June 2008, after the UK government introduced a new points-based immigration scheme.

A second area of development has been in relation to business and funding networks with the diaspora and there have been several initiatives within the Scottish government. The Global Friends of Scotland (or GlobalScot) project referred to above is a mainly business network which aims, firstly, to promote a contemporary image of Scotland internationally through people who feel an affinity to the country; and, secondly, to 'showcase' Scotland's achievements in culture, sport, education and business, through the internet. The network links with a similar initiative with a broader cultural, educational and tourist focus, 'Friends of Scotland'. Another initiative is Scotland Europa, which promotes Scotland's interests within the European Union and which co-ordinates activity with the government's office in Brussels.[5]

There are also a number of similar networks in America. Sir Sean Connery has established a charity also called Friends of Scotland, which acts as a focus for members of the Scottish diaspora in North America. Significantly, the charity opened premises in Manhattan, called Alba House, which has acted as a kind of unofficial Scottish embassy in New York, at the service of Scottish businesses and universities wanting to further their American connections.

Less successful, however, was the Scotland Funds, established in 2005 by members of the Scottish-American business community and MSPs. It aimed to emulate the Ireland Funds, established in 1987 with considerable success in fundraising. But the Scotland Funds closed in August 2008 amid accusations of inept management and having raised little money (*Scotland on Sunday*, 10 August 2008).

The collapse of the Scotland Funds is surprising in view of the apparent goodwill towards Scotland within the business community and the links that had previously been forged. Certainly interviewees appeared to be supportive of this particular kind of fundraising, although a word of warning was sounded by one individual over the degree of Scottish

5   http://www.scotlandeuropa.com; accessed April 2011

involvement; essentially he believed that the impetus had to come from within America:

> Culturally, we're different. Take the whole area of philanthropy, which I'm deeply involved in, both here and there. One of the roles that we're constantly asked to play is to help Scottish organisations fundraise in the United States. And, first of all, you have to deal with the misconception in Scotland that the streets [here] are paved with gold, that money is ready for the asking. You just have to say you're a Scot and the doors are open. It's not true. Fundraising is a really serious business, highly professional, and part of it is trying to get the groups in Scotland to understand that you've got to approach the process scientifically. First of all, you've really got to understand your own organisation. I had a huge, huge problem with the Scotland Fund, when it was started up, because I said, 'Basically, you've got the programme arse backwards.' If you're going to raise money for Scotland, it has to be driven out of America, by Americans. It can't be driven out of Scotland, by Scots. The best model is the American-Ireland Fund, because you have a group of Irish in America, who are committed to raising funds for Ireland but they're not determining how those funds should be used. Working in partnership with an equally impressive group of Irish people, non-sectarian, non-political, who are looking at the needs in Ireland, looking at the best ways to distribute those funds and taking on the responsibility for monitoring how those funds are used. That is the way it works. (N10)

> We want to contribute because we want to help the country but it's also part of who we are. If you're analysing economic or cultural growth, then you have this massive pool of first-, second-, third-generation Scots that actually care enormously about the country and therefore you should tap into them and use them much more extensively when you're trying to look at the people out there, who they are, what they care about, and not make a decision in isolation, back in Edinburgh. (N3)

Business links have continued to be viewed by the Scottish government as being of crucial importance, and the promotion of Scotland's interests in North America has been assisted by the establishment in 2001 of a Scottish Affairs Office, based in Washington DC. Also in Washington, the National Tartan Day committee established a Scottish-American Business Forum in 2002. At its first meeting, it was addressed by Wendy Alexander MSP, then Scottish Minister for Enterprise, who stressed Scotland's science- and skills-based approach to enterprise, in contrast to what she referred to as 'Braveheart, Brigadoon and bagpipes'.[6] The following year, a similar forum was established in New York, under the aegis of the American-Scottish Foundation.

Scottish ministers have continued to visit North America, to expand business opportunities. In October 2005, the then First Minister Jack McConnell visited the USA and Canada, where he met business leaders including those, such as Donald Trump, with Scottish ancestry. He announced that activity in Canada would continue in 2006 in collaboration with the British High Commission, and he clearly saw Canada as the focus of his attempts to attract both migrants and investment (The Herald, 28 October 2005). McConnell had previously argued that one of the significant impacts of devolution had been the opportunity to form such international relationships, with Scottish government policy 'increasingly becoming separate from the activities of the Foreign and Commonwealth Office' (Sunday Herald, 2 October 2005). It could be said that the courting of American business leaders reaped some reward when, in 2008, Donald Trump decided on a significant investment in north east Scotland, involving a golf course, associated leisure facilities, a hotel and housing.

Tartan Day has already been discussed in Chapter 4. This is, of course, an event with its origins in America and not in Scotland but it has gradually been embraced by homeland Scots and the Scottish government because of the opportunities that it offers. During 2003–4, the Scottish Parliament's European and External Relations Committee undertook an inquiry into the promotion of Scotland overseas and received a significant number of submissions either from or about the diaspora.[7] What was striking in the responses was the large number of individuals who referred to Tartan Day as being the event that most engaged the diaspora in America but which was seen as being inadequately supported by the Scottish government.

6 http://www.scotland.gov.uk/News/Releases/2002/04/1418; accessed April 2011
7 The various responses referred to here have been published on the Scottish Executive website. Available at http://www.scottish.parliament.uk/business/committees/europe/reports-05/eur05–01–01.htm (accessed April 2011).

In 2008, Tartan Week gradually became referred to as Scotland Week and the incoming SNP government in Edinburgh made considerable efforts to support it. Reporting on Scotland Week to the Scottish Parliament, the First Minister Alex Salmond spoke of the importance of the continuing links with America and of the various cultural and heritage events attended or hosted by Scottish ministers, including a Washington reception attended by the speaker of the House of Representatives, Nancy Pelosi. But there was also a focus on business and the First Minister stated that:

> Our relationship with the United States and Canada is as much, if not more, about enhancing economic and cultural ties in the future as it is about celebrating historic ties of country and kin. The government's message to our friends all across North America is that Scotland is a country on the move, that we are a nation with ambition and that we are utterly determined to maximise our economic potential. (Report to Scottish Parliament, 16 April 2008)

This broader focus, which has moved beyond issues of history and heritage, is reflected in the government's strategy for expanding its involvement with the United States (Scottish Executive, 2006), The strategy was known to some interviewees who welcomed it:

> If you look at the articulation of the strategy of US–Scotland relations four years ago, the strategy was articulated in a document called 'Tartan Week'. 'Tartan Day' actually — it wasn't even a week. Tartan Day is an event. It's not a strategy. So it's a real copout to say that's our strategy. Since then, just a few months ago, a new US strategy was published by the Scottish Executive. It has some gaps in it, but ... the nice thing is it's a document that contains a lot of pertinent information, key things to build from. (N3)

> ....

> What informs all the work that we now do in the US is the strategy for our engagement in the US, published last October, when the First Minister was in town. So we see Tartan Week as having two roles. It's a vehicle for taking forward the objectives set out in that strategy. There are seven objectives. The primary ones, I think, that Tartan Week allows us to achieve are the first one which is about improving the profile and understanding of Scotland in the US, and the other main objective is the objective about boosting tourism numbers. So they're

the two primary objectives in our strategy that Tartan Week helps us with. There may be a small impact on other objectives like trade, like educational links, but I think primarily it's about profile-raising and improving understanding of Scotland and also about boosting tourism. (N8)

Homecomings and tourist developments

We have already seen that, for many in the Scottish diaspora, heritage and family roots are hugely important and significant numbers of expatriates travel to Scotland regularly to explore their heritage and undertake genealogical research. It therefore makes good business sense for the country's tourist industry to recognise this and to promote 'heritage' or 'roots' tourism as a key part of their strategy. In previous years, this was an underdeveloped area of Scottish tourism but has now become an important niche tourism market (Scottish Executive, 2000).

Perhaps the most obvious examples of heritage events, with a strong emphasis on genealogy, are clan gatherings. A number of clan societies have now established clan museums offering a focus for visitors, as well as the opportunity to explore family histories. Examples include: the Clan Donald Centre at Armadale in Skye; the Clan Cameron Museum at Achnacarry, near Fort William; the Clan Macpherson Museum at Newtonmore; and the Clan Gunn Heritage Centre at Latheron in Caithness. In addition, many clans use a historic castle or family home as a focus for clan gatherings and to welcome overseas visitors. Dunvegan Castle in Skye is a good example as it is the seat of the Clan MacLeod and hosts the Clan MacLeod Parliament every four years, a gathering initiated by Dame Flora MacLeod in 1956. Such clan visits can re-establish kinship ties through:

> becoming acquainted with the clan's origin, myths, slogans, stories and symbols; visiting the clan lands and those collective 'sites of memory' associated with events in clan history; participating in clan marches and ceremonials; and even researching one's family history — locating one's personal lineage within the broader clan genealogy. (Basu, 2005, p. 146)

A number of Scottish tour companies have come to realise the enormous market offered by the diaspora and have begun to run a range of clan tours.

Typically these are of three or four days' duration, starting in Glasgow or Edinburgh, travelling through clan territories and visiting clan castles and museums on the way. Some bus tour companies have developed alternative historical tours for visitors, such as ones that focus, for example, on the Highland Clearances.

A more recent development within Scotland has been the 'Homecoming' event. Such events are commonplace in North America, usually involving former residents and alumni being welcomed back by their high schools, colleges and universities. In Europe, they have been relatively rare but the concept has now been adopted in relation to the welcoming back to their homeland of members of the diaspora. Sometimes, homecomings have operated at a fairly local level, notably in the Orkney Homecoming of 1999, a packaged event in which 150 Canadians of Orkney descent travelled back to the islands off the north coast of Scotland. The Homecoming included a programme of tours and excursions, genealogy investigations and various other activities including a gala evening (Basu, 2004).

In 2009, the concept was used at a national level as the Scottish Year of Homecoming, timed to coincide with the 250th anniversary of the birth of Robert Burns, the national poet. Homecoming Scotland 2009 was made up of a series of events designed to encourage members of the Scottish diaspora to visit Scotland. The celebrations, organised by EventScotland and VisitScotland (the tourist bodies) on behalf of the Scottish government, and part-financed by the European Regional Development Fund, based their publicity around the claim that 'for every single Scot in their native land, there are thought to be at least five more overseas who can claim Scottish ancestry'.

In addition to events focusing on Burns's anniversary, other key themes of the Homecoming were Scotland's contributions to the world, including golf, whisky, invention and innovation (focusing on the Scottish Enlightenment), and the country's culture, heritage and people. Some occasions such as Highland Games, music and literary festivals take place every year but had additional branding for Homecoming Year. In addition, there was also a large number of other events that took place. One high-profile event targeted specifically at the diaspora was a Clan Convention, comprising clan chiefs and leading representatives of Scottish clans, which met to discuss the role of the clan in the twenty-first century, and which took place at the Scottish Parliament.

Perhaps the centrepiece event of the year was The Gathering 2009, which took place in July in Holyrood Park in Edinburgh. This was a clan gathering that included Highland Games, a parade up the city's Royal Mile and a clan pageant on the Castle Esplanade. At the time of writing, it is difficult to evaluate the success of such events, or indeed the Year of Homecoming itself. Economic analysts agreed that the Homecoming brought 72,000 additional visitors to Scotland and boosted the Scottish economy by £31.6 million. But there is some dispute about the number of additional jobs created and the situation has been complicated by the fact that The Gathering (2009) Ltd, the company responsible for the Edinburgh event, actually went bankrupt. Nevertheless, the Scottish government believed that the Homecoming was sufficiently worthwhile to repeat the exercise in 2014. This will coincide with the Commonwealth Games in Glasgow, Scotland's hosting of the Ryder Cup, and the 700th anniversary of the Battle of Bannockburn. It is likely that a third event could take place in 2020, to celebrate the 700th anniversary of the Declaration of Arbroath.

Another initiative which is aimed at celebrating the Scottish diaspora is the development of a Museum of Emigration. The idea was developed by a group comprising the Scottish National Archives, National Library and National Museums and the steering group engaged with equivalent emigration museums, such as Ellis Island in New York. In April 2007, for example, a meeting was held at Ellis Island, under the title of 'Journeys from Scotland to America', with a range of American historical institutions, to discuss ideas for taking the project forward. The election of a Nationalist government in Scotland in May 2007, committed to the museum, was also significant. The museum will not have a building but will operate on an online basis, as a virtual resource for historians and genealogists. An initial exhibition on Scottish emigration was held in the National Library of Scotland as part of the Homecoming Year.

Conclusion

It is clear that, in recent years, Scotland and the Scottish government have sought increasingly to engage with the diaspora, following the lead shown by Ireland. While the diaspora is an important resource for

Scotland, in terms of business links, tourist development and general international friendship, it is equally important that it is not seen as a resource to be exploited.

There is a growing recognition now that the diaspora wishes to retain ties with Scotland and is keen to work with homeland Scots. Those who were interviewed as part of this research, and are in regular contact with Scots in America, referred to the pride that American Scots had in their roots and their positive attitude towards Scotland. In that sense, Scotland has a real advantage compared with many other nations who need to promote themselves in the US.

Devolution has been particularly important in that the existence of a government in Edinburgh has now allowed Scotland to engage directly with its diaspora. However, Scotland, unlike Ireland, is not an independent country and this has led to long debates about national identity and the extent to which Scots feel more or less Scottish or British (Moreno, 1988; Brown *et al.*, 1996). Too often, Scottish identity is defined by simply not being English (Devine and Logue, 2002) and this negative approach to identity is not one which can easily be communicated internationally. The position was ably articulated by an MSP:

> The real trick in dealing with the Scottish diaspora is for change at home. For too long, Scottish identity — from a Scottish perspective — was defined by what we were *not*. That is what has to change. That is what *is* changing. That is why I fully support Scotland looking outwards and that's why it's important for us to interact with our global communities, because it turns us from being a small nation of five million people on the periphery of Europe to being a people of forty to eighty million scattered around the globe, but with a homeland in Scotland. We move from being a wee player on an isolated, peripheral part of the world stage to being actually a major contributor with a community that's centre stage.
>
> So I think the change that is happening in how we view Scottishness here will help. If we have a perception that what defines us is not being English, that is basically a chip on both shoulders, that is also denigratory towards our culture, then clearly we're going to laugh at our expatriate communities. If we define Scottishness as being something positive, as being who we are — whether that's people who

come from Poland or Asia, that they're all Scots — then that veers towards a concept of values, that we have a different perception of the world north and south of the border in a variety of matters. I think it's a two-way process, that we will benefit as much from interacting with our expatriate communities as they will with us.

The diaspora are desperate to retain an affinity and affection. They want to be involved and it's been us in Scotland. We've seen ourselves almost like a hedgehog. Because we're worried about being assimilated from south of the border, we have become very prickly. We've circled the wagons. That's it! 'Heid doon!' We're going to protect the rest of us that remain standing here. The only people that can be Scots are those few of us who are still on our feet here in our native land. I think once we lighten up and realise that you can be Scottish and live abroad, that being Scottish isn't about not being English, I think we'll get a better relationship with the diaspora. (S2)

The Year of Homecoming in 2009 has been a significant initiative by the Scottish government to engage with the diaspora and may be a step on the road towards a greater self-confidence at home and a smaller 'chip on the shoulder' about not being English. Although it is too soon, at the time of writing, for there to be agreement on the impact of the Homecoming, it does appear to reflect a relationship between Scotland and its diaspora which is one of greater maturity.

Chapter 8

Conclusions

The Scots as diaspora

The introduction to this book described some of the work that has been undertaken by scholars on the nature of diasporas, their formation and their various characteristics. The Scots fit into some categories of diaspora creation but not perhaps into others. Some Scots emigrated unwillingly as a result of events such as the Highland Clearances or through involvement with, for example, the Jacobite cause. But many others emigrated through individual initiative, aiming to better themselves, and a considerable number had a significant impact on business and industry in the countries to which they moved.

Unlike many other European migrants to the United States, the Scots spoke English, they were educated and they were Protestant. They were not therefore marginalised in terms of their class, income, language or religion and so it became relatively easy for them to enter mainstream American society. It is unsurprising that writers such as Esman (2009) can claim that Scottish and Scots-Irish immigrants found it unnecessary to form diaspora communities and so they did not behave like many other diasporas.

Esman, of course, is not strictly correct in his assertions. It is certainly true that Scottish identity has been part of the American mainstream and that Scots themselves have become very assimilated into American society, to the extent that Erickson (1972) could describe them as 'invisible' immigrants and Rethford and Sawyers (1997) as 'quiet' immigrants. But that has meant that American Scots have perhaps had to work harder to emphasise their differences from other Americans and to maintain their sense of Scottishness. The Scots may not have formed diaspora 'communities' in the way that groups such as the Irish or Italians did, but they did form Scottish organisations — in significant numbers. The earliest organisations had a charitable aim, to assist indigent immigrants, but over the years they became primarily social and cultural in nature. Partly this reflects the decline in immigration from Scotland, so there were fewer indigent Scots in need of help. Partly it reflects the growing significance of 'symbolic ethnicity' in Gans' (1979) phrase, and the numbers of American Scots searching for their roots and participating in activities related to their heritage. As such numbers increase and as awareness of ethnic and cultural diversity is heightened, there is an increasing demand for such diversity to be recognised (Hollinger, 1995).

Such developments reflect what has happened in many other diaspora communities in America and elsewhere, with increased leisure time providing the opportunity for this growing interest in heritage. Some organisations may, on the surface, appear not to be especially healthy, with relatively small and rather ageing memberships, but often these older members are the very individuals with the time and money available to keep societies going and to preserve the American Scots' sense of heritage. In the case of events such as Highland Games, there has been an actual expansion in their numbers, often to areas with very limited Scottish traditions. And the establishment of National Tartan Day has provided a hugely important focus for celebrations of Scottish ancestry and heritage, a very tangible recognition of the significance of the Scottish-American community.

The developments in America are also reflected in other parts of the world and, while this book is about the United States, the study of diasporas and the ways in which they develop and change is a growing research area elsewhere. There are significant Scottish diasporas, for example, in Australia and New Zealand (Prentis, 2008; Hewitson, 1998; Brooking and Coleman, 2003), where a continuing interest in Scottish heritage may also be found.

The expatriate Scottish identity

For members of the Scottish diaspora — in North America as well as elsewhere — a continuing sense of Scottishness is a key element of their identity. There is an ongoing interest in Scottish ancestry, an attachment to the Scottish homeland and, often, regular visits there. Academic researchers have increasingly explored aspects of national identity, particularly perhaps in Scotland itself and particularly since political devolution (for example, Kiely *et al.*, 2001; Reicher *et al.*, 2009) but there has perhaps been less engagement with the 'hyphenated' identities found within the Scottish diaspora. What is the significance of a Scottish identity, for example, for those who maintain an emotional or symbolic link with a place to which, in some cases, they may have never been?

I have already shown that the numbers of individuals within the United States claiming a Scottish identity were 5.4 million at the 2000 Census, making the Scots the eighth largest ancestral grouping in the country. The size of this grouping raises interesting questions as to how these identities are maintained, acted out and represented. Given also that most Americans will have a range of ancestries depending on where their family members migrated from, then how do individuals construct identities for themselves? Why is a Scottish identity seen as being increasingly desirable and 'popular'?

Part of the answer, of course, lies in the apparent rootlessness of many Americans and the need, according to Waters (1990, p. 150), to be 'from somewhere'. Thus, as discussed in Chapter 1, individuals have increasingly embraced a kind of symbolic ethnicity which, in some cases, reflects one's ancestral inheritance but which may also reflect personal choice. Such choices also change throughout an individual's lifetime. Some aspects of one's identity may be fixed, such as gender, skin colour and so on, but other aspects including a person's affiliation to a given group will shift over time (Maalouf, 2000).

One should, however, beware of assuming that all Americans are somehow in search of their roots. John Garvey (1996) provided an amusing account of a conversation with his daughter who needed to know something about her heritage for a school project. She was unhappy with the knowledge that she was simply 'American' while he was frustrated by the demands of multi-cultural education. So for many families, heritage and ancestry are not especially important. Maybe it is only with the increased leisure time which often accompanies retirement that individuals really immerse themselves in diaspora activities.

Although Scottish identity has never apparently been as popular a choice within America as, for example, an Irish identity, it does appear that it is gaining in popularity, perhaps assisted by events such as Tartan Day. Certainly, Scottish identity has always been part of the American mainstream and has never been culturally marginalised as say the Polish or Italian identities have been in the past (Zumkhawala-Cook, 2005), so perhaps it is an identity that Americans are increasingly 'choosing'. Again, one should beware of such choices. As Waters (1990) pointed out, when individuals of multi-ethnic descent, with no obvious attachment to any one ethnicity, develop an almost *ad hoc* relationship with one in particular, then this raises questions about the sincerity of that attachment in the long term.

Nevertheless, there is indeed evidence that people are actually *choosing* to be Scottish. Sullivan (2009) in her study of the Royal Caledonian Society of Melbourne, drew attention not only to the relatively small numbers of members actually born in Scotland, but also to the growing contingent of members who had apparently no immediate relationship with Scotland 'beyond their own decision to identify personally with the diasporic acts of their often-distant Scottish ancestors'. Certainly this appeared to be the case in my own research with members and sometimes office-bearers of Scottish societies admitting to having virtually no Scottish connection but participating because of being attracted to some of the activities such as Scottish music and dancing.

There is, of course, a reverse position of Scots working in America who choose *not* to be part of diaspora organisations, perhaps because they see it as a hindrance to their desire to become fully part of American society. Several interviewees spoke to me of their knowledge of Scots working in America, who might have brought some new life to diaspora organisations, but they had proved unwilling to join. In New York, where many interviewees were actually Scots-born, organisations such as the New York Tartan Army, which facilitated the following of the Scottish national football team, were, for some, more appropriate organisations to belong to than the more traditional diaspora societies.

Thus an individual's sense of identity is extraordinarily complex. Within the Scottish homeland itself, this sense of identity may be important on particular national occasions but is not something about which Scots have to think too hard. As Kiely *et al.* (2001, p. 34) have suggested 'in their everyday interactions, people's national identity is often seen to be of little immediate relevance'. Thus for much of the time an individual's national identity is a part of their sense of self that can become naturalised and absorbed into his or her mundane and banal everyday practices.

As Billig (1995) has pointed out, our identities are constantly reinforced by the national symbols we see all around us, including flags, banknotes, coins and newspapers — the 'continual "flagging" or reminding of nationhood'. Thus Scots living in Scotland can incorporate, adopt and consistently maintain a national identity without having to try too hard. The most subtle comments, accents, oblique references to a shared past, joking interactions, and references to popular culture can locate and cement individuals into the subtle web of identifiers and markers that associate them with a particular identity — in this case a national identity. Edensor (2002, p. 139) put it well when he suggested that:

> National identity is, then, partly sustained through the circulation of representations of spectacular and mundane cultural elements … the gestures and habits, and examples of tradition and modernity which are held in common by large numbers of people.

Thus a national identity can become something that is mundane, taken-for-granted and not often thought about too deeply. One does not have to try too hard to be, for example, Scottish on a daily basis; one simply *is* Scottish.

For American Scots, it is not possible to take one's Scottish identity for granted in this way and so there has to be a much greater effort expended in maintaining that identity. This is an issue that has been explored quite extensively in this book and I have sought to show the continuing — and often increasing — importance of Scottish organisations and of grand spectacles such as Highland Games and National Tartan Day as part of this process.

Thus American Scots sometimes struggle to hold on to a meaningful semblance of a Scottish identity. The identity that they have is not rooted or embedded in a social context that can drift into the constant background of their lives, as is the case with homeland Scots. So, given this, one can perhaps understand the importance of symbols and ceremonies and their role in identifying and maintaining a Scottish identity. For American Scots, certain activities take on huge significance, including a search for roots, visits to Scotland, internet access, membership of Scottish organisations, travel to Highland Games, the wearing of Scottish dress — these are all ways in which people can become Scottish. Such activities involve effort, time, contacts and money and so, unsurprisingly, they have tended to become the preserve or concern of the middle classes. This was a fact not lost on many of those I interviewed, who would probably have recognised the truth of Novak's (1971) description of them as 'Saturday ethnics'.

As has been discussed within the pages of this book, American Scots' identities are primarily historical in outlook, so they tend to focus on history and heritage. Their interests are more likely to be genealogical than say political. That is not to invalidate them in any way. It is certainly the case that some homeland Scots find the deep-rooted fascination of American Scots with aspects of Scottish history slightly puzzling, as such history does not impact on most Scots' everyday lives. But this simply reflects the points made above in relation to Scottish identity, in that homeland Scots rarely need to think about such things. Scottish history and identity are simply *there,* in one's background.

The position was succinctly described by an interviewee in New York:

So the groups of organisations which you find in the States are usually around the nostalgia model. It's usually around the kilts and the heritage. 'I'm a Cameron', 'I'm a MacDonald', or whatever. And within those, they're divided into two. There's the ones organising the Highland Games and the other ones like St Andrews Club here which is where, if we have a Scottish connection, we get together. The comment to be made is that this is not a Scottish-only thing. Part of the characteristic of Americans — probably less so Canadians — is that they seek their identity. They want to know if they're Italian Americans, African Americans, whatever, so they find a connection even if it's two or three generations remote. They feel they want to investigate it. I would say that's almost universal in all the places I've lived in the States. So I don't think it's driven from the Scottish end. I think it's driven from the American end. (N3)

But as Sarup (1996, p. 40) suggested, identities are fabricated, that is, they are both invented and constructed. Thus, 'The past figures importantly in people's self-representations because it is through recollections of the past that people represent themselves to themselves.' Historical representations, of course, are themselves often inventions. According to Samuel (1998, p. 12):

In foundation myths, visual artifices of the kind practised by court painters are more than matched by verbal apocrypha. In the case of

Scotland, the deceptions are so frequent and so strategic that one is tempted to suggest that all the leading items in the national pantheon, with the honourable exception of the Declaration of Arbroath (1320), can be traced back, ultimately, to be fakes.

Another writer who specialised in debunking historical myths was Hugh Trevor-Roper. He wrote extensively about Scotland, arguing that:

> ... in Scotland, it seems to me, myth has played a far more important part in history than it has in England. Indeed, I believe that the whole history of Scotland has been coloured by myth; and that myth, in Scotland, is never driven out by reality, or by reason, but lingers on until another myth has been discovered, or elaborated, to replace it. (Trevor-Roper, 2008)

Both Samuel (1998) and Trevor-Roper (2008) probably overstated their case but their point is well made. That is, that one should not dismiss American Scots' constructions of Scotland or Scottishness as being somehow less authentic, a form of false consciousness or bad faith. Such constructions of identity have to be understood in the context within which they emerge and the way in which they are used. There has been a tendency by some Scotland-based authors to present American Scots as delusional and therefore to be treated with derision, while some Scottish newspapers portray them as romantic buffoons (Hague, 2006). I have tried very hard not to do this but instead to listen to what individuals had to say and to report and record their views as fairly as possible.

Certainly there are many traditions that have emerged which may be referred to in America as Scottish traditions but which would not be so recognised in Scotland itself. They are essentially Scottish-American traditions. I have already referred to events such as the Kirkin' o' the Tartan, to the presence of clan tents and clan parades at Highland Games, to Tartan Day itself, and to episodes such as that surrounding the establishment of the 'Lone Shieling' in Nova Scotia (see Chapter 3). Some diaspora traditions are actually transported back to Scotland. Allison (2005), for example, writing as a National Trust guide at the Culloden battlefield, referred to American Scots visiting Culloden and dipping their bonnets in the Well of the Dead as a kind of toast to those killed in the battle; this appears to be a tradition that has evolved exclusively within the Scottish emigrant community.

Part of the reason for this divergence between Scottish and Scottish-American traditions is simple geographical distance as, before the days of cheap transatlantic air travel and the internet, contact between Scotland and its diaspora was limited. But it means that the diasporic identity can often be stereotyped and bear limited resemblance to reality. By way of an example, during July 2010, the *Herald* newspaper in Glasgow carried an obituary for Scottish entertainer Billy Meek. Although born in Scotland, he was virtually unknown in his native country as he had emigrated to Canada after the Second World War. But his career developed in Toronto and he became a household name on Canadian television, usually playing an amiable but drunken Scotsman, keen to scrounge a free drink. Thus the characters he portrayed in Canada were Scottish stereotypes, and his success was purely the result of his appeal to a diaspora audience and not a homeland Scottish one.

Similar stereotypes can be seen in literature, and Hague and Stenhouse (2007) have drawn attention to the ways in which Scots are often portrayed in American novels. Romantic novels may have titles such as *The Thorn and the Thistle, The Irresistible MacRae* or *Border Fire,* while there are also racier titles such as *Devil in a Kilt.* One of the most successful authors of recent years is Diana Gabaldon, whose *Outlander* series involves time travel back to the Highlands in the 1700s, and some Highland hotels now lay on special events to encourage the many followers of Gabaldon to travel back to Scotland themselves and immerse themselves in the local area and in local history.

Such stereotypes have surfaced again relatively recently with the launch in America of a Celtic-themed sports bar and restaurant chain entitled 'The Tilted Kilt'. The company employs scantily-clad servers in kilts, although the food and drink appear to have an Irish as well as a Scottish theme. The intention of the company appears to be to pander to what Americans know — or think they know — about Scotland.

In the course of this book, I have sought to show that some things are changing and the internet in particular is allowing American Scots to maintain a connection with Scotland and to inform themselves about Scotland in a way that was previously impossible. Despite the availability of such information, it is clear that some stereotypes persist and there often remains a disconnect between a Scottish and a diasporic Scottish identity.

A continuing connection

One of the most striking things about the Scottish diaspora within America, as evidenced by the various interviews undertaken, is the continuing connection to Scotland itself. The vast majority of interviewees had visited Scotland at some point, some visited regularly, all were in contact with Scotland and with Scottish organisations, and all were, to a greater or lesser extent, informed about developments taking place in Scotland.

While recognising that, for many people, the links were often nostalgic, there was also a significant number of individuals who wished to obtain a wider and more up-to-date perspective on Scotland. One individual, a movie fan, spoke at length of some of the Scottish films he had seen — many of which were far from romantic:

> My goal is to travel every year [to Scotland]. I would like to attend a Hogmanay in Edinburgh for example and see what that's like, social things. Movies are a good thing to see. *Trainspotting, Sweet Sixteen*[1] and everything are a little intense, but I don't want to get a picture of Scotland that I am just comfortable with. I want the truth, I want the facts. They have drug problems just like everybody else and they have thugs and monsters just like we do. So I don't want it watered down. (C8)

Another individual was a keen Gaelic learner. He recognised that learning Gaelic in Colorado, with almost no opportunity to make use of the language, might seem odd to some people, but he was unapologetic about pursuing an activity that gave him a great deal of pleasure. He pointed to the considerable amount of money which he spent in Scotland on visits to Gaelic summer schools and the contribution which he was therefore making to the Scottish economy:

> From my perspective, I hope to live another maybe twenty years, and I hope to maintain my interest in Scottish things, and Gaelic in particular, and, if I do that, I expect that maybe I will live there for the summer perhaps half a dozen times. On a typical trip to Scotland, I spend probably $6,000, and I know how many Americans are doing that. My reason for doing that is largely Gaelic. I'm interested in Scotland, and its culture and its music, but the trips are motivated by my desire

---

1 The film *Trainspotting* was released in 1996, and *Sweet Sixteen* in 2002.

to learn and speak Gaelic. And when I hear certain critics bemoaning the expenditure of amounts of money to support Gaelic, well here I am contributing, loosely speaking, $30,000 or $40,000 towards that. Gaelic is there and available to me, and so that's money that I'm putting into the Scottish economy as an individual. I don't know how many there are like me, but probably quite a lot. I would be very positively motivated by national support for Gaelic in Scotland and demotivated if that support fails ... The kind of people that come there to study Gaelic tend to be people who are well educated, have a lot of discretion with respect as to how they spend their time and their money. This means they are economically in good shape and are by no means second-class citizens. They are the kind of people that you would want coming in, if your business is tourist related. So to treat the people who are coming in to learn Gaelic as anything less than your most preferred tourists is probably short sighted. (C12)

As discussed in Chapter 7, there is now a growing recognition of the value to Scotland of its diaspora. In part, this is a result of devolution and the establishment of a Parliament and government in Edinburgh, which have allowed the country to engage directly with its diaspora in a way that was not previously possible. Events such as the 2009 Year of Homecoming and the attendance of Scottish government ministers at Tartan Day celebrations are examples of this, while there has been a growth in heritage tourism. The Scottish clans have apparently been given an enhanced role in this, as a means of tapping into Scottish diasporic identities. One high-profile event during 2009 was a Clan Convention, comprising clan chiefs and leading representatives of Scottish clans, which met at the Scottish Parliament to discuss the role of the clan in the twenty-first century. Additionally, a number of Scottish tour companies ran a range of tours to clan territories and castles (Sim, 2011b, forthcoming). Thus in some respects, Scottish tourism itself has started to look backwards, in order to welcome Scots from overseas back to Scotland. This is a pattern consistent with other diasporas, who have increasingly been viewed as assets, contributing to the home country.

However, in one important respect, the Scottish diaspora differs from many others and that is in relation to its political role. The United States is, in the view of Huntington (2004), 'the world's number one diaspora hostland' and the sheer diversity of American society means that diasporas can play a significant role in developing relations between the United States and other countries. Diasporas can often exert influence beyond the conventional economic and diplomatic channels and they can also play a role in the homeland itself. This may perhaps be illustrated by the size of the 'Jewish vote' in America and the influence that it has exerted in relation to American relations with Israel.

But perhaps because the Scots were never a marginalised group within the United States, they have hardly ever become involved in campaigning or political organising. This contrasts particularly with Irish Americans who, over a long period, raised funds for political activities within the north of Ireland (Esman, 2009, p. 124). There are some prominent Scottish nationalists around — Sir Sean Connery amongst them — but as a political movement Scottish nationalism has never really been important in America. Some of the individuals interviewed for this book expressed an interest in Scottish political matters and sometimes a sympathy for Scottish nationalism, but many members of the Scottish diaspora appear relatively uninterested.

This absence of political activity within the Scottish diaspora illustrates another important difference between the Scots and other diasporas. Most diasporas have a connection to a particular nation state or, in the case of the Jews or the Irish, have been instrumental in the creation of a state to which they could return if necessary (Huntington, 2004). The Scots, perhaps like the Catalans, already have a national homeland but one that is not actually a state — and indeed Scotland has often been referred to as a 'stateless nation' (McCrone, 2001b). Things may change, of course, and this book has explored the impact that political devolution within the UK and the establishment of the Scottish Parliament have had on the diaspora. If Scotland were to become independent, then the relationship with the diaspora might take on additional significance.

One area in which there has been significant development has been in relation to genealogical research. The enthusiasm for such research within diaspora communities is beyond doubt but now across Scotland — and Britain as a whole — there has been a significant growth in interest in genealogical research, in 'roots' and in family histories. There are now a number of magazines, books and internet sites available to help individuals trace their ancestors, and records of births, marriage and deaths are increasingly available online, for wide use. A particularly popular television programme in the UK from 2004 onwards has been the BBC's *Who Do You Think You Are?*, in which celebrities are assisted in researching their family trees. An American version was launched in March 2010.

In a collaboration between the General Register Office for Scotland, the National Archives of Scotland and the Court of the Lord Lyon, there is now a website entitled 'Scotland's People'[2] on which have been loaded certificates of births, marriages and deaths, Census records, parish registers and copies of wills and testaments. Initial searches are free, while copies of documents may be downloaded for a modest sum. There is also a related magazine entitled *Discover my Past, Scotland* (and an equivalent publication for England). Such websites and publications serve to enhance and to simplify the search for one's roots.

Writers of fiction and popular journalists have been particularly successful in tapping into this growing interest in 'roots', often reflecting the UK's growing multi-culturalism. Both Sarfraz Manzoor's *Greetings from Bury Park* about a Pakistani boy growing up in Luton, England (Manzoor, 2007) and Ziauddin Sardar's (2008) *Balti Britain* explored the multiple identities of Asians living in Britain. Monica Ali's (2003) novel *Brick Lane* was set amid the Bangladeshi community of east London. And Andrea Levy's (2004) book *Small Island* described the arrival of a family into London from Jamaica; in her 1999 work *Fruit of the Lemon,* the principal character returned to Jamaica to explore her family roots. Such books exemplify the increasing interest that seems to exist in different family histories, cultures and backgrounds.

The interest shown by members of the Scottish diaspora in its roots is, of course, reflected in other diasporas. McCain and Ray (2003), for example, pointed to a re-enactment of the voyages of Danish immigrants to the United States, through a sailing of seven sailing ships from Esbjerg to New York in 2001, to the legacy travel of Italian Americans, and various journeys by Jewish Americans in search of their family histories.

As well as genealogy, this book has referred to the continuing desire for business links between the diaspora and Scotland. This emerged from

2   http://www.scotlandspeople.gov.uk; accessed April 2011.

some of the interviews reported in this book, and there are a number of organisations on both sides of the Atlantic dedicated to developing business links. In the United States, some charitable foundations have a specific focus on raising funds for Scottish organisations and, during the Year of Homecoming in 2009, some conferences held in Scotland sought to develop these connections still further.

At various levels, the importance of these connections was well understood, both in America:

> If we don't work to keep the ties alive, with each passing generation they slip away, and if there's no infusion of new blood then it's going to be difficult for Scotland to draw upon the diaspora in the way that it wants. So that's why I get so concerned when Scotland doesn't effectively work with us to make sure that we remain viable, because, if we go, organisations such as ours, and the St Andrew's societies etc, if they don't remain viable and connected, then they're going to lose out. That's a big issue for me. (N10)

And in Scotland:

> People left this country in hardship and in sorrow, because it had forsaken them, or because they'd been driven from it — whether because it was the Highland Clearances or whether because it was the factory shut. But they didn't turn against this country — they retained an affinity for it. There's something amazing about that and we should be grateful. (S2)

At the time of writing, therefore, it seems likely that such links, between the Scottish homeland and the diaspora, will develop further.

Looking to the future

So what might the future be for the Scottish diaspora? Firstly, within the United States, the diaspora may change in size. Research has shown that individuals within the US sometimes change their responses to the ancestry question in the Census and so the size of ancestral groups may alter over time (Alba, 1990). At present, the Scots occupy eighth place in the ancestry league table and it will be interesting to analyse the results of the American 2010 Census, which will appear in the near future.

Secondly, previous Census analysis showed that the Scottish diaspora is an ageing group and it seems inevitable that Scottish organisations

within America will be characterised by an increasingly older membership. However, there are indications from the interviews carried out for
this book that there is a younger generation still interested in their Scottish
heritage and willing in some cases to take on the running of these organisations and societies. Certainly Ray (2005a; 2005c) has suggested that,
within America, things Celtic have become more fashionable in recent
years, so perhaps a Scottish-American identity will continue to be popular.
She also suggested that the Scottish heritage movement as a whole may be
seen as a revitalisation movement, an attempt to create a more satisfying
state of existence by recreating traditions and claiming 'roots' (Ray, 2005a;
2005c).

Thirdly, it is likely that the Scottish diaspora in America will continue
to develop and strengthen its ties with the homeland, aided by the
relatively straightforward nature of travel between the US and Scotland.
This appears to be in contrast to the more distant diaspora in Australasia.
In her recent study of the Caledonian Society of Melbourne, Sullivan
(2009, p. 134) noted that:

> Overwhelmingly, the Caledonian Society's members, both Australian
> born *and* Scottish born, tended to frame their ideas of Scotland around
> the romantic imagery of clans, bagpipes, tartan, haggis, and a rural
> idyll — all of the stereotypical clichés which are commonly associated
> with Scotland by those who are not from there.
>
> Most prevalent among those perceptions was the idea of Scotland
> as a clan-based society, whose hallmarks of a simple rustic lifestyle and
> an abiding loyalty to one's own kind permeated the responses given by
> both the Australian *and* Scottish members.

In this case, the sheer distance from Scotland and the difficulties of travelling home meant that the diaspora viewed it through a particularly nostalgic lens. Sullivan's (2009) work certainly suggested a very strong romanticism which may be slightly less evident in North America.

Zumkhawala-Cook (2008) wrote of the influence of heritage, suggesting that diasporic Scottish identity is:

> less and less about life in Scotland to the great-great-grandchildren
> of Scottish émigrés in Auckland, Johannesburg, Ottawa or Palm
> Beach who are enrolled members of a clan society or attend the local
> Highland Gatherings.

But this is rather too simplistic. The diaspora, as has been shown, is not necessarily ill-informed about life in modern Scotland. Nor can all diasporas — whether in Auckland or Ottawa — be treated as the same.

Indeed, the Scottish diaspora in America also sits in contrast to that in England. Research in England (McCarthy, 2007; Munro and Sim, 2001; Sim, 2011a) revealed a diaspora where Scottish organisations are shrinking as membership ages, with few younger individuals apparently willing to become involved. Of particular interest is the fact that the children of members appear in the main to have adopted an exclusively English identity and do not identify to any great extent with their Scottish ancestry. It seems important therefore to distinguish between the different Scottish diasporas — from the weak 'near' diaspora in England to the stronger, more distant overseas diasporas. But the strength of the overseas diasporas is itself affected by distance from the homeland and the ability to travel back to Scotland.

Fourthly, it is possible that the relationship between America as a whole and Scotland may become more complex, with possible implications for the future 'popularity' of a Scottish-American identity. On the one hand, there have been a number of recent Scottish emigrants to America who have made a significant mark on the country and in the process have perhaps been ambassadors for Scotland. One example is the entertainer Craig Ferguson, who became hugely popular as the host of CBS's *The Late Late Show*. Another is the actor Alan Cumming who achieved success on Broadway and was the grand marshal of the New York Tartan Day Parade in 2009. Both individuals have taken out American citizenship — in Cumming's case so that he could vote for Barack Obama in the 2008 presidential election. Another Scot who has achieved success in America is the singer Susan Boyle, following her appearance in 2009 on the television show *Britain's Got Talent*.

On the other hand, there is no doubt that the release by the Scottish government in 2009 of Abdelbaset Al-Megrahi, the man convicted of the Lockerbie bombing, was hugely unpopular in America. Although the release was made on compassionate grounds following diagnosis of terminal prostate cancer, nevertheless the event led to an investigation by the US Senate's Foreign Relations Committee and strained relations between America and Scotland. So Scotland has been viewed in both a positive and negative light recently and it is not at present clear how attitudes will develop.

Within Scotland itself, relationships with the diaspora have undergone a number of changes. As discussed in Chapter 7, there have been a number of developments that have enhanced the links between Scotland and its diaspora. The development of a diaspora strategy that actively encourages heritage tourism has led to major events such as the 2009 Year of Homecoming. At the time of writing, the Scottish government has decided to hold a second Year of Homecoming in 2014, to coincide not only with the 700th anniversary of the Battle of Bannockburn but also with the Glasgow Commonwealth Games and Scotland's hosting of the Ryder Cup. It has been suggested that a third Year of Homecoming may be held in 2020 to coincide with the 700th anniversary of the Declaration of Arbroath. The decision to make Homecoming events relatively regular suggests that Scotland itself has become more welcoming of diaspora Scots and more relaxed about issues of identity and its relationship with the diaspora.

There is undoubtedly a hope within Scotland that, if members of the diaspora travel regularly back to Scotland, they might be tempted to invest there. This is not viewing the diaspora as a 'cash cow' but nevertheless being aware of the resource potential of the diaspora. To an extent, this view was vindicated when businessman Donald Trump travelled back to Scotland to visit his late mother's home (in Lewis) and announced that he was going to make a major investment in a golf resort north of Aberdeen. The development has not been universally popular with some local people concerned at damage to coastal dunes amongst other things, but the business community in the north east has welcomed the scheme.

Individuals such as Trump are Americans but have a strong sense of their ancestry. There is perhaps an increasing awareness of how this leads into a kind of dual identity for many members of the diaspora, being both Scots and Americans at the same time. This sense of dual identity has been neatly summarised by Craig Ferguson (2009, p. 268) in his reflections on being a Scot who had taken out American citizenship:

> I am the child of two parents and two countries. My mother put the blue in my eyes and my father gave me grit. Scotland made me what I am and America let me be it … I didn't become any less Scottish when I became an American. The two are not mutually exclusive. I am proud of my heritage. I will always be Scottish in my heart, but my soul is American.

Perhaps, at the end of the day, Scotland and its diaspora are actually moving closer together. Homecomings and the like are designed to make the diaspora welcome, while devolution has provided Scotland with a government able to make these things happen. Scotland seems more comfortable now in its own identity and no longer cringes at the use of tartan. Indeed, the wearing of kilts at weddings and social occasions is now commonplace. And, while Tartan Day may be a diaspora invention, there are now Tartan Day celebrations taking place in some parts of Scotland itself. The diaspora may have celebrated St Andrew's Day when it was more or less ignored at home, but since the passing of the St Andrew's Day Holiday (Scotland) Act in 2006 there has been a significant increase in the number of celebrations in Scotland taking place on that day.

Scotland and its diaspora may not yet have the relatively close relationship enjoyed between the Irish and the Irish diaspora but Scotland's relationship is undoubtedly changing. At the time of writing, it is not easy to predict what that relationship will be in, say, ten years' time, but it appears likely that ever closer links will be forged.

Appendix: Summary of interviewees

The interviews quoted in the text all have a prefix letter. The letter C denotes that they were carried out in Colorado in October/November 2003. The letter N denotes that they were carried out in New York in April 2007. Interviews with the prefix letter S were carried out in Scotland, usually in 2007.

The following provides a summary of the individuals interviewed, including their gender, approximate age, birthplace and occupation or interest in Scotland. The organisations they are involved with are generally not named in order to preserve anonymity.

C1   Male, fifties. American born. An office-bearer in a Scottish country dancing group.
C2   Male, fifties. American born. A participant in a number of Scottish country dancing groups.
C3   Female, fifty. American born. A Gaelic learner and member of An Comunn Gàidhealach America.
C4   Male, fifties. American born. An office-bearer of the local St Andrew Society.
C5   Female, fifties. American born. Assists with the organisation of one of the larger Highland Games in Colorado.
C6   Male, fifties. Scottish born. Employed at the British Consulate and with links to various Scottish organisations and Scottish business.
C7   A male and female, married and both in their late fifties. American born. Members of the St Andrew Society and clan organisations and with children involved in dancing and piping.
C8   Male, fifties. American born. Member of St Andrew Society and convener of clan organisation in Colorado.
C9   Male, early seventies. Scottish born. Attends Highland Games and some Scottish events but with limited direct involvement.
C10   Female, early seventies. Scottish born. Attends some Scottish events but less involved than previously.

C11 A male and female, married and both in their fifties. Both American born. Members of St Andrew Society and involved in musical and Celtic study groups.

C12 Male, fifties. American born. A Gaelic learner and with an interest in genealogical research.

C13 A male in his thirties and female in her forties, married and both American born, and teenage son, American born. Involved in clan organisations and Highland Games.

C14 Female, seventies. American born. Involvement in genealogical and clan research and local Highland Games.

C15 A male aged fifty and female in her forties, married and both American born. Involved in genealogical research and assist with organisation of local Highland Games.

C16 A male and female, both in their seventies. Both American born. Both involved in various organisations, including St Andrew societies.

C17 Female, early seventies. Scottish born. Member of St Andrew Society and interested in Scottish dancing but less involved than previously.

C18 Female, fifties. American born. Regular visitor to Scotland but only recently joined Scottish organisations.

C19 Female, forties. Born in Nigeria but brought up in Scotland. Moved relatively recently to America and only recently joined Scottish organisations.

C20 Male, seventies. Scottish born. Member of St Andrew Society and interested in Scottish dancing but less involved than previously.

C21 Male, fifties. American born. A Gaelic teacher and member of An Comunn Gàidhealach America.

N1 Female, twenties. American born. Working in higher education and involved in the playing of traditional music.

N2 Male, seventies. American born. Involved in a heritage organisation within the United States connected to Scotland.

N3 Male, late forties. Scottish born. A businessman, with an involvement in arts and cultural activities connected to Tartan Day.

N4 Male, fifties. American born. A Gaelic learner and member of An Comunn Gàidhealach America.

N5 Male, late thirties. Scottish born. A member of the New York City Tartan Army.

N6 Male, late sixties. American born. An office-bearer of a Scottish organisation based in New York City.

N7 Two males, one aged eighty, the other in his sixties. Both Scottish born. Office-bearers in a Scottish-American club based in New Jersey.

N8   Male, early forties. Scottish born. A civil servant employed by the Scottish government, working in the United States.

N9   A male and female, married and both in their sixties. Scottish born. Members of a Scottish country dancing organisation in New York City.

N10   Male, late sixties. English born. A businessman and office-bearer of a Scottish organisation based in New York City.

N11   Male, late fifties. Scottish born. A member of a Scottish football supporters organisation in New York City.

N12   Female, late thirties. Canadian born with Scottish ancestry. Strong interest in genealogical research.

N13   Female, late thirties. Scottish born. Family connection to Scottish organisations in New York, and interest in genealogy.

N14   Two males, one fifties and Scottish born, one early seventies and American born. Both involved in organisation of Highland Games and clan societies.

N15   Female, seventies. Scottish born. Member of country dance group and author of historical articles in Scottish heritage magazines.

S1   Male, fifties. Scottish born. Working in higher education with an office in the United States to recruit American students.

S2   Male, early fifties. Scottish born. Member of the Scottish Parliament with a strong interest in the Scottish diaspora.

Bibliography

Alba, R. D. (1985) 'The twilight of ethnicity among Americans of European ancestry: the case of the Italians', in Alba, R. D. (ed.) *Ethnicity and Race in the USA. Toward the Twenty-First Century,* London: Routledge and Kegan Paul, pp. 134–58

Alba, R. D. (1990) *Ethnic Identity: The Transformation of White America,* New Haven: Yale University Press

Ali, M. (2003) *Brick Lane,* London: Doubleday

Allaway, R. (2001) 'West Hudson: a cradle of American soccer'. Available from http://homepages.sover.net/~spectrum/hudson.html (accessed April 2011)

Allen, J. P. and Turner, E. J. (1988) *We The People. An Atlas of America's Ethnic Diversity,* New York: Macmillan

Allison, H. (2005) *Rivers Running Far: The Story of Those Who Went Away,* Kinloss: Librario

Anwar, M. (1979) *The Myth of Return: Pakistanis in Britain,* London: Heinemann

Archdeacon, T. J. (1983) *Becoming American. An Ethnic History,* New York: Free Press

Ascherson, N. (2002) *Stone Voices: The Search for Scotland,* London: Granta

Aspinwall, B. (1984) *Portable Utopia: Glasgow and the United States 1820–1920,* Aberdeen: Aberdeen University Press

Aspinwall, B. (1985) 'The Scots in the United States', in Cage, R. A. (ed.) *The Scots Abroad: Labour, Capital, Enterprise 1750–1914,* London: Croom Helm, pp. 80–110

Bailyn, B. (1986) *Voyagers to the West. A Passage in the Peopling of America on the Eve of the Revolution,* New York: Alfred A. Knopf

Basu, P. (2004) 'My own island home: the Orkney Homecoming', *Journal of Material Culture,* Vol. 9, No. 1, pp. 27–42

Basu, P. (2005) 'Macpherson Country: genealogical identities, spatial histories and the Scottish diasporic clanscape', *Cultural Geographies,* No. 12, pp. 123–50

Basu, P. (2007) *Highland Homecomings: Genealogy and Heritage Tourism in the Scottish Diaspora,* London: Routledge

Beals, M. (2005) 'Caledonian Canaan: the Scotch-American Company of Farmers (SACF) and Scottish cultural identity in colonial New England', *International Review of Scottish Studies,* No. 30, pp. 42–85

Berry, J. (1992) 'Acculturation and adaptation in a new society', *International Migration,* No. 30, pp. 69–85

Berthoff, R. (1953) *British Immigrants in Industrial America,* New York: Russell and Russell

Berthoff, R. (1982) 'Under the kilt: Variations on the Scottish-American ground', *Journal of American Ethnic History,* No. 1, pp. 5–34

Berthoff, R. (1986) 'Celtic mist over the South', *Journal of Southern History,* Vol. 52, No. 4, pp. 523–46

Billig, M. (1995) *Banal Nationalism,* London: Sage

Blaustein, R. (2003) *The Thistle and the Brier: Historical Links and Cultural Parallels between*

Scotland and Appalachia, Contributions to Southern Appalachian Studies Series, Vol. 7, Jefferson, NC: McFarland

Bowman, M. (1995) 'Cardiac Celts: images of the Celts in contemporary British paganism', in Harvey, G. and Hardman, C. (eds.) *Paganism Today,* London: Thorsons, pp. 242–51

Boyle, M. and Motherwell, S. (2005) *Attracting and Retaining Talent: Lessons for Scottish Policymakers from the Experiences of Scottish Expatriates in Dublin,* Glasgow: Scottish Economic Policy Network.

Brah, A. (1996) *Cartographies of Diaspora: Contesting Identities,* London: Routledge

Brooking, T. and Coleman, J. (ed.) (2003) *The Heather and the Fern: Scottish Migration and New Zealand Settlement,* Dunedin: University of Otago Press

Brown, A., McCrone, D. and Paterson, L. (1996) *Politics and Society in Scotland,* Basingstoke: Macmillan

Brown, E. H. (2005) 'Erasing the hyphen in German American', *Reviews in American History,* Vol. 33, No. 4, pp. 527–32

Bruce, D. (1996) *Scotland the Movie,* Edinburgh: Polygon

Bruce, D. A. (1996) *The Mark of the Scots; Their Astonishing Contribution to History, Science, Democracy, Literature and the Arts,* New York: Birch Lane Press

Bruce, D. A. (2000) *The Scottish 100: Portraits of History's Most Influential Scots,* New York: Carroll and Graf

Bruce, D. A. (2002) 'Comment on "National Tartan Day"', *Scottish Affairs,* No. 40

Buettner, E. (2002) 'Haggis in the raj: private and public celebrations of Scottishness in late imperial India', *Scottish Historical Review,* Vol. 81, No. 2, pp. 212–39

Bumsted, J. M. (1999) 'Scottishness and Britishness in Canada, 1790–1914', in Harper, M. and Vance, M. S. (eds.) *Myth, Migration and the Making of Memory. Scotia and Nova Scotia c.1700–1900,* Halifax: Gorsebrook Research Institute for Atlantic Canada Studies, pp. 89–104

Butler, K. D. (2001) 'Defining diaspora, refining a discourse', *Diaspora,* Vol. 10, No. 2, pp. 189–219

Byron, R. (1999) *Irish America,* Oxford: Clarendon Press

Calder, J. (2006) *Scots in the USA,* Edinburgh: Luath Press

Cameron, I. (1998) *The Jimmy Shand Story,* Edinburgh: Scottish Cultural Press

Campbell, D. and MacLean, R. A. (1974) *Beyond the Atlantic Roar: A Study of the Nova Scotia Scots,* Toronto: McClelland and Stewart

Cantrell, J. P. (2006) *How Celtic Culture Invented Southern Literature,* Gretna, LA: Pelican Publishing

Carlson, R. A. (1987) *The Americanisation Syndrome: A Quest for Conformity,* London: Croom Helm

Chhabra, D., Healy, R. and Sills, E. (2003) 'Staged authenticity and heritage tourism', *Annals of Tourism Research,* Vol. 30, No. 3, pp. 702–19

Charlesworth, S. J. (2000) *A Phenomenology of Working Class Experience,* Cambridge: Cambridge University Press

Child, I. L. (1943) *Italian or American? The Second Generation in Conflict,* New Haven: Yale University Press

Cohen, R. (1997) *Global Diasporas: An Introduction,* London: UCL Press

Conzen, K. N. (1976) *Immigrant Milwaukee, 1836–1860. Accommodation and Community in a Frontier City,* Cambridge, MA: Harvard University Press

Cowan, E. J. (1999) 'The myth of Scotch Canada', in Harper, M. and Vance, M. S. (eds.) *Myth, Migration and the Making of Memory. Scotia and Nova Scotia c.1700–1900,* Halifax:

Gorsebrook Research Institute for Atlantic Canada Studies, pp. 49–72

Cowan, E. J. (2005) 'Tartan Day in America', in Ray, C. (ed.) *Transatlantic Scots*, Tuscaloosa, AL: University of Alabama Press, pp. 318–38

Crane, T. C., Hamilton, J. A. and Wilson, L. E. (2004) 'Scottish dress, ethnicity and self-identity', *Journal of Fashion Marketing and Management*, Vol. 8, No. 1, pp. 66–83

Devine, T. (1994) *Clanship to Crofters' War: The Social Transformation of the Scottish Highlands*, Manchester: Manchester University Press

Devine, T. (1999) *The Scottish Nation, 1700–2000*, Harmondsworth: Allen Lane

Devine, T. and Logue, P. (eds.) (2002) *Being Scottish. Personal Reflections on Scottish Identity Today*, Edinburgh: Polygon

De Vos, G. A. (1995) 'Ethnic pluralism: conflict and accommodation. The role of ethnicity in social history', in Romanucci-Ross, L. and de Vos, G. A. (eds.) *Ethnic Identity: Creation, Conflict and Accommodation*, Walnut Creek, CA: AltaMira Press

Dezell, M. (2002) *Irish America: Coming into Clover*, New York: Anchor Books

Didcock, B. (2007) 'The wild drovers', Glasgow: *Sunday Herald* (Seven Days section) 14 January, pp. 12–13

Dinnerstein, L. and Reimers, D. M. (1975) *Ethnic Americans. A History of Immigration and Assimilation*, New York: Dodd, Mead

Dobson, D. (1994) *Scottish Emigration to Colonial America, 1607–1785*, Athens, GA: University of Georgia Press

Donaldson, E. A. (1986) *The Scottish Highland Games in America*, Gretna, LA: Pelican Publishing

Donaldson, G. (1966) *The Scots Overseas*, Westport, CT: Greenwood Press

Donaldson, G. (1980) 'Scots', in Thernstrom, S. (ed.) *Harvard Encyclopedia of American Ethnic Groups*, Cambridge, MA: Harvard University Press, pp. 908–16

Dunn, C. W. (1953) *Highland Settler: A Portrait of the Scottish Gael in Nova Scotia*, Toronto: University of Toronto Press

Eckstein, S. (2002) 'On deconstructing and reconstructing the meaning of immigrant generations', in Levitt, P. and Waters, M. C. (eds.) *The Changing Face of Home. The Transnational Lives of the Second Generation*, New York: Russell Sage Foundation, pp. 211–15

Edensor, T. (2002) *National Identity, Popular Culture and Everyday Life*, Oxford: Berg

Erickson, C. (1972) *Invisible Immigrants. The Adaptation of English and Scottish Immigrants in Nineteenth-Century America*, Coral Gables, FL: University of Miami Press

Eriksen, T. H. (1993) *Ethnicity and Nationalism: Anthropological Perspectives*, London: Pluto Press

Esman, M. J. (2009) *Diasporas in the Contemporary World*, Cambridge: Polity Press

Ewing, W. and Russell, M. (2004) *Stop the World: The Autobiography of Winnie Ewing*, Edinburgh: Birlinn

Farley, R. (1991) 'The new census question about ancestry: what did it tell us?', *Demography*, Vol. 28, No. 3, pp. 411–29

Fenton, S. (1999) *Ethnicity, Racism, Class and Culture*, Basingstoke: Macmillan

Ferguson, C. (2009) *American on Purpose: The Improbable Adventures of an Unlikely Patriot*, New York: HarperCollins

Finlayson, I. (1987) *The Scots. A Portrait of the Scottish Soul at Home and Abroad*, New York: Atheneum

Forrester, A. T. (2003) *Scots in Michigan*, East Lansing: Michigan State University Press

Fraser, M. (n.d.) 'Canada's Scots and Tartan Day celebrations'. Available from Electric

Scotland website http://www.electricscotland.com/canada/tartan_day.htm (accessed April 2011)

Fry, M. (2002) *The Scottish Empire,* Edinburgh: Birlinn

Fry, M. (2003) 'Bold, Independent, Unconquer'd and Free'. How the Scots made America Safe for Liberty, Democracy and Capitalism, Ayr: Fort Publishing

Gans, H. J. (1979) 'Symbolic ethnicity: The future of ethnic groups and cultures in America', *Ethnic and Racial Studies,* Vol. 2, No. 1, pp. 1–20

Garvey, J. (1996) 'My problem with multi-cultural education', in Ignatiev, N. and Garvey, J. (eds.) *Race Traitor,* New York: Routledge, pp. 25–31

Gerber, D. A. (2006) 'A network of two: Personal friendship and Scottish identification in the correspondence of Mary Ann Archbold and Margaret Woodrow, 1807–1840', in McCarthy, A. (ed.) *A Global Clan: Scottish Migrant Networks and Identities Since the Eighteenth Century,* London: Tauris Academic Studies

Germana, M. (2003) 'Historical places of interest, books, tourism and advertising: Scottish icons in contemporary Halifax (Nova Scotia), *International Review of Scottish Studies,* No. 28, pp. 22–46

Gibson, R. (2003) *Plaids and Bandanas: From Highland Drover to Wild West Cowboy,* Edinburgh: Luath Press

Gillanders, F. (1968), 'The economic life of Gaelic Scotland today', in Thomson, D. S. and Grimble, I. (eds), *The Future of the Highlands,* London: Routledge and Kegan Paul, pp. 95–150

Ginsburg, N. (1994) 'Ethnic minorities and social policy', in Clasen, J. and Freeman, R. (eds) *Social Policy in Germany,* Hemel Hempstead: Harvester Wheatsheaf, pp. 191–206

Giulanotti, R. and Robertson, R. (2006) 'Glocalisation, globalisation and migration: the case of Scottish football supporters in North America', *International Sociology,* Vol. 21, No. 2, pp. 171–98

Gjerde, J. (ed.) (1998) Major Problems in American Immigration and Ethnic History, Boston: Houghton Mifflin

Glazer, N. and Moynihan, D. P. (1963) *Beyond the Melting Pot. The Negroes, Puerto Ricans, Jews, Italians and Irish of New York City,* Cambridge, MA: MIT Press

Gordon, M. M. (1964) *Assimilation in American life. The Role of Race, Religion and National Origins,* New York: Oxford University Press

Gordon, M. M. (1978) *Human Nature, Class and Ethnicity,* New York: Oxford University Press

Graham, I. C. C. (1956) *Colonists from Scotland: Emigration to North America 1707–1783,* Ithaca, NY: Cornell University Press

Greeley, A. M. (1971) *Why Can't They Be Like Us? America's White Ethnic Groups,* New York: E. P. Dutton

Greeley, A. M. (1974) *Ethnicity in the United States: A Preliminary Reconnaissance,* New York: Wiley

Hague, E. (2001) 'Haggis and heritage — representing Scotland in the United States', in Horne, J. (ed.) *Leisure Cultures, Consumption and Commodification,* Brighton: Leisure Studies Association Publication, No. 74, pp. 107–29

Hague, E. (2002a) 'The Scottish diaspora. Tartan Day and the appropriation of Scottish identities in the United States', in Harvey, D. C., Jones, R., McInroy, N. and Milligan, C. (eds.) *Celtic Geographies: Old Culture, New Times,* London: Routledge, pp. 139–56

Hague, E. (2002b) 'National Tartan Day: rewriting history in the United States', *Scottish Affairs,* No. 38, pp. 94–124

Hague, E. (2002c) 'Rejoinder to "Comment on National Tartan Day"', *Scottish Affairs*, No. 40, pp. 149–50

Hague, E. (2006) 'Representations of race and romance: The portrayal of people of Scottish descent in North America by British newspapers, 1997–1999', *Scottish Affairs*, No. 57, pp. 39–69

Hague, E., Giordano, B. and Sebesta, E. H. (2005) 'Whiteness, multi-culturalism and nationalist appropriation of Celtic culture: The case of the League of the South and the Lega Nord', *Cultural Geographies*, No. 12, pp. 151–73

Hague, E. and Sebesta, E. H. (2008) 'Neo-Confederacy, culture and ethnicity: A white Anglo-Saxon Southern people', in Hague, E., Sebesta, E. H. and Beirich, H. (eds.) *Neo-Confederacy: A Critical Introduction*, Austin TX: University of Texas Press, pp. 97–130

Hague, E. and Stenhouse, D. (2007) 'A very interesting place: Representing Scotland in American romance novels', in Schoene, B. (ed.) *The Edinburgh Companion to Contemporary Scottish Literature*, Edinburgh: Edinburgh University Press, pp. 354–61

Haley, A. (1976) *Roots: The Saga of an American Family*, Garden City, NY: Doubleday

Hall, S. (1990) 'Cultural identity and diaspora', in Rutherford, J. (ed.) *Identity: Community, Culture, Difference*, London: Lawrence and Wishart, pp. 222–37

Halter, M. (2000) *Shopping for Identity. The Marketing of Ethnicity*, New York: Schocken Books

Handlin, O. (1973) *The Uprooted: The Epic Story of the Great Migrations that Made the American People*, Boston: Little, Brown

Hanham, H. J. (1969) *Scottish Nationalism*, London: Faber

Harper, M. (2003) Adventurers and Exiles. The Great Scottish Exodus, London: Profile

Harvey, D. C., Jones, R., McInroy, N. and Milligan, C. (eds.) *Celtic Geographies: Old Culture, New Times*, London: Routledge

Herman, A. (2001) *The Scottish Enlightenment. The Scots' Invention of the Modern World*, London: Fourth Estate

Hewitson, J. (1993) *Tam Blake & Co. The Story of the Scots in America*, Edinburgh: Canongate

Hewitson, J. (1998) *Far Off in Sunlit Places: Stories of the Scots in Australia and New Zealand*, Edinburgh: Canongate

Hollinger, D. A. (1995) *Postethnic America: Beyond Multi-culturalism*, New York: Basic Books

Hollinger, D. A. (1998) 'Postethnic America', in Katkin, W. F., Landsman, N. and Tyree, A. (eds.) *Beyond Pluralism. The Conception of Groups and Group Identities in America*, Urbana, IL: University of Illinois Press, pp. 47–62

Hook, A. (1999) From Goosecreek to Gandercleugh: Studies in Scottish-American Literary and Cultural History, East Linton: Tuckwell Press

Howe, I. (1977) 'The limits of ethnicity', *New Republic*, 25 June, pp. 17–19

Hughey, M. W. and Vidich, A. J. (1998) 'The new American pluralism: Racial and ethnic sodalities and their sociological implications', in Hughey, M. W. (ed.) *New Tribalisms. The Resurgence of Race and Ethnicity*, Basingstoke: Macmillan, pp. 173–96

Hunter, J. (1994) *A Dance Called America. The Scottish Highlands, the United States and Canada*, Edinburgh: Mainstream

Hunter, J. (2005) *Scottish Exodus: Travels Among a Worldwide Clan*, Edinburgh: Mainstream

Huntington, S. P. (2004) *Who Are We? America's Great Debate*, London: Simon and Schuster

Hutchinson, E. P. (1956) *Immigrants and Their Children, 1850–1950*, New York: Russell and Russell

Bibliography

Ignatiev, N. (1995) *How the Irish Became White*, New York: Routledge

James, S. (1999) 'The American right and Scottish nationalism', World Socialist Web Site. Available at http://www.wsws.org/articles/1999/feb1999/scot-f03.shtml (accessed April 2011)

Jarvie, G. (1991) *Highland Games: The Making of the Myth*, Edinburgh: Edinburgh University Press

Jarvie, G. (2005) 'The North American émigré, Highland Games and social capital in international communities', in Ray, C. (ed.) *Transatlantic Scots*, Tuscaloosa, AL: University of Alabama Press, pp. 198–214

Jeffery, C. (2008) 'Where stands the Union now? Scottish-English relations after devolution', in Devine, T. (ed.) *Scotland and the Union 1707–2007*, Edinburgh: Edinburgh University Press, pp. 195–209

Jenkins, R. (1997) *Rethinking Ethnicity: Arguments and Explorations*, London: Sage

Jones, M. A. (1974) *The Old World Ties of American Ethnic Groups*, London: H. K. Lewis (inaugural lecture at University College London, 17 January 1974)

Jones, M. A. (1976) *Destination America*, London: Weidenfeld and Nicolson

Karras, A. L. (1992) *Sojourners in the Sun. Scottish Migrants in Jamaica and the Chesapeake, 1740–1800*, Ithaca, NY: Cornell University Press

Kay, B. (2006) *The Scottish World: A Journey into the Scottish Diaspora*, Edinburgh: Mainstream

Kiely, R., Bechhofer, F., Stewart, R. and McCrone, D. (2001) 'The markers and rules of Scottish national identity', *Sociological Review*, Vol. 49, No. 1, pp. 33–55

Krickus, R. (1976) *Pursuing the American Dream. White Ethnics and the New Populism*, Bloomington, IN: Indiana University Press

Kymlicka, W. (1995) *Multi-cultural Citizenship. A Liberal Theory of Minority Rights*, Oxford: Clarendon Press

Landsman, N. (1982) 'The Scottish proprietors and the planning of East New Jersey', in Zuckerman, M. (ed.) *Friends and Neighbors: Group Life in America's First Plural Society*, Philadelphia: Temple University Press, pp. 65–89

Leonard, S. J. and Noel, T. J. (1990) *Denver: Mining Camp to Metropolis*, Niwot, CO: University Press of Colorado

Levy, A. (1999) *Fruit of the Lemon*, London: Headline Review

Levy, A. (2004) *Small Island*, London: Headline Review

Leyburn, J. G. (1989) *The Scots-Irish: A Social History*, Chapel Hill: University of North Carolina Press

Lieberson, S. and Waters, M. C. (1988) *From Many Strands. Ethnic and Racial Groups in Contemporary America*, New York: Russell Sage Foundation

Light, D. B., Jr. (1985) 'The role of Irish-American organisations in assimilation and community formation', in Drudy, P. J. (ed.) *The Irish in America: Emigration, Assimilation and Impact*, Cambridge: Cambridge University Press, pp. 113–41

Lockwood, G. J. (1991) *Beckwith: Irish and Scottish Identities in a Canadian Community*, Beckwith, ON: Corporation of the Township of Beckwith

Logan, J. (1998) *It's a Funny Life*, Edinburgh: B and W Publishing

Lynch, P. (1999) *SNP: The History of the Scottish National Party*, Cardiff: Welsh Academic Press

Maalouf, A. (2000) *In the Name of Identity: Violence and the Need to Belong*, New York: Penguin

MacArthur, C. (2003) *Brigadoon, Braveheart and the Scots: Distortions of Scotland in*

Hollywood Cinema, London: I. B. Tauris

MacAskill, K. and McLeish, H. (2006) *Wherever the Saltire Flies*, Edinburgh: Luath Press

MacDonald, J. R. (1992) 'Cultural retention and adaptation among the Highland Scots of Carolina', unpublished PhD thesis, Edinburgh: University of Edinburgh

MacGregor, G. (1980) *Scotland. An Intimate Portrait*, Boston: Houghton Mifflin

MacLennan, H. (1960) *Scotchman's Return and Other Essays*, New York: Charles Scribner's Sons

MacLeod, A. (2001) *No Great Mischief*, London: Vintage

Manzoor, S. (2007) *Greetings from Bury Park: Race, Religion and Rock 'N' Roll*, London: Bloomsbury

McCain, G. and Ray, N. M. (2003) 'Legacy tourism: The search for personal meaning in heritage travel', *Tourism Management*, No. 24, pp. 713–17

McCarthy, A. (2006a) 'Ethnic networks and identities among inter-war Scottish migrants in North America', in McCarthy, A. (ed.) *A Global Clan: Scottish Migrant Networks and Identities Since the Eighteenth Century*, London: Tauris Academic Studies, pp. 203–26

McCarthy, A. (2006b) 'Scottish national identities among inter-war migrants in North America and Australasia', *Journal of Imperial and Commonwealth History*, Vol. 34, No. 2, pp. 201–22

McCarthy, A. (2007) 'The Scots' Society of St Andrew, Hull, 1910–2001: Immigrant, ethnic and transnational association', *Immigrants and Minorities*, Vol. 25, No. 3, pp. 209–33

McCarthy, P. (2000) *McCarthy's Bar: A Journey of Discovery in Ireland*, London: Hodder and Stoughton

McCrone, D. (2001a) 'Who are we? Understanding Scottish identity', in di Domenico, C., Law, A., Skinner, J. and Smith, M. (eds.) *Boundaries and Identities: Nation, Politics and Culture in Scotland*, Dundee: University of Abertay Press

McCrone, D. (2001b) *Understanding Scotland: The Sociology of a Nation*, London: Routledge (second edn)

McKay, I. (1992) 'Tartanism triumphant: The construction of Scottishness in Nova Scotia, 1933–1954', *Acadiensis*, Vol. 21, No. 2, pp. 5–47

McMahon, P. (2002) 'Fall of a First Minister: McLeish's mission to woo Sean Connery', *The Scotsman*, 28 January.

McWhiney, G. (1988) *Cracker Culture: Celtic Ways in the Old South*, Tuscaloosa, AL: University of Alabama Press

Meyer, D. (1961) *The Highland Scots of North Carolina, 1732–1776*, Chapel Hill: University of North Carolina Press

Miles, R. (1993) *Racism After 'Race Relations'*, London: Routledge

Momeni, J. A. (1984) *Demography of Racial and Ethnic Minorities in the United States. An Annotated Bibliography with a Review Essay*, Westport, CT: Greenwood Press

Montero, D. (1980) *Japanese Americans: Changing Patterns of Ethnic Affiliation over Three Generations*, Boulder, CO: Westview Press

Moore, L. (2006) 'Education and learning', in Abrams, L., Gordon, E., Simonton, D. and Yeo, E. J. (eds.) *Gender in Scottish History Since 1700*, Edinburgh: Edinburgh University Press, pp. 111–39

Moreno, L. (1988) 'Scotland and Catalonia: The path to home rule', in McCrone, D. and Brown, A. (ed) *Scottish government Yearbook 1988*, Edinburgh: Edinburgh University Press, pp. 166–81

Mork, G. R. (1996) 'Scots', in Taylor, R. M. Jr and McBirney, C. A. (eds.) *Peopling Indiana:*

The Ethnic Experience, Indianapolis: Indiana Historical Society, pp. 498–507

Morrison, C. (2003) 'Culture at the core: Invented traditions and imagined communities. Part 1: Identity formation', *International Review of Scottish Studies,* No. 28, pp. 3–21

Morrison, D. B. (ed.) (1956) *Two Hundredth Anniversary (1756–1956) of the Saint Andrew's Society of the State of New York,* New York: St Andrew's Society

Moss, K. (1995) 'St Patrick's Day celebrations and the formation of Irish-American identity, 1845–1875', *Journal of Social History.* Vol. 29, No. 1, pp. 125–48

Munro, A. and Sim, D. (2001) *The Merseyside Scots: A Study of an Expatriate Community,* Birkenhead: Liver Press

Nagel, J. (1994) 'Constructing ethnicity: Creating and recreating ethnic identity and culture', *Social Problems,* No. 41, pp. 1001–26

Nairn, T. (1977) *The Break-Up of Britain,* London: New Left Books

Neidert, L. J. and Farley, R. (1985) 'Assimilation in the United States: An analysis of ethnic and generation differences in status and achievement', *American Sociological Review,* No. 50, pp. 840–50

Newton, M. (2001) *We're Indians Sure Enough: The Legacy of the Scottish Highlanders in the United States,* Auburn, NH: Saorsa Media

Newton, M. (2004) '"This could have been mine': Scottish Gaelic learners in North America', *e-Keltoi* 1. Available at http://www4.uwm.edu/celtic/ekeltoi/volumes/vol1/1_1/newton_1_1.pdf (accessed April 2011)

Newton, M. (2005) 'Afro-Gaelic music in America', *History Scotland,* Vol. 5, No. 2, pp. 43–7

Novak, M. (1971) *The Rise of the Unmeltable Ethnics. Politics and Culture in the Seventies,* New York: Macmillan

Parenti, M. (1967) 'Ethnic politics and the persistence of ethnic identification', *American Political Science Review,* No. 61, pp. 717–26

Paterson, L. (2002) 'Is Britain disintegrating? Changing views of "Britain" after devolution', *Regional and Federal Studies,* Vol. 12, No. 1, pp. 21–42

Payne, P. L. (1996) 'The economy', in Devine, T. and Finlay, R. J. (eds.) *Scotland in the Twentieth Century,* Edinburgh: Edinburgh University Press, pp. 13–45

Pires-Hester, L. (1999) 'The emergence of bilateral diaspora ethnicity among Cape Verdean-Americans', in Okpewho, I., Davies, C. and Mazrui, A. (eds.) *The African Diaspora: African Origins and New World Identities,* Bloomington, IN: Indiana University Press, pp. 485–503

Pittock, M. (1998) *Jacobitism,* Basingstoke: Macmillan

Portes, A. and Rumbaut, R. G. (1990) *Immigrant America, A Portrait,* Berkeley: University of California Press

Prentis, M. (2008) *The Scots in Australia,* Sydney: University of New South Wales Press

Radhakrishnan, R. (2003) 'Ethnicity in an age of diaspora', in Braziel, J. and Mannur, A. (eds.) *Theorising Diaspora: A Reader,* Oxford: Blackwell, pp. 119–31

Ray, C. (2001a) *Highland Heritage: Scottish-Americans in the American South,* Chapel Hill, NC: University of North Carolina Press

Ray, C. (2001b) 'Comment on "The Confederate Memorial Tartan" (*Scottish Affairs* No. 31)', *Scottish Affairs,* No. 35, pp. 133–8

Ray, C. (2003) '"Thigibh!" means "Y'all come!" Renegotiating regional memories through Scottish heritage celebration', in Ray, C. (ed.) *Southern Heritage on Display: Public Ritual and Ethnic Diversity Within Southern Regionalism,* Tuscaloosa, AL: University of Alabama Press, pp. 251–82

Ray, C. (2005a) 'Transatlantic Scots and ethnicity', in Ray, C. (ed.) *Transatlantic Scots,*

Tuscaloosa, AL: University of Alabama Press, pp. 21–47

Ray, C. (2005b) 'Scottish immigration and ethnic organisation in the United States', in Ray, C. (ed.) *Transatlantic Scots,* Tuscaloosa, AL: University of Alabama Press, pp. 48–95

Ray, C. (2005c) 'Bravehearts and patriarchs: Masculinity on the pedestal in Southern Scottish heritage celebration', in Ray, C. (ed.) *Transatlantic Scots,* Tuscaloosa, AL: University of Alabama Press, pp. 232–62

Redmond, G. (1971) *The Caledonian Games in Nineteenth-Century America,* Rutherford: Fairleigh Dickinson University Press

Reicher, S., Hopkins, N. and Harrison, K. (2009) 'Identity matters: On the importance of Scottish identity for Scottish society', in Bechhofer, F. and McCrone, D. (eds.) *National Identity, Nationalism and Constitutional Change,* Basingstoke: Palgrave Macmillan, pp. 17–40

Rethford, W. and Sawyers, J. S. (1997) *The Scots of Chicago. Quiet Immigrants and Their New Society,* Dubuque, IA: Kendall Hunt

Richards, E. (1999) *Patrick Sellar and the Highland Clearances: Homicide, Eviction and the Price of Progress,* Edinburgh: Polygon

Richards, E. (2000) *The Highland Clearances: People, Landlords and Rural Turmoil,* Edinburgh: Birlinn

Roberts, D. (1999) 'Your clan or ours?', *Oxford American,* September-October, pp. 24–30

Robinson, M. (1995) 'Cherishing the Irish diaspora', Address to the Houses of the Oireachtas, 2 February. Available at http://www.oireachtas.ie/parliament (accessed April 2011)

Rubinstein, S. P. (1981) 'The British — English, Scots, Welsh and British-Canadians', in Holmquist, J. D. (ed.) *They Chose Minnesota. A Survey of the State's Ethnic Groups,* St Paul: Minnesota Historical Society Press

Safran, W. (1991) 'Diasporas in modern societies: Myths of homeland and return', *Diaspora,* Vol 1, No. 1, pp. 83–99

Samuel, R. (1998) *Theatres of Memory (Volume 2): Island Stories: Unravelling Britain,* London: Verso

Sardar, Z. (2008) *Balti Britain: A Journey Through the British 233Asian Experience,* London: Granta

Sarup, M. (1996) *Identity, Culture and the Postmodern World,* Edinburgh: Edinburgh University Press

Sawyers, J. S. (1997) *Famous Firsts of Scottish Americans,* Gretna, LA: Pelican Publishing

Sawyers, J. S. (2000) *Celtic Music. A Complete Guide,* Cambridge, MA: Da Capo Press

Schlesinger, A. M. Jr (1991) *The Disuniting of America,* Knoxville, TN: Whittle

Scott, P. H. (1999) *The Boasted Advantages: The Consequences of the Union of 1707,* Edinburgh: Saltire Society

Scottish Executive (2000) *A New Strategy for Scottish Tourism,* Edinburgh: Scottish Executive. Available at http://www.scotland.gov.uk/Publications/2000/02/4936/File-1 (accessed April 2011)

Scottish Executive (2004) *New Scots: Attracting Fresh Talent to Meet the Challenge of Growth,* Edinburgh: Scottish Executive. Available at http://www.scotland.gov.uk/Publications/2004/02/18984/33666 (accessed April 2011)

Scottish Executive (2006) *Scotland's Strategy for Stronger Engagement with the USA,* Edinburgh: Scottish Executive. Available at http://www.scotland.gov.uk/Publications/2006/10/16134953/0 (accessed April 2011)

Sebesta, E. H. (2000) 'The Confederate memorial tartan: officially approved by the

Scottish Tartan Authority', *Scottish Affairs*, No. 31, pp. 55–84

Shain, Y. and Barth, A. (2003) 'Diasporas and international relations theory', *International Organisation*, No. 57, pp. 449–79

Shepperson, G. (1981) 'The Scot around the world', in Orel, H., Snyder, H. and Stokstad, M. (eds.) *The Scottish World: History and Culture of Scotland*, New York: Harry N. Abrams, pp. 229–52

Sim, D. (2011a) 'The Scottish community and Scottish organisations on Merseyside: development and decline of a diaspora', *Scottish Journal of Historical Studies*, Vol. 31, No. 1, pp. 99–118

Sim, D. (2011b, forthcoming) 'Scottish devolution and the Scottish diaspora', *National Identities*

Smith, D. M. and Blanc, M. (1996) 'Citizenship, nationality and ethnic minorities in three European nations', *International Journal of Urban and Regional Research*, Vol. 20, No. 1, pp. 66–82

Smith, M. P. and Guarnizo, L. E. (eds.) (1998) *Transnationalism from Below*, Edison, NJ: Transaction Publishers

Stein, H. F. and Hill, R. F. (1977) *The Ethnic Imperative. Examining the New White Ethnic Movement*, University Park, PA: Pennsylvania State University Press

Steinberg, S. (1981) *The Ethnic Myth. Race, Ethnicity and Class in America*, New York: Atheneum

Stone, F. A. (1979) 'Connecticut's Kilmarnock Scots', *Connecticut Historical Society Bulletin*, Vol. 44, No. 4, pp. 97–105

Stone, L. and Muir, R. (2007) *Who Are We? Identities in Britain 2007*, London: Institute for Public Policy Research

Strathern, A. and Stewart, P. J. (2001) *Minorities and Memories: Survivals and Extinctions in Scotland and Western Europe*, Durham, NC: Carolina Academic Press

Stratton, J. and Ang, I. (1998) 'Multi-cultural imagined communities. Cultural difference and national identity in the USA and Australia', in Bennett, D. (ed.) *Multi-cultural States. Rethinking Difference and Identity*, London: Routledge, pp. 135–62

Sullivan, K. (2009) 'A diaspora of descendants? Contemporary Caledonian Society members in Melbourne, Australia — a case study', in Fernandez, J. (ed.) *Diasporas: Critical and Inter-disciplinary Perspectives*, Oxford: Inter-disciplinary Press, pp. 127–38

Szasz, F. M. (2000) *Scots in the North American West, 1790–1917*, Norman, OK: University of Oklahoma Press

Thomson, J. C. (1996) *Great Scots! The Scottish-American Hall of Fame*, North Riverside, IL: Illinois St Andrew Society

TNS System Three (2007) *USA Strategy Communications Research*, Edinburgh: Scottish government

Trevor-Roper, H. (1983) 'The invention of tradition: the Highland tradition of Scotland', in Hobsbawm, E. and Ranger, T. (eds.) *The Invention of Tradition*, Cambridge: Cambridge University Press, pp. 15–41

Trevor-Roper, H. (2008) *The Invention of Scotland: Myth and History*, New Haven, CT: Yale University Press

Van Hear, N. (1998) *New Diasporas: The Mass Exodus, Dispersal and Regrouping of Migrant Communities*, London: UCL Press

Van Vugt, W. E. (1999) 'British (English, Welsh, Scots, Scotch-Irish)', in Barkan, E. R. (ed.) *A Nation of Peoples. A Sourcebook on America's Multi-cultural Heritage*, Westport, CT: Greenwood Press

Bibliography

Van Vugt, W. E. (2006) *British Buckeyes: the English, Scots and Welsh in Ohio, 1700–1900*, Kent, OH: Kent State University Press

Vance, M. (2005) 'Powerful pathos: the triumph of Scottishness in Nova Scotia', in Ray, C. (ed.) *Transatlantic Scots,* Tuscaloosa, AL: University of Alabama Press, pp. 156–79

Waters, M. C. (1990) *Ethnic Options. Choosing Identities in America,* Berkeley: University of California Press

Waters, M. C. (1998) 'Multiple ethnic identity choices', in Katkin, W. F., Landsman, N. and Tyree, A. (eds.) *Beyond Pluralism. The Conception of Groups and Group Identities in America,* Urbana, IL: University of Illinois Press, pp. 28–46

Webb, J. (2004) *Born Fighting: How the Scots-Irish Shaped America,* New York: Broadway Books

Weed, P. L. (1973) *The White Ethnic Movement and Ethnic Politics,* New York: Praeger

Wilkie, J. (2001) *Metagama: A Journey from Lewis to the New World,* Edinburgh: Birlinn

Wilkinson, T. J. (2002) 'Scottish hillbillies and rednecks', Electric Scotland. Available at http://www.electricscotland.com/history/world/scottish_hillbillies.htm (accessed April 2011)

Wilson, A. J. (1995) *Irish America and the Ulster Conflict, 1968–1995,* Belfast: Blackstaff Press

Yinger, J. M. (1981) 'Toward a theory of assimilation and dissimilation', *Ethnic and Racial Studies,* Vol. 4, No. 3, pp. 249–64

Zelinsky, W. (2001) *The Enigma of Ethnicity: Another American Dilemma,* Iowa City: University of Iowa Press

Zumkhawala-Cook, R. (2005) 'The mark of Scottish America: Heritage identity and the tartan monster', *Diaspora,* Vol. 14, No. 1, pp. 109–36

Zumkhawala-Cook, R. (2008) *Scotland As We Know It: Representations of National Identity in Literature, Film and Popular Culture,* Jefferson, NC: McFarland

Index